Contemporary *A*
and Digital Cult

Contemporary Art and Digital Culture analyses the impact of the internet and digital technologies upon art today. Art over the last fifteen years has been deeply inflected by the rise of the internet as a mass cultural and socio-political medium, while also responding to urgent economic and political events, from the financial crisis of 2008 to the ongoing conflicts in the Middle East.

This book looks at how contemporary art addresses digitality, circulation, privacy, and globalisation, and suggests how feminism and gender binaries have been shifted by new mediations of identity. It situates current artistic practice both in canonical art history and in technological predecessors such as cybernetics and net.art, and takes stock of how the art-world infrastructure has reacted to the internet's promises of democratisation.

An invaluable resource for undergraduate and postgraduate students of contemporary art – especially those studying history of art and art practice and theory – as well as those working in film, media, curation, or art education.

Melissa Gronlund is a writer and lecturer on contemporary art, specialising in the moving image. From 2007–2015, she was co-editor of the journal *Afterall*, and her writing has appeared there and in *Artforum, e-flux journal, frieze*, the *NewYorker.com*, and many other places.

Contemporary Art and Digital Culture

Melissa Gronlund

Routledge
Taylor & Francis Group

LONDON AND NEW YORK

First published 2017
by Routledge
2 Park Square, Milton Park, Abingdon, Oxon OX14 4RN

and by Routledge
711 Third Avenue, New York, NY 10017

Routledge is an imprint of the Taylor & Francis Group, an informa business

British Library Cataloguing in Publication Data
A catalogue record for this book is available from the British Library

Library of Congress Cataloging in Publication Data
Names: Gronlund, Melissa, author.
Title: Contemporary art and digital culture / Melissa Gronlund.
Description: New York : Routledge, 2016.
Identifiers: LCCN 2016026138 | ISBN 9781138936386 (hardback :
  alk. paper) | ISBN 9781138936447 (pbk. : alk. paper) |
  ISBN 9781315676852 (e-book)
Subjects: LCSH: Technology and the arts. | Arts and society. | Art and the
  Internet. | Digital media—Social aspects.
Classification: LCC NX180.T4 G76 2016 | DDC 701/.03—dc23
LC record available at https://lccn.loc.gov/2016026138

ISBN: 978-1-138-93638-6 (hbk)
ISBN: 978-1-138-93644-7 (pbk)
ISBN: 978-1-315-67685-2 (ebk)

Typeset in Bembo
by Apex CoVantage, LLC

Printed and bound in Great Britain by
TJ International Ltd, Padstow, Cornwall

To the A, B, C team

Contents

Figures

Acknowledgements

Thanks to the many who helped in making material, images, information, and opportunities available: Lawrence Abu Hamdan, Ed Atkins, Karl Baker, Andrew Black, Andrew Bonacina, Melanie Bühler, Freddie Checketts, Stuart Comer, Ben Cook, Mike Cooter, Jesse Darling, Övül Durmusoglu, Rosza Farkas, Martha Fleming-Ives, Rob Horning, Bouchra Khalili, Omar Kholeif, Nsenga Knight, Christopher Kulendran Thomas, Mark Leckey, Olia Lialina, Guthrie Lonergan, Shana Moulton, Maria Muhle, David Panos, Vince Patti, Elizabeth Price, Seth Price, Rachel Reupke, Hannah Rickards, Martha Rosler, Urok Shirhan, Mariana Silva, Mike Sperlinger, Hito Steyerl, Philip Tan, Tamara Trodd, Pauline van Mourik Broekman, Artie Vierkant, VNS Matrix, and Mark Webber.

My personal thanks to my multi-time-zoned support team. The sun never sets when you are addicted to your smartphone: Pablo Lafuente; Libby Graf, Peter Gronlund, and Katherine Zoepf; Belinda Bowring, Jemima Murray, Amalia Pica, Claudia Schenk, and Victoria Siddall. Thank you to the Afterall team for the years of support, and Helena Vilalta, I was as ever privileged by your careful comments and suggestions. My great thanks to Nida de Leon: you were a constant in the most important sphere of activity. Thank you as always to my parents and my brother, and to the littlest two members of our family. Finally, my greatest thanks to Chris, who is the best one could ask for.

Introduction

Beyond the visible image

Twice I've been wrong about the internet.

When I was in high school in New York in the early 1990s, my parents had a technologically savvy friend. He told us about a service he had signed up to, America Online. "If you log on to my computer", he said, "we can find out what the weather is like in Detroit". "Why would you want to know what the weather is in Detroit?" I thought. This thing's a bust.

When I graduated from college, I had only vague ideas of what I wanted to do and used my college career services department to apply for various jobs. One was an alum working out of his house in Westchester County, New York, who was starting an internet company that could put comments boxes on news stories on the web. "You could put a box on this *New York Times* story and feed back on what you think", he explained in my interview. "Why would the *New York Times* care what you think?" I thought. They're the *New York Times*. This thing's a bust.

It goes without saying I hope this isn't the third time I'm wrong about the internet.

This book addresses the profound changes that digital culture has had on contemporary art and sets out the history within which new experiments with digital culture should be seen. As with many movements that invoke the new, or which feel themselves to be part of a sea change, the artwork about the internet and digital technologies since the mid-2000s has sought to present itself as a break from the past. It portrays the world after the internet as so irrevocably changed that the work made within it is changed as well. This book will look seriously at what typifies the art of digital culture and show how it comes out of the tenets that ran throughout the twentieth century. It will also seek to understand the effects that digital culture has had on the infrastructure of the art world and on theorisations of the art object and, most importantly, to look closely at the works themselves and the themes they explore.

*

Art made in response to the internet and digital technologies addresses the changes to identity, to political freedoms, to behaviour, and to codes of representation through the prism of the digital. It is work about the internet, but not necessarily on the internet, and tracks the internet's emergence into the main-stream, particularly as a platform for social media. Art concerned with digital culture tends to be discursive and representational, arguing for a story, setting out a case, or operating as a metaphor for a state of affect engendered by a digital reality. This notion of affect is key: a great number of post-internet works try to get across the new *feeling* of a life lived in the digital era, and the first-person narrator is a major navigator through this territory.

Medium loses its importance, as work appears in one medium only to migrate to another in a different exhibition context. Sculptural works, employing new items of technology in assemblages, become circulated images; videos appear in immersive installations that privilege spectatorship; performances are accumu-lative. Works are also made online, using and critiquing the new social media platforms of the Web 2.0, whose rise is coincident with that of expanded digital culture. Among these crossings of boundaries, one mode is crucial: that of per-formance, particularly the lecture-performance and a mode I call personation. These allow the individual to demonstrate his or her bodily self as against the technology that operates under a register of the omnipotent mind.

The years that this study focuses on, from roughly the mid-2000s to 2016, are those in which the internet and digital technologies move, like debris from an avalanche, into daily life: Facebook is founded in 2004, YouTube in 2005, Twitter in 2006, and the iPhone appears in 2007. The young artists whose work is commonly, though contentiously, referred to as "post-internet art" emerge alongside these developments, and at the same time, concerns related to the internet and digital technologies – patterns of circulation, information, and digital representation – inflect the work of already established critical artists. It is important to underline the feedback loop here, to use a cybernetic term. The internet and digitality become concerns for artists just as the internet and digitality become parts of everyday life.

Indeed, the intersection between daily life and digital culture is precisely the field investigated by art of digital culture.

The digital bleeds into all other categories of life and cultural production: its radical reorganisation of how we live is one reason for the multitude of artistic responses to it as well as to the enthusiasm with which these have been greeted. People are hungry for sense to be made of these widespread changes. In this way, art that responds to digital culture during this time period can be distinguished from technological predecessors. The internet that movements such as net.art treated was a very different internet, and other earlier technological movements were regarded as marginal to the mainstream, sequestered within a technologi-cal ghetto.

The move into the mainstream

It might seem odd that it took until the mid-2000s for the mainstream of contem-porary art to start addressing the internet. At the turn of the millennium, the inter-net and digital technologies were a relatively minor subject in this mainstream, which can be understood as constituted by a Bermuda Triangle of institutions, biennials, and commercial galleries. In the 2000s, moving-image work in the art world was still deeply invested in analogue technologies of 16mm and 35mm celluloid film and its paraphernalia of projectors and the film strip. Tacita Dean's triumphant monument to celluloid film, her Tate Modern Turbine Hall commission *FILM*, was made as late as 2011: that is, it took till 2011 for contemporary art to say, "Analogue film is dead! Long live analogue film". In sculpture, craft-based projects were resurgent, and painting, influenced by mass-production processes, was (and is) still a dominant mode of working. This suggests a conservative rather than avant-garde impulse at the heart of art-making — an implication that artists now seek to show what has been left behind as much as pushing forward with the new. When networks and computers were entering office spaces in the 1960s, one might remember, Conceptual artists became interested in the typewriter, the index card, and other physical effects of administration.

The slowness of art to pick up on digital technologies was one of the factors in a divisive 2012 *Artforum* article by Claire Bishop, "The Digital Divide: Contemporary Art and New Media", which queried why contemporary art was "so reluctant to describe our experience of digitized life" (Bishop 2012).[1] The article caused a furore with the net.art community and that of other artists working in digital media and media arts, who, of course, had been working in the field of digitised life. But Bishop's article, though reflecting a historical inaccuracy of artistic progression, accurately demonstrated the purview of the art mainstream, and the major magazines, art journals, and art academe who track it. The art mainstream's elitism and fence-building is itself something that net.art and other technological movements were keen to challenge; Bishop's article was doubly a slap in the face for them, marginalising these art practices by the very criteria they disavowed.

As internet usage has become ubiquitous, its potential challenge to this gallery–institution–biennial triangle of power has been one of its most exciting prospects. As a circulatory mechanism, it has allowed young artists to bypass curator and gallerist to post work online themselves and to use the internet's capacity for self-organisation and networking to establish new hybrid institutions that fulfil the role of producer, critic, and commercial gallerist alike. The reorganisation of these roles has been one of the claims made for the "sea change" effected by work of this period, and in this study, we will look at these views in detail. The movement of the internet into daily life means potential infrastructural shifts are part and parcel of what is meant by "new technologies", and indeed thought of in this way, we can see how art-making practice was indeed inflected by the internet and new technologies much earlier than the mid-2000s, as well as throughout the 2000s and 2010s in ways that are not related to simply the presence or absence of a digital console in an exhibition setting. By this, I mean the attitude shifts that are consonant with, though not solely determined by, the internet and digital technologies.

For example, my incredulity that the *New York Times* editors might care what is written in a small comments box below an article shows a deference to authority and a passive readership of news and opinion that couldn't be further from engagement with knowledge structures today. Activity on the web is one of participation rather than consumption: commenting, live-blogging, forwarding or posting links, adding to Reddit threads, participating in memes. Exhibitions, particularly biennial openings, engender enormous immediate response on Instagram and Twitter, and curators actively cultivate this mediation. The move towards participation can also be seen in art practice. Artworks that require the participation of the public for their completion are now established art-making modes, whether codified in Relational Aesthetics or as a general aspect of performance, and exhibitions regularly privilege the participation of their viewers. Hans Ulrich Obrist's exhibition "Do It" (1993), which now has now taken place in more than fifty locations and is still ongoing, entirely comprises instruction pieces to be activated by the viewer. Instruction pieces and participation have a long history in art practice (Duchamp's sugar-cube readymade, which he instructed his sister to make in 1917; Yoko Ono's book of instructions, *Grapefruit* (1964); Fluxus more generally in the 1960s), but by the 1990s, one can say they became a normalised artistic mode. It is also significant that the year of the first "Do It" – 1993 – is when the first web browsers were introduced for the general public. "Do It", you might say, is an exhibition for the internet age.

The intersection between art world and wider cultural trends in this example shows the promise of this field of enquiry – how art has responded to the everyday effects of internet and digital technologies – as well as its limitations: how on earth to chart a methodologically sound and achievable path through this vast territory. This is corroborated and compounded by the work itself: the refusal of internet- and digital-related queries to remain within formal parameters is fundamental to the work we are considering. Even delimiting the digital ontologically falters. The digital, as Kerstin Stakemeier (2014) has argued, is a meta-medium, an imaginary, and a social field as much as a description of a binary process of communicating information. Part of my project here will be to typify this sign of "digitality". Work concerned with digital technology freely moves from formal investigations of the medium to socio-economic or affective implications, and back again. Its wide purview also means it directly addresses other societal, economic, and political shifts that have occurred over the same time period of its development – not just the Silicon Valley tech innovations, but the catastrophic political and economic events that bookend and punctuate it: the Iraq War begins in 2003, vastly amplifying Western military engagement in the Middle East; the financial crash of 2008 results in a further widening of the income and wealth gap in the West; the Arab Spring of 2011 puts paid to hopes for stability in the Middle East; and Edward Snowden's revelations about the National Security Agency's (NSA) internet surveillance program, in 2013, initiates a sentiment of deep scepticism and anxiety over the internet that profoundly contrasts with the feeling of optimism it engendered among artists in the 1990s. These events figure heavily in the work produced and will be guiding factors in our discussion of them.

Seeking to situate art responding to digital culture within an art history also poses challenges, as parameters for periodisation have been rendered murky by a lack of clarity over postmodernism, the last fully periodised cultural movement. Postmodernism, when it appeared in the 1980s, was very clear about itself, defined explicitly in reaction to modernism. But the received understandings of both modernism and postmodernism have since shifted. The return to modernism as a theoretical construct, in Roger M. Buergel's edition of Documenta (2007); the artistic (and market-encouraged) return to modernist geometrical forms and abstraction in painting and sculpture in the 2000s and 2010s; the widening of modernism geographically (the idea of many modernisms); and Latour's influential challenge to the very idea of Western modernity (*We Have Never Been Modern*, 1991; English translation, 1993), has undermined a stable identity for the period. The suggestion that postmodernism was merely the tail end of modernism rather than its own movement has also made its characterisations less secure – postmodernism becomes a hiccup rather than a sequential phase, shot through with questions of hyper-reality and appropriation but not one necessarily moving on from its predecessor in any sort of teleological or dialectic progression. The failure to identify what has followed postmodernism – posthumanism? – likewise contributes to the feeling of stasis or progression breaking down. Teleology itself was critiqued under the (chronologically constituted) sign of postmodernism and poststructuralism, and that critique has proved robust and pervasive. The end of "grand narratives" is part of the cultural theory imaginary, alongside the aura and the gaze. This problem of periodisation has led to proclaiming the end of art (David Joselit) or forgetting the art world (Pamela Lee). Peter Osborne, in *Anywhere or Not at All: Philosophy of Contemporary Art* (2013), conceives of contemporary art as a spatial phenomenon, connected to transnational globality as much as a temporal progression or index of time.

This is to suggest that the rather broadsheet-minded allegations of the irruption of the digital moment have their roots in greater anxieties around time and periodisation than just in the notion that life was so very different before we had iPhones. Post-internet art doesn't explicitly promote its connections to technological predecessors such as cybernetics and net.art, nor with other traditions that one might think it would have come out of. Most of the discourses that artists cite are themselves young disciplines: accelerationism, speculative realism, object-oriented ontology. Artworks make connections among music, design, advertising, and film – a dispersion of kinds of culture in the present moment rather than a chain of historical connections.

The notion of the immense, irrevocable, and universal paradigm shift that has been accomplished by the ubiquity of digital and communication technologies forms part of the controversy over "post-internet art", which is seen as alleging radical novelty where there is in fact only artistic rehashing. This has been exacerbated by the parameters for the category of post-internet art being set as a function of age rather than intentionality or shared characteristics. One is forced to imagine an entire swathe of young people so interpellated by internet and digital technologies they are constitutionally different from anyone with wrinkles, even incipient ones.[2] Shows like the New Museum's "Younger than Jesus" (2009), of artists under the age of 33, in New York, or the Serpentine's 89plus Marathon event (2013), in London, comprised of artists born after 1989, and its subsequent 89Plus project set the boundaries of the movement as generational. This is echoed within the rhetoric and reception of post-internet art. Speaking about the New Museum's triennial "Surround Audience" (2015), made up of post-internet artists, the show's co-curator, the artist Ryan Trecartin, framed art-making as a mode of behaviour and as one that deliberately denies historical focus: artists, Trecartin said,

> aren't concerned with the somewhat parochial thinking about what an art practice can or should encompass right now. It's hard to meditate on potential futures when we are still transitioning out of a period that has been culturally obsessed with defining the past through acts of rejection or fetishisation. There are many artists today who are not only looking past older entrenched ways of thinking about art, they are actually *behaving* past it.
>
> (quoted in Burns, *The Guardian*, 2015)

And Holland Carter, the *New York Times* critic, on the same show: "So, if you're expecting a 'digital' show, you won't get one, or not one that advertises itself as such. For most of the participants, the majority born in the 1980s, digital is nothing special, no big deal. It's a given. It's reality" (Carter 2015). It's reality. Reality itself has changed.

Throughout this book, I hope to complicate this rather large claim but also take it on board as a signifying illusion. For Trecartin is right: post-internet work does constantly try to unmoor itself from the past. The notion of its being out of time is part of the work's affective response to a bleak political and economic time. The time of post-internet is one of perennial catastrophe – a present that has turned its back on the elegiac ruins of analogue to find an information age whose promises of democratisation and political emancipation have soured. Historical progression, if it inheres, is in the morally ambiguous form of accelerationism, where crisis arrives as an "apocalyptic messenger" (Stakemeier 2014, 178). Elsewhere, the past appears, Stakemeier writes, "not oriented towards a future perspective, be it utopian or dystopian", but simply "drifting repetitions" (2014, 172). By following a rather straightforward historiography, I want to show how the complex of characteristics evoked by these "drifting repetitions" has been formed, as well as to understand their unique temporality today. Indeed, following Stakemeier, I want to sketch out a state of digitality as a mode of both critique and compromise.

Digitality

The condition of digitality has three main facets: deterritorialisation, the reiterability of information, and a visual basis in the image. These scale from the imaginary into reality: the notion of the internet as deterritorialised, for example, is untrue in the sense of the physical incorporation of the tech companies that provide the platforms and the physicality of server farms and the consoles by which we access material. But an important (and consterning) facet of the internet is the way it takes on board its illusions as reality. The image of deterritorialisation draws from the experience given by the web of information flowing seamlessly from site to site, or from the larger context of increasing globalisation and post-Arab Spring mass migration that the internet is set within. Partially, this is because the real workings of the internet surpass general knowledge and partially because they are deliberately obscured by tech corporations in order to create "user friendliness". The signifying power of illusions also occurs in theories of technology. In her seminal study *How We Became Posthuman* (1999), N. Katherine Hayles, for example, treats the emergence of the category of the posthuman by drawing on the history of cybernetics and science fiction alike.

Similarly, the online image is not infinitely reiterable but gives the impression of being so. This suggests the possibility of infinite semiotic substitution, something symbolised by the reigning post-internet motif of the green screen. Digitality thus reflects a weakening power of the image even as images become ubiquitous. In this way language, that poststructuralist arena of mutating meaning par excellence, becomes less fungible in online circulation than images. This can be seen in everyday experience – activists, for example, take pains to stage the linguistic reading of the image, designing their protest signs with media circulation in mind or by ambushing photo ops with their written messages. Language piggy-backs onto the circulation of the image, with captions inserted into the images themselves such that their reading cannot be re-determined.[3]

This weakening of the image is compounded by a critique of visibility as a political strategy. Where identity politics saw the emergence into visibility as a form of political empowerment, the positive valences of this visibility is countered by the fact that visibility on the internet makes one liable to surveillance and data mining. Responding to this, a number of contra-visibility critiques attempt to understand politics in visual culture when visuality itself is compromised. Hito Steyerl and David Joselit, in separate contexts, have put forward the idea of being "in between the cracks", or in between discourses, where the route towards political emancipation lies in access rather than visibility. This reflects a move beyond the binary of public/private, or audience/individual, and towards the network-centric thinking of a number of networks existing side by side.

Similarly, a number of politically engaged works are invested not in visuality but in embodiment. Works by artists such as Lawrence Abu Hamdan and Bouchra Khalili look at oral speech as a means to connote political representation and belonging. Orality comes to signal embodiment but also, as public speech, entry into the demos and political engagement. These works suggest that the realm of governmentality continues to be associated with offline exertion. A triad of orality, embodiment, and physical indexicality emerges to counteract the weakening basis of visuality and the image as secure signifying forces.

It is worth noting two final points before leaving this argument (for now). First, "offline" is, again, to be taken both literally and metaphorically. One of the ironies of the digital representation of embodied speech is that this representation of embodiment is accomplished on a video that is digitally projected in a gallery or which circulates on Vimeo. Indeed, the networked status of these works is crucial to their accruing influence and value. My rather inelegant use of "offline exertion" is also meant in a sense of being partly imaginary: what I mean by this is that state force is bounded by national borders, over which its jurisdiction is sovereign and that its mode of exercise is the regulation of bodies in space (not that lawmakers send missives with quill feathers on parchment, though I am sure some of them wish they did). This line of thinking owes deeply to Giorgio Agamben, whose analysis of the state of exception has grown more prescient as time goes by. The period 2001–2016 is one of a number of states of exception, from the tactics of Bush's "War on Terror", such as Guantánamo Bay and the practice of extraordinary rendition, to the crises following the Arab Spring in Bahrain, Yemen, Tunisia, Libya, Egypt, and Syria. The Palestinian and Kurdish people can be said to live in a permanent of exception, as do an increasing number of minority groups (Yazidis, the Druze) under the Islamic State (IS). So, too, do African and Middle Eastern migrants in a Europe that is inhospitable towards them or Latin American migrants and people of colour in states in the US whose laws do not safeguard them. These groups live "in between the cracks", but they do not contain the access or self-determination that turns this situation into one of freedom. It is my contention that the state of exception is also part of the online and digital imaginary, where deterritorialisation and infinite substitution creates a similar situation of being beyond the protective reach of the law or without juridical recourse. As we shall see, legal frameworks are a subject often put into play by post-internet works. This is not to make an equivalence between the perceived insecurity of online existence and the real conditions of states of exception, but rather to set into historical context the privileged anxiety engendered by hyper-capitalism, the ascendency of networks, the limited potential for political change, and the liminal role of embodiment and to understand how artworks dealing with digital culture navigate so fluidly among these topics.

A few words on nomenclature

The only subject more heated than the genealogy (or lack thereof) between post-internet art and net.art is the term "post-internet art" itself, which is seen as rightly confusing. The term was coined by the artist and curator Marisa Olson in a 2008 interview to refer to work she made "after" surfing the internet, suggesting a field of personal exploration rather than abstract periodisation (Cornell et al. 2016).[4] It was almost immediately decried on the grounds of basic confusion – it suggests work made after the internet is over, when it denotes the very opposite: work made because the internet is so present. Other monikers were floated – internet-aware work, work "after the internet" (which simply inverts Olson's formulation) – but post-internet seems to have stuck. As I intimated before, the body of work assembled under the moniker of "post-internet" has also been a subject of controversy, greeted with equal parts enthusiasm and scepticism. In some ways, it suffers from the narrative arc of any movement that has the misfortune for enthusiasm to turn into hype. One could read the backlash against it as signalling the close of the moment and could tentatively periodise post-internet as ending in 2014/2015, though I suspect it might be too soon to lay down any dates.[5] Moreover, the usefulness of the label is itself questionable, given how it was resisted, as is frequent with labels, by so many of the artists themselves.

This book is not purely a study of post-internet art, which would provide too narrow a framework of artistic engagement with the internet and digital technologies. But it does address the work, and to do so without re-entering the discussions over the name and what it covers, I take "post-internet" as read and use it to refer to a more or less discrete group of practitioners who began working mostly in New York, London, and Berlin with an – again, more or less – unified aesthetic, from the mid- 2000s to the present. Post-internet work includes work accomplished online as well as facets borrowed from the internet, such as Tumblr image streams, blog posts, the use of green-screen technology, high production values, stock photography, and the imitation of corporate platforms. It entails image production and selection fuelled by algorithms and semi-automated processes and the intertwining of the posthuman and the commodity form. There is a keen interest in banality and the norm and in the accumulation and curation of information as material. It is frequently performative and unrolls through time rather than appearing in isolated instantiations. The internet and digitality are signalled as subjects and also used to inform its working methods of appropriation, curation, and digital manipulation.

In seeking to extend the purview beyond the artists whose work has been associated with the term, I have settled on the wider term "digital culture" as well as the sadly clunky but accurate phrase "art responding to the internet and digital technologies" and at times even "post-internet art and art responding to the internet and digital technologies", when I want to signal that a certain concern is a hallmark of post-internet style. This expansion of nomenclature has allowed me to bring in artists who would not be considered "post-internet" – such as Rabih Mroué, Hito Steyerl, or Nsenga Knight – but whose work responds to the concerns that I argue have been ushered in by the internet and digital technologies.

Why both the internet and digital technologies? Or, rather, why lump them together? The internet is the world of memes; social media; the performance of identity; the need to be switched on all the time; the erosion of barriers between public and private; the terrain of copy-paste culture; and normalised, non-signifying appropriation. The impact of digital technologies includes the ability to doctor images or to create images with no referent: the endless substitution enabled by green-screen technology, 3D printing, and the interchange between an image on the web and material in one's hand. Often these go hand-in-hand: the internet is a forum for circulating images produced by digital technologies, for example. But it would be too generalising, even in this generalising mode, to say all artists concerned with new technologies in the mid–2000s–2016 moment are concerned with both. Ed Atkins, for example, is interested in digital technologies; Steyerl looks at the circulation of information on the internet.

And, of course, Atkins and Steyerl both survey much more than just these two facets: this book is an attempt to sketch out exactly what this "much more" is – to locate and analyse the concerns that pool among these artists. In broadening out the corpus of artists from post-internet to (here we go) artists responding to the internet and digital technologies, it will also attempt to widen the field geographically. In particular I focus on artists working in the Middle East, first because I simply found the most direct interest on their part with the relationship between digital and internet technologies and the everyday, more so than in Latin America (despite that region's strong tradition in electronic art), Africa, and East Asia. The similarity of this type of work in the Middle East to work made in the US and Europe reflects the major political events that occur in that time frame and the internet's role in them: again, the Iraq War, the Arab Spring, the Syrian Civil War, the "War on Terror", and the NSA surveillance tactics. These events sadly bridge NATO countries and countries of the Middle East.

At the same time, I must admit that the work discussed here still betrays a focus on the art world's epicentres. This is mostly reactive: the kind of work made in this vein is concentrated in London, New York, and Berlin. Art responding to things like Instagram is also work of a privileged variety, even if precarity and violence are two of its signal concerns. More systemically, I would argue that the art world is funnel-like in its grasp. I am looking at a particular type of art language in this study, and literacy only comes by moving through the art system. This migration of bodies, information, and education is part and parcel of the post-internet terrain and indeed is thematised and addressed within the work itself.[6]

One last note on this subject is the question of the market. By looking at the art world centres, this also suggests I am looking at work that is traded and sold within an ever-inflationary art market. Where all this money comes from is an exceedingly legitimate question. One reason the moniker "post-internet" fell out of favour was its imbrication with the market: it became a fashionable style churned out for eager collectors. Most of the artists I treat have gallery representation – in itself a clear point of difference with the net.art generation – which, while not disqualifying them from criticality, reflects their circulation within a system that is becoming ever more problematic. Museums, for example, collect and archive art for future generations and spread it from the cognoscenti to a wider public. I am a museum-believer – maybe one of the few remaining – and in Chapter Six, I defend their role in the information age. But they are factors of hyper-capitalism, and one can't be naïve about the sources and functions of capital in the art world. Museums offer tax exemptions and cultural capital to those who have amassed large fortunes by potentially unethical means, giving a democratic face to their undemocratic accumulations. None of the artwork I treat is outside this world of art schools, biennials, galleries, and institutions. And a lot of the work frets about it. The art world as a luxury economy is a real problem, and another hallmark of the work of this moment is its means of coping with this collusion: strategies of disavowal, self-commodification, homoeopathic doses of violence, demonstrations of complicity, and ironic appropriation of corporate or institutional discourses. This paragraph – this *mea culpa* – is no different.

Organisation

One of the motivations for this study was to clearly show the artistic antecedents to post–internet art and art responding to the internet and digital technologies. This seemed particularly necessary because of the liminal position that technological work has occupied, in which it has been seen as a secondary current running alongside (or below) mainstream contemporary art. I wish to trouble this segregation of histories, looking both at the canonical version of twentieth-century art history and the more obviously technological precedents that inform work of the present moment.[7] The first three chapters of this book are devoted to such an art-historical framework; the second two, to a closer analysis of the work itself, focused on circulation and identity; and the last, to the larger economic, political, and technological context within which the work is found. I treat a range of artists and theorists, with some appearing throughout: Mark Leckey, Seth Price, and Hito Steyerl are artistic touchstones, as is the vigorous reappraisal of the category of the image accomplished by David Joselit.

In Chapter One, "Reproducibility and Appropriation in the Twentieth Century: Precursors to the Digital Age", I set out the case for the "immaterial imaginary" or the belief that the internet and digital technologies are a realm of immaterial zeroes and ones – images that appear magically at the touch of a button. I chart out the increasing move towards the image that is spearheaded by technologies of image reproduction such as photography and film, which continues throughout the twentieth century to focus artistic and theoretical interest on the image itself and not on its material substrate. I show how this focus on the image is from the very beginning associated with capitalism, in that the equating of different images within advertising, photomontage, and collaged work mimics the workings of exchange value. I also illustrate how the key mode of working with images and material on the internet and for artists interested in the internet and digital technologies is appropriation, which itself forms part of the move away from a material substrate and towards "pure" image. Appropriation in the hands of contemporary artists, however, no longer carries the radical displacement that it did for Situationist or 1980s Appropriation artists; rather, appropriation now is a means of participation in the life of the image. How one apprehends an image – the mode of visibility – also emerges in this chapter and forms a leitmotif of the book. Rather than visibility being a means of political representation, artists' work with the green screen signals its opposite: visibility as an expression of insecurity.

In Chapter Two, "Cybernetics and the Posthuman: The Emergence of Art Systems", I focus on this narrative of immateriality from a more technological standpoint, looking at how cybernetics complicated Conceptualism's celebrated dematerialisation of the art object and at its prescient analysis of art as producing systems rather than art objects. Contra cybernetics, I also show how the 1960s artistic understanding of "technology" in terms of machine-based works ignores everyday items of technology and the social field, as was explored elsewhere in art of the time, particularly by Martha Rosler. Cybernetics's contributions to information theory have proved more influential than its contributions to artistic practice, particularly the idea of information as something that communicates itself through patterns, rather than a stable entity in itself, and the figure of the posthuman, which forms the focus of the last part of the chapter. The posthuman appears most famously in Donna Haraway's cyborg: the third way, non-gendered man/woman/machine that crystallises early optimism for technology. The cyborg heralds the undoing of gender binaries, as well as the techno-fetish, anti-abjection aesthetic that I show as characteristic of much post-internet work and art responding to digital technologies.

In Chapter Three, "Challenges to Immateriality: Posthumanist Thought and Digitality", I work to debunk the notion of immateriality altogether, or rather, to show how just at the very moment when immateriality might think it has won the day – with historical forces ranged in its favour, relationships conducted via smartphones, and virtual reality a growing entertainment genre – a variety of challenges are mounted against it, from artists, theorists, and philosophers alike. These challenges to the doctrine of immateriality do so in the name of social and economic concerns such as feminism, immaterial labour, and workers' rights; this is no accident but relates to the twinning of the discourse of the image and semiotic capitalism sketched out in Chapter One. At the same time, new philosophies call for a reconsideration of the agency of the object and the importance of networks and systems as a means of comprehending what was formerly structured as subject/object relations, and I argue that discourses such as that of actor-network theory and objected-oriented ontology follow on the discussion of systems delineated in cybernetics.

I also show here how digitality as a mode of exhibition takes on immateriality's set of negative political, economic, and social associations and how it functions as a meta-sign for artistic production. Digitality provides one way towards understanding the vexed relationship between post-internet art and net.art, its most immediate and obvious predecessor, which investigated the potential for code as a medium and the internet as a forum of exhibition and community building in the 1990s and early 2000s. This is fraught terrain, as so many of the concerns within net.art – privacy, circulation, information, representation – are key concerns to post-internet art as well. The distinction is also not entirely clear-cut: a number of artists can be classified both within net.art and post-internet art, and post-internet work at times looks back with fondness to the 1990s as a pre-corporatised, more democratic moment for the internet. Though it is often closely associated with internet site specificity, I show how net.art travelled easily between online and offline publics. Art responding to contemporary digital culture, by contrast, resolves itself contentiously in an offline idiom that counters the way images accrue value – through circulation. This tension,

I argue, is a constituent part of digitality, the meta-sign that uneasily comprises flux and stasis, materiality and immateriality.

The following two chapters look more closely at the artwork itself. Chapter Four, "Violence and the Surveilled Internet", addresses the fact of the image's new capacity for circulation and reiteration through the affective and thematised responses of art to this development. A historical dualism between Jeffrey Deitch's "Posthuman" (1992–1993) exhibition and Mike Kelley's "The Uncanny" (1993) exhibition demonstrates a polarity between circulating image and the notion of the uncanny, while also suggesting a new valence to the latter: not the fear of what might be revealed, but the fear that nothing may remain hidden. Privacy emerges here as a mode of possibility that is under threat. Drawing on what I earlier characterised as a Gothic tendency, I also argue that one of the ways post-internet art counters the anonymity and lack of specificity of online circulation is to exhibit moving-image works with material viewing conditions that have a privileged relationship to the content of the film. The use of specifically Gothic tropes points to, I argue, a concern with changes to notions of privacy and domestic life, and indeed these are recurring sites in which conflicts emerge.

I also address a second facet of circulation: the fact that the internet imaginary obviates against a sense of place: where, for example, do Tweets exist? What is the physical location of a Facebook feed? Artists thematise this illusion of anywhereness (the answer is server farms) via indeterminate portrayals of affect that challenge the here/there binary that was constitutive of ethnographic film. Violence is brought allegorically against the maker of the work, suggesting a homoeopathic dose and further confusing the boundaries of here/there, inside/outside. I also look at the specific connections of the internet to violence: at the web of surveillance and rendition of the "War on Terror" that internet usage is contiguous with and at an internet awash with images of sexual violence against women.

The question of embodiment is picked up in the subsequent chapter, "Identity, Language, and the Body Online". Identity is a major part of the internet imaginary, largely drawn from the conditions of engaging with the internet – the fact that one can appear online without visible character traits. This fluidity is reinforced by shifts in thinking of identity as both more socially produced, and more multiplicitous and fluid, than pre-twenty-first-century conceptions. To examine these claims, I focus on language as the key mode in which identity is expressed and also as a way that the apparently limitless potential for identity passing is in fact curtailed. I concentrate particularly on the rhetorical use of dialogue to show how artists figure the public as a factor inherent to the understanding of identity. I also look at the notion of ironically inhabiting a character, as on YouTube, Instagram, or other forms of social media, in a disquieting genre I call personation. This is a mode of fully inhabiting the role of the performer in a way that leaves no room for self-critique, and as a form of self-commodification, it is related to affirmative attitudes of digital culture towards the commodity.

I also turn to the other of written language, oral speech, to reprise the question of how artists figure politics in a digital idiom. The perceived deterritorialisation of the internet is a key factor here. I show how speech is used to signal ethnic belonging and often appears as a tactic of the dispossessed – those who live in between the cracks of nation-state belonging or who are politically marginalised within hegemonic power structures. Here the voice appears as the metonym for the real body, demonstrating again how the body becomes so important as a bulwark against the many sources of precarity symbolised by digitality, such as finance capitalism, surveillance, non-territoriality, and mass migration, as well as the site these conflicts are pictured upon.

The final chapter of the book focuses on the context that the art object exists within, rounding out our (not exhaustive) grouping of ways to approach the art object. Chapter Six, "The Art World Infrastructure Post-Internet", looks at how the internet has affected the art world, as well as specific changes to art discourse that have developed in response to the way artworks behave on the internet. The real workings of the art market have proved historically difficult to write about in any analytic manner, primarily because its transactions are shielded from public view and because the knowledge competencies required to unpack its workings – or even to know about them – often do not overlap with those of the art world's chroniclers. However, because one of the major changes coincident with the period of post-internet art is the vast inflation of the art market, it seems important to treat it – though briefly – here. Moreover, in line with the increasing philosophical importance of systems and networks, I want to emphasise that the art market is an integral network that both constitutes and is constituted by the art image.

Lastly, I look at the internet's changes to the structure of knowledge production, which has deep potential consequences for how art, whether produced on the internet or off, is thought about and historicised. Here we see a shift from a binary of private/public to questions of network and access – the same terms that recur throughout the study in various ways, particularly in object-oriented ontology (OOO) and actor-network theory discussed in Chapter Three. In the final chapter, we look specifically at the crucial theoretical changes to the artwork under the internet: the effect of circulation, the rise of the author figure, and the de-privileging of the unique artwork. I will show how the early analysis of dispersion has fallen away, almost as a marker of its success. As Seth Price and others note, notions of public and private – the categories through which dispersion was thought – no longer inhere, and the question of art's public has transformed into an understanding of many publics, all with unique modes of engagement. In the absence of white cube parameters, I show how the author figure now ontologically determines a work of art's status as art and show how thinking of transactions, systems, and networks will profoundly change the art world infrastructure.

A final note on context

The 2010s are a moment of pessimism versus the optimism of the 1990s, not just around the internet but in general. The 1990s were a time of the Clintonian and Blairite third ways (thought of, then, positively!), Cool Britannia, a booming economy, the internet as a demos. By the 2010s, the internet is surveilled, corporations provide its dominant pathways, the economy has collapsed due to invisible derivatives, austerity measures are in power, and racist politics are on the rise. As I intimated in the beginning of this chapter, much of the popular writing around post-internet art focuses on its very ontological challenge to the art object and to identity. These are incredible demands to ask of a mode of art-making, rather like giving a Nobel Peace Prize to a president in his first year in office. To appreciate why it might be so, we can turn to an historical example of new technologies from another context: that of the encounter between photographic technologies and Islam at the turn of the twentieth century. The Islamic art historian Finnbar Flood has analysed the entry of the relic of the Prophet Mohammed's sandal into the age of mechanical reproduction (Flood 2016). The Prophet's sandal is an important relic that provides protection and blessings (*baraka*), which are transferred to the pilgrim by means of direct contact with the sandal. Flood shows that, in the 1900s, a lithograph appeared in Beirut of the Prophet's sandal with a note as to the image's mechanical origins. The lithograph, issued by a senior, conservative sheikh, was concerned to legitimise photographic reproductions of the sandal as proper versions of the relic, based on what we would recognise as the technology's indexicality. Text surrounding the outline of the sandal reiterated the *baraka* it would provide, almost boxing it in: the image is at pains to communicate its legitimacy.

Flood shows the nervous motivation for proving the relic's standing was not simply due to the need to come to terms with mechanical reproduction from a standpoint of devotional objects. The desire to secure the status of such objects was a reaction to wider pressures on Islam and the Islamic world, which in the 1900s saw the waning of the Ottoman Empire, European colonialism in the Middle East, and increased secularisation from within. It was an anxious image for an anxious time. This is worth keeping in mind when we consider the state of the West (and that of the Middle East) one hundred years on, when slowing economies, bifurcating class systems, and ecological disasters are sources of widespread anxiety. The circulating questions of the current moment – what is digital reality, what is the image, what is the art object – reflect formal and technological novelties, as well as cultural unease.

Notes

1 A follow-up text commissioned by Lauren Cornell and Ed Halter reflects on the controversy. See C. Bishop, "Sweeping, Dumb, and Aggressively Ignorant! Revisiting 'Digital Divide'", in L. Cornell and E. Halter (eds.), *Mass Effect: Art and the Internet in the Twenty-First Century*, Cambridge, MA: The MIT Press, 2015, pp. 353–55.

2 This is the idea of the digital native. Though if we want to pursue a sociological analysis, I would submit that internet receptability also has much to do with class. In contrast to the ease with which people now share personal information on social media, remember that women were told till only recently, in certain social circles, that their names should only appear in print twice – in their marriage announcement and in their obituary.

3 Bishop points out that the digital is a linguistic medium, something that will become relevant when we talk about the linguistic basis of performances of identity (Bishop 2012).
4 Olson specifies in the interview what she means by the term: "It's the yield of my compulsive surfing and downloading. I create performances, songs, photos, texts, or installations directly derived from materials on the Internet or my activity there".
5 See, for example, Brian Droitcour, "The Perils of Post-Internet Art", *Art in America*, 30 October 2014, or his "Why I Hate Post-Internet Art", from 31 March 2014, originally appearing on his blog *Culture Two*: https://culturetwo.wordpress.com/2014/03/31/why-i-hate-post-internet-art/ (last accessed on 2 May 2016). Droitcour is a perceptive writer on and figure within post-internet art, making these articles more apostasy than external critique.
6 On a personal note, I also wrote this book while living in Abu Dhabi. Though much of my research was accomplished before, this experience has no doubt influenced what I have looked at.
7 Post-internet art's historicisations have been few. At this point in writing the only comprehensive attempt has been the curator Omar Kholeif's exhibition "Electronic Superhighway 2016–1966" at the Whitechapel Gallery in London, which focused largely on technological precursors. (Other projects on post-internet art, such as Ed Halter and Lauren Cornell's edited volume *Mass Effect* [2015]; Melanie Bühler's edited volume *No Internet, No Art* [2015]; and Kholeif's own *Art after the Internet* [2014], look more narrowly at the moment itself.)

Bibliography

Bishop, C. (2012) "Digital Divide: Contemporary Art and New Media". *Artforum*, 51 (2), 434–41.
——— (2015) "Sweeping, Dumb, and Aggressively Ignorant! Revisiting 'Digital Divide'". In: Cornell, L. and Halter, E. ed. (2015) *Mass Effect: Art and the Internet in the Twenty-First Century*, Cambridge, MA: MIT Press, 353–55.
Bühler, M. ed. (2015) *No Internet, No Art*, Eindhoven: Onomatopee.
Burns, C. (2015) "New Museum's Generational Triennial: Wired for the Future". *The Guardian*. 25 February, https://www.theguardian.com/artanddesign/2015/feb/25/new-museum-generational-triennial-wired-future (last accessed on 6 September 2016).
Carter, H. (2015) "Review: New Museum Triennial Casts a Wary Eye on the Future". *The New York Times*. 26 February, http://www.nytimes.com/2015/02/27/arts/design/review-new-museum-triennial-casts-a-wary-eye-on-the-future.html (last accessed on 6 September 2016).
Cornell, L. Olson, M., Arcangel, C., Bell-Smith, M., Staehle, W., Connor, M. and Jones, C. (2006) "Net Results: Closing the Gap between Art and Life Online". *Time Out New York*. 9 February, https://www.timeout.com/newyork/art/net-results (last accessed on 6 September 2016).
Droitcour, B. (2014a) "The Perils of Post-Internet Art". *Art in America*. 30 October, http://www.artinamericamagazine.com/news-features/magazine/the-perils-of-post-internet-art/ (last accessed on 6 September 2016).
——— (2014b) "Why I Hate Post-Internet Art". Available from *Culture Two* [personal blog], https://culturetwo.wordpress.com/2014/03/31/why-i-hate-post-internet-art/ (last accessed on 2 May 2016).
Flood, F. (2016) "Circulating Baraka: Relics as Images across Eras of Mechanical Reproduction". 19 January, NYU Abu Dhabi, Abu Dhabi.
Osborne, P. (2013) *Anywhere or Not at All: Philosophy of Contemporary Art*, London: Verso.
Stakemeier, K. (2014) "Prosthetic Productions: The Art of Digital Bodies on 'Speculations on Anonymous Materials' at Fridericianum, Kassel". *Texte zur Kunst*, 93, 166–82.

1 Reproducibility and appropriation in the twentieth century

Precursors to the digital age

To an ever-greater degree, the work of art reproduced has become the work of art designed for reproducibility.

(Walter Benjamin)

How about siding with objects for a change?

(Hito Steyerl)

The narrative of post-internet art emerging from a technological ghetto, as I sketched out in the introduction, is flawed in a few respects. The battle lines it draws, between technological and non-technological art, ignores the fact that the "mainstream" of contemporary art, by the end of the twentieth century, takes as integral artwork made by technologies of reproduction, namely photography and film, that were themselves seen as beyond the pale of proper art and academia even fifty years ago. Today these two technologies are so normalised as modes of production that the skirmishes that were fought over their legitimacy – as the sixth and seventh arts – are now mere historical curiosities. And they have proved exceedingly important: in the following chapter, I want to argue that it is within the discourses initiated by film and photography that the current understanding of the "image" emerges – as a circulable representation, as a unit of communication, and as lacking a material support.

To do so, I follow film and photography from their early reception not through the history of photography and artists' film but rather through canonical twentieth-century art history, in order to show how the increasing immateriality of the image becomes orthodoxy within art discourse. One of the most intriguing features of digital culture is that it picks up on and hastens strategies and theories that were in place before the advent of digital technologies. I deliberately take a long view here, looking at how a set of political and social associations have been built up around the digital image – and how these assumptions form the terms of contemporary critical artwork responding to digital technologies.

I thus centre on immateriality and materiality as foundational currents that run throughout the twentieth century. I also hope to demonstrate that this movement away from materiality occurs in tandem with and is accelerated by appropriation – which we can now think of as the conventional response to the category of the image – and at how economic critique was embedded within the rhetoric of the reproducible image from the very start.

Immateriality and appropriation

In charting a history for post-internet art that can be plotted without re-writing the histories of twentieth-century art, nor rehearsing the vast scholarship on artistic engagement with digital media, it is important to keep in mind the push and pull between facets of twentieth-century art that recur in digital culture but yet were inaugurated before the idea of an email chain, a forward, or a Tweet were a sparkle in anyone's eye. An email chain, a forward, and a Tweet – as processes of iteration and publicity – are further steps along a sequence of technologies initiated in the twentieth century. The question of whether they are different in degree or in kind is one of live debate: in my view, the changes wrought by the internet differ in degree only, and we would do well to look back at the theorisations around technologies to show how many of its signal concerns build upon and deepen well-established trends. Imagine a narrative of thinking about images, where, in the beginning of reproductive technologies such as photography and lithography, the image exists as an object to be regarded, held, and saved. The image moves throughout the twentieth century further away from this objecthood and closer to pure image, as in Baudrillard's account of the simulacra as the defining paradigm for late capitalism or Peter Osborne's and Hito Steyerl's linking of contemporary art and its fantasies of immateriality to neoliberal speculative capitalism. In everyday use, rather than being a memory-image, or a repository of memory, images are now "live". They exist as items of social communication, as fodder to be taken up and changed, and as means of participation in a social commons.

The twentieth century, the first century in which mass-circulated images became possible, came to terms both with the sheer power of images as a form of communication and with their technologies of production. Early theorisations of modernism and of photography and film frequently used metaphors of immateriality. As a symbol for the loss of a stable grounding for concepts, immateriality reflected modernity's challenges to older, erstwhile stable ways of living – its "maelstrom of change", as David Harvey put it (Harvey 1989, 11). T. J. Clark, for example, notes how "steam" became an abiding subject within modernist painting and sculpture, appearing as an image of abstraction, eventhood, and power (Clark 2002, 156–57). Marx famously described the change to social relations under modern industry as "all that is solid melts into air" (Marx and Engels 1848/2010, 16). And, in the same way that Clark's ruminations on steam came as a reaction to the newfound cultural importance of information in the early 2000s – "the idea of the world being newly robbed of its space-time materiality by a truly global, truly totalizing apparatus of virtualisation" (Clark 2002, 173) – we might also think of the recent prevalence of Marx's pronouncement within the work of artists, academics, and curators. "All that is solid melts into air" has given the title not just to Marshall Berman's popular book on modernism (1982) but also to a 2008 video by Mark Boulos, a 2008 sculpture by Jimmie Durham, a 2009 group show curated by Dieter Roelstraete, Jeremy Deller's 2013–2014 touring exhibition, a 2015 text by Naeem Mohaiemen, to name just a few. We can say that the end of the 2000s and the beginning of the 2010s were very interested in the idea of immateriality, indeed.

It is worth noting how Conceptualism instituted immateriality as a response to work informed by systems and information, but also how dematerialisation differs from immateriality. "Dematerialisation" remains the watchword for Conceptual art, made famous by Lucy Lippard's book *Six Years: The Demate-rialization of the Art Object from 1966 to 1972* (1973/1997), and first coined by the art critic Oscar Masotta in Buenos Aires in 1967 to describe Happenings and "communicational" art.[1] Dematerialisation implies an action: something that had materiality has lost it – a narrative underscored by the dates included in Lippard's title and by her layout of the book as a year-by-year account, as if charting through time the progressive loss of materiality by the art object. "Immateriality", by contrast, suggests an always-already state of a loss of materiality: things that began in the ether and remain there, such as video game avatars, digitally drawn creations, and virtual reality. Much of post-internet art is concerned with parsing the effects of living in a realm that has no materiality to speak of: a social life lived in chat rooms, social media, email, and Skype; artwork created in software programs; and pop culture received, added to, and participated within online. As Clark also noted, the rise of information means the rise of the *visualisation* of knowledge (Clark 173), and in Chapter Two, I will note how this impulse to visualise knowledge, particularly in the work of cybernetic artists who were contemporaneous to and often exhibited alongside Conceptualist artists, provides a different gloss to the story of art's 1960s dematerialisation. Importantly, the look back at immateriality is also motivated by the sheer focus on materiality in a number of contemporary critical artworks, and in Chapter Three, I will complete this argument by showing how a critical strand of art concerned with digital technologies has been concerned to the show the illusion of immateriality: the material things (computers, servers, cables, chairs, fingers) that enable this so-called immateriality to flourish.

First, however, I wish to show how appropriation exacerbates the tendency towards immateriality. Appropriation is commonly assumed to be the main strategy of production in digital culture. In many ways, it is barely worth remarking upon: taking something, doing something to it, and doing something else to it is simply a way of acknowledging that artists take images and objects already found in the world as their field of artistic material, much as artists used paint and plaster formerly. Given this ubiquity, it has ceased to contain the critical and oppositional edge from when it was used as one strategy out of many. Legal concerns around the appropriating of images and footage belonging to other individuals or to corporations do not have much purchase; overhangs of the ethos of hacksterism, sympathy with sites like Napster and

Pirate Bay and the idea that information should be free; and the general sense of the internet being open for the taking – taking and sending on images is also now part of everyday communication – obviate any sense of transgression that the re-use of internet material might contain. It is worth debating whether the term "appropriation" still bears meaning or whether it should be confined to its historical use as a strategy for the readymade, detournement, or the "Pictures" generation in 1980s New York, in the way that one speaks now of the "historical avant-garde". This change likewise hinges on materiality: there is a substantial difference between the appropriation of images from the web, for example, and Sturtevant's long, painstaking process of remaking other artists' physical works and installations.

As we will see with the rhetoric around early film and photography, appropriation is also closely linked with the move towards mass production techniques and exchange value in capitalist economics. This is at play, for example, in the 1960s by the "atlas" works of Gerhard Richter and, later, Hanne Darboven; Andy Warhol's screenprinted mass-media images; and, crucially to our project, the Appropriation artists of the 1980s. Again in all of these, the image appears as dismembered from its material support and original context. They create what can be termed "lateral hierarchies", where images are reiterated or set side-by-side with others so that their meaning is produced relationally as well as occurring integrally. The kind of thinking inherent to lateral hierarchies, the notion of chains of equation, also parallels the action of reducing everything to an exchange value. As Allan Sekula wrote about archives, "The *semantic availability* of pictures in archives exhibits the same abstract logic as that which characterises goods in the marketplace" (Sekula 1983/2003, 444). Advertising also gives rise to the "mass image", following mass production and the idea of the mass as a political force. This too finds its aesthetic articulation in chains of lateral hierarchies, such as Warhol's use of the screenprint technique to mirror the mass production of consumer goods and the circulation of images of fame.

Appropriation is not only part of the methodology of works concerned with digital technologies but also informs their areas of focus. The interest in subcultures, for example, has been facilitated by the fact that rare, historical, and unusual images and footage are easily available via search engines and able to be re-used in artworks. They also point away from the making of objects and towards a state of fluid production that we will see is crucial to the genre of post-internet art. As Seth Price wrote in *Dispersion* (2002/2008), one of the earliest and most influential accounts of how the internet would transform both artistic practice and its public (and which we will return to throughout this study):

> With more and more media readily available through this unruly archive, the task becomes one of packaging, producing, reframing, and distributing; a mode of production analogous not to the creation of material goods, but to the production of social contexts, using existing material.
>
> (Price 2008)[2]

As Price identified, the circulation of a work becomes more important, and even part of the work itself, both in its production and in what we can understand as an image's "life".

The normalisation of appropriation as a strategy also relates to the so-called context collapse of the internet. When Duchamp conceived the idea of the readymade – the first serious gesture of appropriation art – he radically switched in context from an item of everyday use into an artwork. Duchamp's attempt at exhibiting the infamous urinal at the Independent Show in 1917 was imbued with artistic attention: the soft curvature of the porcelain vessel, the femininity of the shape, and the fact that it operates as a vessel for male fluid, as well as the fountain-like function that gave it its name – all these allow *Fountain* to stand as an aesthetic object, within a history of artistic production. But it was also a prank. Duchamp submitted it to the show anonymously, though he knew members of the jury well, and he chose an object knowingly indecent. The radicality of his gesture, as does not need to be reminded, was based in his mental decision to turn it into an object, a transformation that was underlined by choosing such a mundane item as its object.

But what happens when this context is missing? When the urinal is neither indecent nor the Armory Show policed? The term context collapse is often used to describe the situation in which an online image or comment is moved from one context to another and, in the process, loses the parameters that gave it its meaning. While this is a feature particularly acute on the internet, the anxieties over an object's transference from its site of origins to another place in which these origins are illegible is not new: art museums of the West, since their emergence in their current form in the 1700s, have taken religious and ritual objects from Western churches and non-Western civilisations and exhibited these in the secular halls of formal appreciation. Chris Marker and Alain Resnais made a film in 1953 in which they alleged the "death" of the African statues in such a process of transference, in *Les Statues meurent aussi* (*Statues Also Die*). In his book on photography *Le Musée Imaginaire* (*Museum without Walls*, 1965), André Malraux compared the loss of context engendered by the museum to the effects of photography, which, like the internet now, accelerated the process of context shift, bringing a wider scope of artworks into the dominant narrative of art history. For Malraux, this was a source not of anxiety but of optimism:

> When seen through the ambiguous unity of photography, the Mesopotamian style, from the *Fertilities* of the tombs to the cylinder seals, to the bas-reliefs, to the statues and bronze plaques of the nomads, seems to take on a creative existence of its own.
>
> (Malraux 1965, 160)

And context collapse becomes a signal feature of appropriation used as a radical tool. In a note on his use of stolen films, Guy Debord writes, "these stolen fiction films, external to my film but brought into it, are used, *regardless of whatever their original meaning may have been*, to represent *the reification of the 'artistic inversion of life'*" (Debord 1989/2003, 222, emphasis in original).

Within current use, context collapse provokes similarly varied reactions: from an unremarkable by-product of how we access images (Google Images, for example, aggregates images and offers them to the user with the original ["original"] link a second click away) to something regarded with fear, as a proxy for the loss of other stable phenomena. The fact that the origins of an image are already distanced means the capacity of the image to signify autonomously becomes of even greater importance. This is something Malraux intimated

Figure 1.1 Aby Warburg, *Bilderatlas Mnemosyne* (*Mnemosyne Atlas*), 1929, panel 28/29.

© The Warburg Institute, University of London. The images shows the panels photographed in situ, in the reading room of the Kulturwissenschaftliche Bibliothek Warburg in Hamburg where they were assembled

when he discussed the lack of context of photographed artworks and objects in the imaginary museum of his illustrated art book: *style* would become paramount. One could isolate a fragment from a whole and find in that a beauty or splendour the context might have otherwise effaced. "We can study Gothic figures separated from the profusion of the cathedrals, and Indian art freed of the luxuriance of the temples" (Malraux 1965, 106). The lack of context adds as much as it takes away.

A similar project, and equally famous, to Malraux's imaginary museum is Aby Warburg's *Bilderatlas Mnemosyne* (*Mnemosyne Atlas*, 1924–1929), in which the German art historian laid reproductions of artworks from across different periods on his study floor, finding a recurrence of certain gestures and postures. He used these visual clusters to demonstrate the *Pathosformeln*, or expressive formulas of emotion, that he argued ran throughout artworks from Antiquity to the Renaissance to the present – universal impulses held across human history and geography that spurred on the production of art. Like Malraux with his imaginary museum, Warburg explored the idea that the appropriation and transference of artworks as physical objects to images could produce new meaning: images could be circulated more freely, juxtaposed, and compared laterally to discover traits that artworks' separation by time and geography had previously kept hidden.

Early theories of technology

When photographic technology was first invented in France in the mid-1800s, it was quickly picked up and used for family photographs, police profiling, amateur landscapes, and illustrated magazines – a grouping of uses that has remained largely consistent to this day. Though it was excluded from the fine arts, its impact on art was nevertheless enormous: it helped free painting from its duty of representing the past, either as history painting or in portraits of prominent figures, and opened painting to be the exploration of inner desires, the expression of self, or the execution of self-reflexive and formal experiments.

Cultural commentators of the time focused both on photography's ability to capture the present faithfully and its capacity to be reproduced: the capacity of images themselves to be reiterated. Walter Benjamin, endlessly cited in studies of the impact of technologies on art, assessed the central problematic of photography both as "original/copy" but also, I want to underline, as "object/image". His terms of "cult value" and "exhibition value", categorisations that underscore the Marxist methodology of the "Work of Art in the Age of Mechanical Reproduction" (1936/1998), I suggest, are deeply attuned to materiality. "Cult value" denotes an artwork physically embedded in its site: "Certain statues of gods are accessible only to the priest in the cellar" (Benjamin 1936/1998, 225). "Exhibition value", on the other hand, is a new category that describes an image that may travel. Benjamin was explicit on the relation of photography and film to exhibition value, writing that they are "the most serviceable exemplifications of this new function" (Benjamin 1936/1998, 225). In the notes to his text, he emphasises that the link between aura – a concept related to the uniqueness of each artwork, i.e. as opposed to a reproduced artwork – and cult value can be articulated in terms of objecthood, by extending to the aura the spatio-temporal specificity characteristic of materiality: "The definition of the aura as a 'unique phenomenon of a distance however close it may be' represents nothing but the formulation of the cult value of the work of art in categories of space and time perception" (Benjamin 1936/1998, 243, fn5). Works of exhibition value lose the specificity inherent in cult value, though this may be supplanted via captions (Benjamin 1936/1998, 226), and one may only speculate about a world of pure exhibition value – pure imagehood – as Benjamin is vague about the consequences for the image in this context. He writes, "By the absolute emphasis on exhibition value the work of art becomes a creation with entirely new functions", but never details what these "new functions" are (Benjamin 1936/1998, 225).

The fragmented and arbitrary aesthetics of photomontage in Weimar Germany are perhaps an answer to this question: the reproduction of images used in illustrated magazines and advertisements to provoke commodity desire. These photographs were arrayed in a system of sign exchange that mirrored the exchange value of goods that they advertised, and this new function for images was quickly reflected in contemporary artistic work. Their disjunctive apparition in the work of Dadaist montage, for example, imitated the experience of flipping through a newsmagazine, with images of war alongside cigarette advertisements, the promotion of beauty ideals as a means to sell commodities, and the construction of social subject positions (as critiqued by, for example, the work of Hannah Höch). With its use of collaged advertisements as material, Dadaist photomontages underlined the fact that consumerism was a photographically supported enterprise. This facet also marks other artistic work of the time: the sheen of the fetish that marked consumer objects, for example, appears in the sharply polished style of Neue Sachlichkeit photographer Albert Renger-Patzsch, which revealed the natural world as a commodity for purchase.

One cannot understate the changes coincident with the world of early photography: sudden advances in transportation, new conceptions of time, large-scale urbanisation and capitalism, alongside the changes in forms of documentation that they directly address. Benjamin's "Mechanical Reproduction" text is as much a study on photography and film as it is about shifting forms of low and high entertainment and the emergence of the audience of the working classes. Widespread consumer use of early photography and film also coincided, in Germany, with the years in which National Socialism was gathering its support, and Benjamin's contemporary Siegfried Kracauer, for example, discussed the mechanisms of film in "The Mass Ornament" (1927) alongside the incursion of advertisements and Nazi party rallies. The weighting Benjamin, Kracauer, and others placed on the memory-image to hold together stable, physically located systems of meaning shows how the image can be understood as much more than a new means of technology: the stability implied by material embeddedness is extrapolated to stand for an older form of societal relations.

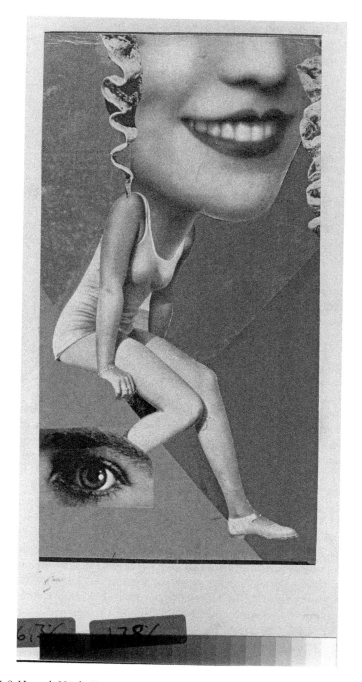

Figure 1.2 Hannah Höch, *Für ein Fest gemacht* (*Made for a Party*), 1936, collage, 36 × 19.8 cm.
Collection of ifa (Institut für Auslandsbeziehungen), Stuttgart © VG Bild–Kunst, Bonn, 2016

The shift when images become liberated by reproductive technologies to circulate freely – in Benjamin's exchange value – is thus read in remarkably strenuous terms. In the essay "Photography" (1927), Kracauer connected the proliferation of images enabled by the technologies of mass reproduction to a loss of memory: he predicted a "blizzard of images" that would obliterate one's own ability to remember (a premonition of the contemporary belief that technology effaces natural abilities). He opened his essay with a vivid set piece, asking the reader to imagine an old photograph that shows a young starlet, twenty-four years old, in a fancy hotel. The woman is now a grandmother, living in a flat with a view onto the old part of town, and for her grandchildren, only "oral tradition" – the stories of their parents – connects her to the starlet she used to be. The image alone says nothing. More than that, it is a source of humiliation. The grandchildren poke fun at the old-fashioned crinoline peeking out from under the starlet's skirt, at her hairstyle and cinched waist. She is a figure of amusement to them. Rather than proving an ineffable link to their past, the photograph works against the creation of affective bonds within the family: Kracauer creates an opposition between the memory-image and the photograph-image, pointing out the degradation of a photograph's value once memory is no longer there to supply the visual contents with meaning.

Kracauer's reading became influential to a text by Benjamin Buchloh relating the "memory crisis" of 1920s Germany, glimpsed in works such as Warburg's *Mnemosyne Atlas* and Höch's Dadaist news-image collages, to Gerhard Richter's post-World War II *Atlas* (1965–ongoing), a vast compendium of different images from varied sources that Richter organises together by subject.[3] In unpacking Richter's *Atlas*, Buchloh uses Kracauer to underline the connection between the early photograph and the family marker: the photograph as a source and an emblem of kinship that signalled the stable territory of family, political territory, and the geographic cultural tradition within which individuals are ensconced. Buchloh writes of the

> realisation that – with the rise of media culture – the subject would no longer be primarily constituted within the models of continuity formerly provided by ethnicity and family, nation-state and culture, tradition, class and social customs. Not even the bodily site of the mnemonic appeared any longer as a guaranteed referent, encroached upon as it was by the rapidly shifting fashion system. Instead, newly constructed signs and languages, residing and operating outside of all the mnemonic forms of experience that the family figures had represented, would now enter the mnemonic field, binding the desire for identity in different representational registers altogether.
>
> (Buchloh 1999, 140)

The grandmother – the "bodily site of the mnemonic" – has given way to the semiotic system of meaning production of illustrated magazines and advertisements, and the private constitution of identity has given way to the public. These new systems of meaning production, in the 1920s as well as in post–World War II Germany, functioned to erase memory – stakes higher for post-war Germany with its threatened whitewashing of the events of the Third Reich. This is the world that Richter tests, seeing whether images of events as horrific as the concentration camps can hold their meaning within a system of levelling of meaning.

Buchloh also intimates how the incursion of capitalism was associated, explicitly or implicitly, with the US. He specifies, for example, how Richter claims as his influences US artists such as Robert Rauschenberg, Roy Lichtenstein, and Andy Warhol, though the *Atlas* is comprised mostly of everyday images found in German pop culture. This ambivalence allows Richter's *Atlas* to be both "specifically German" in its "repression of historical memory" (Buchloh 1999, 141) but also marked by the idea of sign exchange promulgated by Rauschenberg's collages and American consumer capitalism. The identification of the language of consumerism with the US becomes a powerful strand throughout twentieth-century art, from Jean-Luc Godard to Sigmar Polke to David Lamelas to Martha Rosler, in which the US often appears as a bastion of pure capitalism, where exchange value trumps social or sentimental bonds. This is perhaps obvious to point out, but it adumbrates the set of concerns that also coalesce around immateriality: artistic, personal, economic, as well as nationalistic and political. Particularly during the 1970s and the Vietnam War, political critique in Europe, Latin America, and elsewhere was largely political critique directed against the US. This remains so for the critique against digital immateriality, which will come to include US government surveillance and the Snowden leaks and Western involvement in the Middle East and the Arab Spring.

The thinking of the media image in relation to memory approaches the free circulation of images differently than for the "Pictures" generation. While the latter centred on the questions of semiotics and original/copy, early analyses of the circulation of images focused more on the loss of the image's original resonance – which would be only privately available to those who took or posed for the photograph – as it entered into a system of sign exchange. The post-internet fixation on and critique of immateriality builds on both these traditions: it is deeply invested in the postmodern critique of a landscape in which images are to be taken as reality, but it also resurrects the "I" as the mediating figure who navigates this landscape and on whom its effects are personally felt.

The question of memory, in Buchloh's sense as that which guards against the groundlessness of the free circulation of images, is today crucial. Post-internet art seeks to performatively enact a condition of contextlessness, while also to assiduously provide the mnemonic function so missing from atlas works or, equally, from gridded search results on the internet. Artworks often provide microhistories or examples of media archivism, following one item through its (frequently technological) chain of existence, such as Hito Steyerl's video-essay *Lovely Andrea* (2007), about a photograph of the artist in bondage that she seeks to recover;[4] Lawrence Abu Hamdan's installation *Double-Take: Officer/Leader of the Chasseurs/Syrian Revolution Commanding a Charge* (2014), which uses Théodore Géricault's painting *Officer of the Chasseurs Commanding a Charge* (1812) to tell the story of a wealthy Syrian businessman who commissioned a version of the original painting that replaced its French imperial officer with Sultan Basha Al-Atrash, the leader of the Syrian uprising against the French in 1925–1927; or Mark Leckey's re-staging of the first TV broadcast of Felix the Cat, in the lecture-performance *In the Long Tail* (2009). Conversely, Anicka Yi, in the installation *7,070,430K of Digital Spit* (2015) sought to "bottle" the scent of forgetting, working with a perfumer to summon the smell of no memory, created by invoking the smell of a foetus in the womb and of an Alzheimer's patient, alongside re-stagings of her work from the past five years. Memory, in all of these, is of profound concern.

And in all the "I" is salient, whether as subject or in the role of detective. The past is transformed into cultural tradition when it reaches an individual; crinolines become not laughable but tender remembrances if one can remember one's grandmother swishing about in them. Artists speak, as we shall discuss further, from a standpoint of an "I", and often literally so, with the lecture–performance becoming a key genre within post-internet art. This "I" transforms the memory crisis inherent in the contextless vista of the internet into a personal crisis: the question of identity and the reading of history as private as well as public. Steyerl searches for *her* photo in the video *Lovely Andrea*; Yi complements the smell of forgetting with her own works; Leckey tests Felix the Cat for how it makes him, his body, feel.

Kracauer's situation of the supplanting of memory images by photographic images, and Benjamin's exhortation that the photograph always needs captions, anticipates the terms around context collapse of post-internet art: the trading of memory for a system in which meaning is fragmentary and only partially available. It accounts too for the radical performativity of identity that is assumed within digital culture, where one is taken to be able to (or to have to) generate new identities online, created by postings, links, likes, and one's network of friends. Identity online is produced not by "ethnicity and family, nation-state and culture, tradition, class and social customs", but by the cumulative effects of daily activity. This means that though one's ethnicity, nationality, cultural traditions, and class inform and determine the way one thinks, context is internalised and relative to each user. In Chapter Four, of course, we shall test how true this is.

Postmodernism

The understanding of an image without context also serves to distinguish post-internet art from its most closely overlapping discourse and its most immediate predecessor, postmodernism, which also grappled with questions of ahistoricity, appropriation, and the simulacra. Indeed many of the concerns that post-internet art addresses are to be found within postmodernism, though they are tackled in different ways. It is within the moment of postmodernism that the image becomes radically freed from its material support, its origin, and even its referent, in the work of the "Pictures" generation, and it is for postmodernism that Jean Baudrillard develops his concept of the simulacra, where appearances precede reality. Indeed the simulacra has become ubiquitous, though problematically, as a metaphor for the internet. However, despite their contiguities, I would like to draw a distinction between postmodernism and post-internet work and to do so around the mediating figure of the "I", who again transforms an objective condition of contextlessness into a question of personal identity and cultural tradition, as much as the condition of the simulacra engendered by the notion of the copy without an original.

The work of the "Pictures" generation is indelibly influential on post-internet art. The group of artists working mainly in New York in the 1970s and '80s took as their field of material the innumerable and ideology-laden images circulating around them. They sought to interfere in this fabric of images by the use of images: critiquing originality by re-photographing or reusing artistic or advertising imagery, by photographically inhabiting stereotypes given by pop and media culture, or by fragmenting well-known images to suggest a dismembered and fractured subjecthood. Rather than interfering in the material world, they accomplished their critique through the world of images, in much the same way as their contemporary Baudrillard asserted that the appearance of things was now tantamount to their reality. Like post-internet artists do now, their quoted and appropriated images were forced to function on their own in order to reveal new or secret meanings: in Richard Prince's Marlboro man, for instance, an image of a cowboy riding across a vista is denuded of its advertising function – the "Marlboro" logo is erased – making the work an exposition of the construction of American male identity. Cindy Sherman created a series of cliché poses of movie heroines, showing how the poses performed as free-floating signifiers, irrespective of the characters they were tied to: not the narrative of a story but an image and a pose make someone a damsel in distress.

The Appropriation artists' all-out assault on the concept of originality – which it read variously as complicit with power structures, white and patriarchal definitions of authority, and with the market – becomes important to the point of normalisation for post-internet artists, who live in an era in which the re-photographing of images and the re-use of others' documents is, as was mentioned before, methodology rather than oppositional statement. In Oliver Laric's *Versions*, an ongoing project within which three videos have been released under the same name (2009, 2010, 2012), Laric portrays all of art history as a story of re-use, in a flow of influence and adaptation from artwork to artwork: the poses of Greek sculpture re-appear in Roman sculpture (Warburg would have loved it); the iconoclasm of the Reformation creates new sculptures, which appear in tourist photographs; the Madonna becomes Lady Justice by replacing the Christ figure that she holds with a pair of scales. A work's importance, he argues, is given not by its uniqueness but by its level of presence: "an image viewed often enough becomes part of collective memory". Laric's *Versions* itself takes part in this project, with each new video iteration being dubbed a new "version" of the argument.

A by-product of the "Pictures" generation critique was to entirely remove the idea of media support for the image, such that it could function even more free-floatingly as image. This is perhaps obvious in thinking of postmodernism's fascination with the world of images, but this notion proves an important step in the illusion of immateriality that emerges within digital culture. The "Pictures" generation's critique linked originality with the image's objecthood. For instance, in Douglas Crimp's seminal essay on the movement, he discusses Sherrie Levine's *Untitled* (1978), an image, taken from a magazine, of a woman with long hair in braids holding up a young girl, which Levine projected in the cut-out shape of John F. Kennedy's well-known profile. Crimp asks,

> Shown as a slide projection last February at the Kitchen, the mother-and-child/Kennedy picture was magnified to a height of eight feet and diffused through a stream of light. This presentation of the image gave it a commanding, theatrical presence. But what was the medium of that presence and thus of the work? Light? A 35-mm. slide? A cut-out picture from a magazine? Or is the medium of this work perhaps its reproduction here in this journal? And if it is impossible to locate the physical medium of the work, can we then locate the original artwork?
>
> (Crimp 1979, 87)[5]

Here, "medium" retains its etymological origins in referring to the physical medium through which an idea is communicated. Crimp's rhetorical questioning of the kind of medium draws not on a discourse of medium specificity nor even on the notion that the medium is particularly significant; rather, it is a proxy for "original", with the suggestion that the Levine copy here exists only in the realm of immaterial imagehood. (It is perhaps handy that it is a projection.) He claims this lack of origin and of physicality precisely as the radical potential of the work. The phenomenological conditions of the image's projection (the "exhibition value" of the work) count more than its origins in this account; and the work's subversion of myth comes from the way the two images – the happy maternal dyad and the profile of the iconic president – are read through each other: the mother and child fill in the Kennedy profile, which itself delineates the domestic scene, to create a network of desire, status, and ultimately patriarchy as emblematic of the normalising American experience.

Appropriation becomes ever more a performative practice, one in which the end product is reproducible (as far as the art market allows) and the image's material support even more irrelevant. Sherman's film stills, for example, derive their power from her inhabitation – her total absorption into – the role evoked by the setting around her. In a clear echo of Baudrillard's simulacra, the cliché of movie starlet, the wisecracking dame, the innocent ingénue precedes and determines her performance of the role. The support of the image is irrelevant – its number is delimited for market purposes – but Sherman's *image* is the work.

Figure 1.3 Sherrie Levine, *Untitled [President Profile]*, 1979, glass slide, slide projector, 365.8 × 213.4 cm.

Courtesy David Zwirner, New York, Simon Lee Gallery, London, Jablonka Galerie, Cologne

The simulacra

Indeed it is worth noting just how important *images* became in the 1980s and '90s. The isolation of the image from any material support also surfaces in the formulation of "image theory" at the time, most notably by the University of Chicago professor W.J.T. Mitchell, whose suite of books *Iconology: Image, Text, Ideology* (1987); *Picture Theory: Essays on Visual and Verbal Representation* (1995);

and *What Do Pictures Want? The Lives and Loves of Images* (2006) have analysed the signifying power of images over the course of three decades. Mitchell seeks to show how images signify in a visual language distinct to verbal interpretation. Here the immaterial workings of language (pace Derrida) become the homology for the image, rather than the image as embedded within a physical support or historical tradition of painting, sculpture, and drawing. Other thinkers in the evolving field of image theory, such as Gottfried Boehm and his theory of *Bildwissenschaft* in Germany, likewise sought in the same period to understand how iconic knowledge could be produced as distinct from verbal meaning.

This is further set within by popular claims of the "age of the visual". In the Introduction to *What Is an Image?*, a roundtable discussion of image theory, James Elkins echoes accepted understandings of contemporary life's saturation with the image,

> We are said to live in an especially visual culture: we may see more images in our lifetimes than any other culture has, we may be able to assimilate more images per minute than any other culture. Visuality is said to be characteristic of late capitalist first-world culture, and it has even been claimed that we have come to think and experience primarily through the visual.
>
> (Elkins and Naef 2011, 2)

Mitchell and Boehm each coined the term of the "pictorial turn" in the early 1990s, while Rosalind Krauss introduced the idea of the "visual turn" in a caustic essay on visual studies, "Welcome to the Cultural Revolution" (1996). By the 1990s, that is, the field of iconology emerges as an indication both of the terrific prevalence of images and also of the need to think through images as a particular category demanding a particular response from its beholder.

Questions of tactility and embodiment are raised within these theories (e.g. Mitchell, in Elkins and Naef 2011, 28), but overall the image was conceived of as immaterial and all-powerful. As Krauss writes, "*image*, its material structure has collapsed and, disembodied, it now rises as Imaginary, hallucinatory, seductive" (Krauss 1996, 92).[6] Krauss details the emergence of visual studies as a discipline focusing on reception of images rather than their production. Like image theory, visual studies worked to unite disparate fields under the broad sign of what can be perceived with the eye: art history, semiotics, pop-cultural studies, cartography, etc. – a dissolution of the barriers between disciplines that reflected the broadening of areas of artistic interest. "Images" become a way not only to remove the material support of an image but also to confront an art corpus that itself shifted away from art history and towards any images whatsoever.

Within the theorisation of visual studies, images retain the association with semiotics and late capitalism that we saw from Weimar Germany onwards, here exemplified by spectacle. Krauss writes elsewhere:

> If in an earlier version of commodity culture the mobility of exchange-value relentlessly replaces the embeddedness of use-value, in its latest

manifestation, then, both of these yield to the phantasmagoria of Spectacle in which the commodity has become image only, thus instituting the imperious reign of pure sign-exchange.

(Krauss 1999, 291)

This particular critique draws on Baudrillard, who in his 1981 account of the historical ages of capitalism, defines the era of postmodernity as the era of the simulacra, one in which all reality has been reduced to signs regulated by desire. To illustrate this idea, Baudrillard uses the famous fable from Jorge Luis Borges of a map that is intended to indexically represent its territory, but which grows ever larger, to the size of the empire itself, as it continues on this quest: it cannot escape its fundamental referentiality. It is the desire of the map for real presence that constitutes virtuality: the simulacra does not simply denote the reduction to sign but the ascendency of desire for the sign to be reality.

In Baudrillard's conception, the simulacra emerges as a third order in the progression of capitalism, following representation as a placeholder for the object itself (the pre-modern period) and, second, the mass-production copies of objects, where representation becomes commodity (the industrial period). In the third, the postmodern period, the distinction between original and representation breaks down. The simulacra thus reflects a three-stage move from use value to commodity to hyper-reality, or pure equivalence: we are not simply alienated from a sentimental mode of "reality" but the notion that our need for objects comes from our use of them in order to live. The "artificiality" of postmodern existence is not only the trading in signs (such as copies of the real, like Disneyland as the "miniaturised pleasure of real America" [Baudrillard 1981, 12] or the fake Lascaux cave that has been erected five hundred metres from the original for tourists to visit), but the artifice that either centre of entertainment should be necessary for actual life. Capitalism engenders desire for objects: rather than *needing* a mass-produced shovel, a commodity, to clear away the snow from the fields, one *desires* consumer objects. Within this logic, it is the desire for the object to be a source of real need rather than one of desire that constitutes the state of virtuality. The simulacra, the field of this virtuality, is thus not only made up of images or signs, but discourses, behaviour, and unconscious thought.

The application of the term *simulacra* in an internet context often misreads Baudrillard's definition in simply seeing the simulacra as a network that is taken for reality. The simulacra has become a common way to describe specific instances when something happens on the internet that crosses over into offline life – where appearance affects reality, and back again. One may think of the "intruder" meme, where a young black man in Alabama, Antoine Dobson, was interviewed on TV about an intruder who came into his sister's apartment and tried to apprehend her. His recounting of the episode to a local news station was so stylised and lyrical that it went viral, and soon a second video circulated, in which his account had been filtered through Autotune and given the melody and hooks of a pop song. Soon enough, this second iteration appeared on iTunes as a track for sale, and, according to the website knowyourmeme.com, sold more than 10,000 copies in its first two days of availability. A few days later, the North Carolina A&T University marching band took to its school's football stadium playing the tune, and Dobson tried (unsuccessfully) for a reality TV career. The meme circulated not just on the internet but offline, in the channels of commercial pop music, band repertoire, and celebrity.

In many ways, the remarkableness that something happening "online" should affect life "offline" is an updating of the notoriety of when "life mimics art": a reversal of the way the order should happen (art should follow life, online life should mimic offline life) and a miscegenation of ontological boundaries of "reality" and (for lack of a better term) "virtuality", whether virtuality is between the pages of a novel or travelling along an internet meme. The use of Baudrillard, rather than an art/life binary, in this context – even or especially if misapplied – is a means to suggest the vertiginousness of the layers of signs, and the understanding of the internet as set within a context of advertising, celebrity culture, and advanced stages of capitalism. The "image" as it emerges as an imaginary in the 2010s contains these valences of being both a reflection of reality and something that supplants the real, as well as something that is an element of the real itself.

At the same time, Baudrillard's writing also engenders the confusion over hyper-reality. His analysis of it – where the representation of reality is indistinguishable from reality itself – points to a key strand of thinking in the doctrine of the immaterial: the very basic way in which "reality" is often understood simply as coterminous with "objecthood". In this context, this means that causal chains that are understood to be "virtual" – whether the manipulation of digital information (typing an email, selling a stock option) or even the unloading of a bomb from an airplane by means of a button – can be considered to not affect reality, precisely because the effects on reality remain so far removed from our field of comprehension, vision, or other forms of apperception. This is another way of reading Baudrillard's famous claim about the first Iraq War, when he alleged, in three subsequent articles for the French newspaper *Libération*, that the Iraq War did not take place. ("La Guerre du Golfe n'a pas eu lieu".) Baudrillard's articles intended to focus attention on the dematerialised means of warfare and its relation to the larger economic superstructure. Warfare, he argued, was being played out on a simulacral plane, where the appearance of warfare was indistinguishable from the war itself – a claim he elaborated by pointing to the disinformation and deterrent economic strategies leading up to the war, the war's decoy campaigns and its "orgy" (Baudrillard 1991/2009, 57) of aerial bombardment, and the use of the mass media to broadcast images of the war. It was warfare not of flesh and blood but of changes to information patterns. Baudrillard linked these to the functioning of late-stage capitalism:

> Just as wealth is no longer measured by the ostentation of wealth but by the secret circulation of speculative capital, so war is not measured by being waged but by its speculative unfolding in an abstract, electronic and informational space, the same space in which capital moves.
>
> (Baudrillard 1991/2007, 56)[7]

We shall see in the following chapter how information patterns – here, the circulation of capital rather than capital itself – have become both symptom and cause of the ideology of immateriality; in this case, it becomes fodder for Baudrillard's assertion that a war that resulted in tens of thousands of deaths did not happen. As claims go, even made knowingly, that is a pretty audacious syllogism between dematerialised tools and unreal consequences – note how even the idea of aerial bombardment (rather than, one supposes, hand-to-hand combat) becomes for Baudrillard a further example of dematerialisation – and suggests both the strength of the illusion of immateriality and the protective privilege inherent in it. The technophilia of histories of technology and the almost lurid fascination that hyper-reality holds often mask individual triumphalism: the notion that one's own engagement with technology and consumer capitalism are part of universal stages of history helps overshadow the fact that the move away from use value is only available to those not living in subsistence or simply more impoverished conditions.

Not a version, not a copy: the introduction of the digital

In the 1980s and '90s, a number of events occurred that are grouped in rhetoric. The US, the UK, and other Western economies began relaxing financial regulations: with the "Big Bang" under Thatcher in 1986, UK stock market regulations were restructured to allow for more liquidity, and famously in 1999 the US revoked provisions of the Glass-Steagall Act (1933) that prohibited commercial banks from using their depositors' money to make investments. These looser rules engendered finance capitalism – profiting from the investment of money rather than the production of goods – and ultimately the (truly vertiginous) suite of derivatives and imaginary assets whose repackaging of debt caused the 2007/2008 financial crash. By the 2000s, Western economies had also completed their shift from manufacturing to service economies, accompanied by what Luc Boltanski and Ève Chiapello (1999) called "the new spirit of capitalism" in their work of the same name: the rise of the informal worker, the erosion between work and private time, and the rise of computers in office life.[8]

In the 1990s, too, digital photography and film, which were in production since the 1960s, became workable, cost-effective, and available to consumers and artists. The first commercially available digital camera appeared in 1990, the Dycam Model 1, which retailed to consumers at $995, took pictures in black-and-white in 320×240-pixel resolution (equivalent to 0.077 megapixels) and stored 32 photos on its memory card. The drop in price and rise in specs since have been enormous. By 2003, digital cameras were outselling analogue cameras, and one could buy a model with 2MB of storage for as low as $100. It was also in the late 1990s and early 2000s that digital film became widely accepted in Hollywood.

And the 1990s was also, of course, the period when the internet began to be used by consumers. AOL – the service by which my family's tech-savvy friend offered to look up Detroit's weather – was founded in 1985 and took off in the early 1990s. Geocities, one of the first web-hosting platforms and an important one for artists, was founded in 1994. AltaVista, that old search engine, appeared in 1995. In the art world, this was the period of net.art, the largely site-specific exploration of internet and digital means of making new artworks and discursive projects. Net.art, which we will look at more closely in Chapter Three, was marginalised by the mainstream art world, which – perhaps in reaction to the emerging technologies' affront on both medium and materiality – was at that period deeply invested in analogue technologies and in the signifying potential of artwork's medium, particularly for work of the moving image.[9] The medium of an artwork was often overly advertised, called attention to in ways were extraneous to the already legible fact of its material support – like determining someone is British because he or she happens to blurt out "bollocks" rather than their obvious and continuously available British accent. The technological means of displays of film and video were included in the galleries rather than being hidden behind in a projection booth. Sixteen-millimetre cameras whirred; television monitors sat atop plinth-like stands; LED projectors hovered in view. One might think here of the work of Hilary Lloyd, Emily Wardill, or Kutluğ Ataman. This is obviously quite a quick overview, but the point is clear: as digital and internet technologies were taking shape in the 1990s, the dominant strands of art-making displayed little curiosity towards or engagement towards them. (This is the period Bishop was referring to in "Digital Divide" [2012].) One might speculate that this is an almost retrograde reaction to digital technologies – and for moving-image work this holds water, as the cheapness of digital film formed a direct threat to analogue ways of working. But for other types of practices, it is more accurate to say that engagement overall with the internet and digital technologies was still largely specialised, and participation in them was confined to those, like net.artists, who knew how to code or work within a non-user-friendly terrain.

Most early (1990s) theorisations and artistic uses of digital technology occurred in the worlds of long-form film and film and media theory, as can be seen, for example, in enquiries as varied as those by Pedro Costa and David Lynch or Lev Manovich and Sean Cubitt.[10] These critiques were founded on both ontology and metonymy (reading the digital as a cypher for something else) and have significantly affected the digital and internet imaginary of today. They helped create the picture of an immaterial, consequence-free environment, where information can be infinitely replicated and forwarded on without any change to the information or to its users; a sense of freedom in the virtuality and anonymity of actions online; a privileging of reception rather than origins; and the ability to build virtual worlds of pure visibility without referent. The film theorist Vivian Sobchack, for example, framed the film strip as an indexical, physical, stable mark of the past, in contrast to the continual refreshing of pixels on a screen, creating a phenomenological condition of absolute presentness for digital media.[11] (This comparison also holds true vis-à-vis video as it appeared in the 1970s, which was a function of electronic beams hitting a cathode ray display and was stored on magnetic tape.) Film and photography, seen by early theorists of film and photography as engendering modes of equivalence and a lack of materiality, suddenly become emblems of materiality itself. The early coupling of reproducible medium and economic discourse reappears, in heightened terms: the vertiginousness of digital video, for example, was seen as a parallel for finance capitalism. Writing later, Steven Shaviro argues, "Just as the groundless figures of digital video are no longer tied to any indexical referents, so too the endlessly modulating financial flows of globalised network capitalism are no longer tied to any concrete processes of production" (Shaviro 2010, 31). The digital media historian Charlie Gere notes the affinities between early digital and internet culture and the contemporaneous movements of poststructuralism and deconstruction, each of which moved away from a stable referent and towards chains of influence and free-floating signifiers (Gere 2002/2009, 154–80). Social and economic fears were again mirrored in new technological developments.

For artwork responding to digital technologies today, however, medium is downgraded in favour of the information it contains. This might be a peculiar observation for a grouping of work in which a mediumistic category – digital and internet technologies – provides its very title, but I hope to show that the undermining of medium both forms part of the illusion of the digital imaginary as groundless and reflects the fact that medium, meanwhile, has come to be understood as a social rather than ontological phenomenon. The film theorist Francesco Casetti refers to medium as a cultural form, defined by the "type of experience that it activates" (Casetti 2012). It describes a certain type of social behaviour – the taking, sharing, and archiving of a picture – as much as the material through and on which this action occurs. This can be glimpsed in the popular usage of photography as well as the artistic, which is supported by the way technology companies have integrated reproductive media onto consumer devices: creating an illusion of a continuity of medium and coding it as familiar. An icon of an analogue camera opens the camera function on the iPhone, while a digital re-creation of a shutter opening and the sound of its closing denote the taking of a picture. Manovich pointed out digital cameras' usage of analogue effects as early as 1995 in his article "The Paradoxes of Digital Photography". Since then, the atavistic shutter has surpassed any function of being a helpful crossover to smooth the transition from analogue to digital and is now an accepted icon of the medium of photographic-ness, whether digital or analogue. Instagram likewise engenders a confusion of digital and analogueness, trading off nostalgia for analogue photography with filters that suggest rematerialised, tactile photography produced in a darkroom, although no feature exists for printing the pictures one uploads. The nomenclature around "sharing" photographs, from a physical "photo album" (also the name for the iPhone's means of organising its photos) to social-media networks, also remains the same.

The changes to the demotic use of photography are most accurately as described as social changes stemming from technological advancements. The complex ontological critique of the differences between digital and analogue photography is not available to most people, and though the digital's changes to photography as a social medium obviously have to do with new technologies, actual usage reflects these technologies' second-stage effects. These include the merging of the phone with the camera as something one always carries around; the negligible cost of taking photographs (or the fact that this cost is hidden elsewhere) versus the cost and hassle of printing photographs; and the normalising of remote communication. Photography has become performative, as Julian Stallabras said about tourist photographs in an interview with Trevor Paglen (Stallabras 2011). One takes a photo, he says, of the Eiffel Tower to prove one has been there, not to obtain an image of the site itself. Social-media platforms such as Instagram have shifted photography from its mnemonic function to one of immediate social interaction. Photography also reflects an acquisitional impulse, which one could argue has become more widespread in late capitalism where style is a means of self-definition. Taking a photograph is akin to consumption: one engages with a scene by taking a representation of it for oneself. The business of printing pictures and putting them in a photo album is only rarely and laboriously done. Images are instead used as items of communication: people respond to Instagram posts with emoticons.

Thinking of these usage changes more broadly also dovetails with how post-internet art understands digital technologies: not as subject in themselves but for the effects they have had on subjectivity and daily life. As I said before, medium is downgraded in post-internet work, meaning that the distinction between analogue and digital film, PDF and Word document, cinema or TV projection, matters very little. For example, a work such as Erica Scourti's video project *Life in AdWords* (2012–2013) is visible on her website, as a video projection in a gallery setting, and, in a longer format, as a video file prepared for screenings at experimental film festivals. Even more so than for Levine's portrait of the mother and child, it would be difficult to say what the medium of this work is (her website lists it as "webcam video", which signals the means of production rather than the exhibition), or to understand the work's exhibition context as legible in any way. It is radically un-site-specific, though – significantly – it is always digital. This picks up on and furthers the sense of the post-medium condition that Krauss identified in 2000, in *Voyage on the North Sea: Art in the Age of the Post-Medium Condition*, in which Krauss delineates the move away from medium's modernist roots as a shift general to contemporary art.[12]

In an influential text on post-internet work, "The Image Object Post-Internet" (2010), the artist Artie Vierkant draws two major conclusions from the lack of importance of the means of realisation of a work: first an undermining of the significance of an original source, and second an increased importance of the point of reception. "A source video exists", he writes. "The idea of a source video exists. But the way the object is instantiated denies both the necessity of an original and adherence to the representational norms that follow the creation of 'video' as both technical device and terminology" (Vierkant 2010). Vierkant proposes an almost Romantic model of endless production, where instead of a divide between producer and viewer, the audience participates in the production of work: "mass media and the world of 'the screen' *is* our communal space". This is a drastic re-reading of the act of appropriation by which most post-internet work is made: all material is fair use, because it is ever in use.

While materiality/immateriality takes on a binary, Manichean aspect, medium appears as flexible, plastic. The work is taken to be the image or the information, and this information is fluid: it can take the shape of whatever vessel contains it. Both Laric and Steyerl quote Bruce Lee on the properties of water in two different videos (Laric's *Versions*, 2012, and Steyerl's *Liquidity, Inc.*, 2014): "water can flow, or it can crash". Steyerl excerpts the longer quotation, which bears repeating for what it indicates about contemporary perceptions of information:

> You must be shapeless, formless, like water. When you pour water in a cup, it becomes the cup. When you pour water in a bottle, it becomes the bottle. When you pour water in a teapot, it becomes the teapot. Water can flow, and it can crash. Become like water, my friend.

This downgrading of medium, and its corollary that information should be the "fluid" that transfers from vessel to vessel, is a key factor in the illusion of immateriality. It doesn't matter if I make another copy of a video from my desktop or if I forward it on to someone else. It is just code, seamlessly transferred from user to user. If I open my video in DivX and you on a Mac's DVD Player, we will watch the same movie. It might matter for copyright, or for containing the art market, but speaking about an artwork ontologically, the information counts more than the vessel. The downgrading of medium has a political dimension; Cadence Kinsey, for example, has written on how the notion itself of a medium as technologically determined relates to hierarchies of high modernism, which can be potentially restructured by post-internet work (Kinsey 2013). At the same time, I also want to insert almost a placeholder in this passage: for moving away from a focus on the means of exhibition is as problematic as saying the Gulf War didn't take place, and as much as art is concerned with suppression of materiality, it is also concerned with the revelation of this suppression – a laying bare of the device, to use an old modernist chestnut. The demonstration of the falsity of the illusion of immateriality is a leitmotif of art that is concerned with digital technologies, even while it agrees that information is conceived both of as fungible and of ontological priority.

Look but don't touch

The priority of information poses a profound question – if there is no set material framework to instantiate information, how do we apprehend it? Indeed, the rise of images is paralleled by a rise in the claims made for visibility. In the final section of this chapter, we will discuss how visibility as a political tool of representation is ambivalently and even contradictorily addressed by art concerned with the internet and digital technologies. Within critical artworks, visibility shifts in political valence, as its potential is compromised on the internet by revelations of NSA surveillance and social media's wholesale conflagration of privacy as a curtain behind which one can test unformed, exploratory, and inconsistent behaviour. In what follows, I will set out two hypotheses: first look-ing at the motif of the green screen to begin in earnest our investigation of the personal anxieties, political compromises, and economic critiques inherent in contemporary art's treatment of what was formerly its most basic condition: visibility. And second, through the work of Mark Leckey, we will conclude the chapter's argument of the twentieth century's art-historical move towards image. Leckey's work shows how digital technologies, though not foreseen in the early twentieth-century imaginary, allow a radical completion of the dema-terialisation initiated then – but also how this completion, putatively argued, falters and fails.

Visibility, by the 1990s, becomes linked with the rhetoric of political representation – both in the popular sense of a minority group "gaining visibility" as a tool for and reflection of enfranchisement, greater social valu-ation, and political rights, and in more specific art-critical and philosophical senses. The art historian T. J. Clark (1973/1999) analysed the entry of the middle and working classes into the field of visibility as the subject matter of nineteenth-century French realism, appearing, for example, in Courbet's depiction of peasants, the working class, and the bourgeois – a visibility that went hand-in-hand with the political rights they gained throughout that century and specifically agitated for in 1848. Broadly speaking, the French political philosopher Jacques Rancière – such an important figure to the art world of the 2000s – conceived in *Le Partage du sensible* (2000; *The Politics of Aesthetics*, 2006) of politics as a regime of the sensible, or that which is appre-hended by the senses, with the entry into politics understood as the entry into sensible apprehension, primarily by vision. These and other isolations of visibility have arguably developed in reaction to the contemporary focus on information and the fact that code, invisible to the eye, determines so much of daily life, from social-media platforms to workplace activity. Vision becomes a way of making sense, a guiding metaphor for navigating a world as a mate-rial being just as more becomes invisible, with the flows of information and money beyond sight.

The theorist Nicholas Mirzoeff has developed the field of critical visuality studies in response to these changes. This critique is again set in the context of the rise of the image and the importance of vision as a way to orient ourselves cognitively and perceptually. Visuality, as Mirzoeff defines it, is less the idea that the world unfolds in images but rather that we *think* in images: "Visual culture does not depend on pictures but on this modern tendency to picture or visualize existence" (Mirzoeff 1999/2005, 5). In his 2011 volume *The Right to Look: A Counterhistory of Visuality*, Mirzoeff extends this critique to the realm of warfare and governance, reading the assertion and maintenance of power as a function of visuality. Linking visuality and authority, he traces a genealogy in which visuality begins as a concept with the slave plantation, which mapped the territory in order to give the overseer complete (visual, absolute) author-ity over the complex. This phase, which he labels one of "oversight", transi-tioned in the mid-nineteenth century to that of imperial visuality, or where the "cultured" dominated the "primitive". The contemporary condition is one of "post-panoptic visuality" in which a variety of image sets – satellite imagery, infrared, CCTV surveillance, drones – produce an array of visualisations that can be themselves be invisible. Visuality is thus not simply a visualisation of the social field but an identity with authority, as he writes in an essay on critical visuality studies: it is

> a regime of visualisations, not images, as conjured by the autocratic leader, whether the plantation overseer, the general, the colonial governor, the fascist dictator, or the present-day "authoritarian" leader. It is also the attribute of bureaucratic and structured regimes, from the imperial administration of vast swathes of the world's surface in the nineteenth century [to] the U.S.-led military global counterinsurgency of today.
>
> (Mirzoeff 2013, xxx)

Against this, Mirzoeff poses the "right to look", or the "claim to a subjectivity that has the autonomy to arrange the relations of the visible and the sayable" (Mirzoeff 2011, 1). Drawing on Rancière's consideration of the social field as one of the sensible, Mirzoeff elevates visuality into the means by which power is distributed but also by which it can be challenged.

It is beyond the scope of this work, which confines itself to contemporary art, to adequately treat Mirzoeff's argument, particularly as fascinating and complex as it is. I bring it up here to show how important and broadly applied thinking through images has become and the sophistication by which visibility and visuality are theorised. It is also worth mentioning that despite the terminology of "visuality", in Mirzoeff's study, and the main means of understanding Rancière's points as visual (buttressed by his proximity to visual culture), both Mirzoeff and Rancière broaden their categories of apprehension beyond the visual towards the sensible.[13] At the same time, I want to note that, within the subset of the field of visual culture of the art world, the idea of the visual as a privileged mode of perception is largely against the grain of how images and visibility are emerging within contemporary artists' treatment of the internet. Images are seen as degraded by their overuse and are perceived of in terms of networks and circulation that defy visualisation – indeed one of the problems we will see in work responding to digital technologies is exactly how to represent such flights of capital and information. The move towards the object as witness in projects such as Eyal Weizman's Forensic Architecture and oral embodiment as a form of political enunciation come also in response to the over-concentration of belief in the visual register. Art's focus on information and data also forces it to think not through images, but again through circulation and networks – glimpsable through performance, argument, and representations of their affective resonances.

Invisibility, moreover, emerges as an (ambivalent) political tool. Internet activists gain freedom by remaining imperceptible to power structures, as suggested by Steyerl's video *How Not to Be Seen: A Fucking Didactic Educational .MOV File*

(2013), which claims invisibility as having both an emancipatory and an anti-democratic function. As Steyerl narrates in the video:

> Ways to be invisible: invisible by disappearing; living in a gated community; living in a military zone; being in an airport, factory or museum; . . . invisibility cloak; being a superhero; being female and over 50; surfing the dark web; being a dead pixel; . . . being a disappeared person as an enemy of the state.

The category of visibility can be roughly mapped on here to nation-state jurisdiction and compliance with its laws, versus sites of deterritorialised flights of capital such as duty-free zones in airports or museums built of tax-exempt donations, or political states of exception such as military zones or extraordinary rendition. The terms Steyerl sets up here of the non-state, deterritorialised category will become of great importance to this study as it moves forward, and it is important to note the liminal position it implies: again, both a political tactic and precarity. She defines invisibility via the metaphor of a target, in which being unseen implies protection from military weaponry. Comparing the decommissioned targets printed in the Utah desert on which analogue surveillance planes focused their lenses, she notes that digital satellite surveillance can now perceive much greater resolution: the goal is, she argues, to remain smaller than this resolution size, or smaller than a pixel as it moves through the web – a digital version of flying under the radar.

An often-reproduced suite of images from *How Not to Be Seen* shows Steyerl, the protagonist of the video-essay, in a black kimono, standing in front of the black-and-white geometric patterns that cameramen use to focus their lenses, and which also recall the New Aesthetic, the style that James Bridle coined as the image of digitality (binary colouring, right angles and straight lines, the impression of representing data).[14] In one image from this scene, the text "I AM COMPLETELY INVISIBLE" partially obscures Steyerl's face, masking out her eyes. In another, she seems to rub away her skin to reveal the digital substrate below – the same geometric patterning as is behind her, as if she were a digital layer who could easily be erased. In another image, she draws resolution targets on her own skin, in dashes like war paint, through which the unmistakeable glow of the green screen shines through. I want to focus on this last emblem, that of the green screen, which has become a signal motif of art responding to digital technologies, to further demonstrate how visualisation has become a sign of anxiety, representing images not as stable entities but as in perpetual motion. Indeed, to fully complete the reading of *How Not to Be Seen*, we must think also of the reproduced images it has generated, which now circulate on networks of art press, internet searches, and exhibition information material. This is not to simply say that Steyerl's desire to be "COMPLETELY INVISIBLE" ends up accelerating her visibility, which, in making for an image with visual punch, of course it does, but also to show that the proliferation of these images moves beyond the "didacticism" of the second part of the title. These images travel

Figure 1.4 Hito Steyerl, *How Not to Be Seen: A Fucking Didactic Educational .MOV File*, 2013, HD video, single screen in architectural environment, 15 minutes, 52 seconds, Edition of 10, with 2 APs.

Figure 1.5 Hito Steyerl, *How Not to Be Seen: A Fucking Didactic Educational .MOV File*, 2013, HD video, single screen in architectural environment, 15 minutes, 52 seconds, Edition of 10, with 2 APs.

beyond her video to become parts of different arguments and to be given new meanings, despite the video's ironic attempt to lock them down in some kind of linguistic precision. Her .MOV file is not only didactic, it's fucking didactic, and it's not only fucking didactic, it's educational, which is the same thing. But when the images join an external circulating network what they signify – what is "seen" – is contingent.

The green screen

The green screen is vividly connected to questions of visibility and invisibility, and precarity and affect, particularly as they are experienced by the artist. It dramatises both the work's digitalness and the artist's participation – in production and daily life – in the digital state. Technically, the green screen is another term for chroma-keying, a post-production technique that allows one to isolate and delete one colour from the image on screen. Everything that particular colour is then replaced by a second image or a composite of images. It is mostly used to change the background of an image, and is the same technology that was long used by weathermen to show different weather maps in the course of news segments, and by special effects teams in feature filmmaking, before it became more readily available via computer software. It was accomplished for analogue film via the technique of "travelling mattes", a difficult process that allowed two images to be combined into one. (Travelling mattes typically used blue as the colour to be keyed out, known as blue-screening. Blue and green are used as they are furthest away from the human skin tone and thus have the least effect on the film's rendition of the human face. Green screens are most often used for shooting inside studios, and blue screens when outside.) Video editing software has now turned this once technically expert procedure into an automated one: green-screening can be done by anyone holding up something coloured green (a screen, a bolt of fabric, a T-shirt) behind them and a touch of a button.

Starting in around the mid-2000s, the green screen emerges as typical feature of art that is interested in the internet and digital technologies – both as a tool and, more importantly, as a subject in itself, a metonym for the plasticity of information and the malleability of apparent realities. The green screen points not to a dichotomy between fiction/reality but to the internet's state of "infinite substitution", as the artist David Panos has put it (Panos 2013, pers. comm.). The green screen can be anything that is screened onto it: a map of Wyoming in the snow, Abu Dhabi in the heat, a modernist bedroom, a dusty vista, a kitschy front room. Its role in post-internet art is to symbolise a paradigmatic axis of signification eternally in flux – a chain of possibilities for meaning in a sentence that never rests on one. This is, not coincidentally, also part of the like-for-like substitution of capitalism: a picturing of the imaginary of exchange value.

The green screen signals unreality: a non-space of digital resolution of unnatural bright green, whose lack of shadows or light source further inhibits naturalism or a sense of depth. Its placeholder-like status is at times literally enacted. Laric's video *Touch My Body (Green Screen Version)* (2008) used Mariah Carey's video for her single "Touch My Body" as material. The original is structured as a dream sequence where a dorky computer technician (played by Jack McBrayer, best known as Kenneth from the sitcom *Thirty Rock*) is invited to frolic with the celebrity whose bandwidth he is charged with increasing. Laric crudely chroma-keyed out the entire background throughout the video, leaving poor Carey writhing in the middle of monochromatic non-space in a procession of flimsy outfits. He then posted *Touch My Body (Green Screen Version)* on YouTube with the instructions to add backgrounds to the green screen he left "empty", with the result of a variety of versions being added, from one entirely comprised of watermarked stock images to horror genres ("Mariah of the Dead"). (One thing Laric's gambit does is to open up a literal space for an infinite variety of male fantasies.)

The green screen, in its picturing of a void waiting to be filled, also speaks to a space of subjectification, of policies of erasure or of becoming the unwitting mouthpiece for others. One of the characters in the artist Ryan Trecartin's operatic cast is the girl Twi-Key (from the video *Ready (Re'Search Wait'S)*, 2009–2010), who is named after the chroma-key technique. Twi-Key is constituted by being visually keyed out, such that she is covered by text that is spoken in the video or which relates to elements in the movie. (Trecartin has described her as an office oracle, in reference to the fact that surroundings speak through her.) In a perceptive article on Trecartin's responsiveness to foreign and US domestic conflict, Kareem Estefan notes how the colour used to chroma-key Twi-Key is black, rather than the typical green or blue:

> Twi-Key acts as a blank screen onto which Trecartin projects images and text; mining and magnifying the vexed terrain of invisibility and blackness, he uses her figure as ground . . . the composited character inhabits a racialised position of servitude, objectification, and reflectiveness.
>
> (Estefan 2014)

I think we could go further and look at race as a specifically visual example of political subjectification and suggest that the very emblem of the chroma-keyed screen is that of a racially constituted subject. It is defined only by what it is not, in the same way that blackness is constituted by being not-white. It is the placeholder waiting to be projected upon. Indeed one might think of the physical displacement of religious or cult statuary to museums and private collections as a kind of green-screen-ification of their cult value: radical displacement, eradication of histories, and a de-coupling of relations between figure and ground that suggests the mutability of context as experienced by the black subject. In the way that whiteness can determine the space around it – a white person can feel confident in most situations – blackness must adapt. The lack of context of ground invades the territory of the figure, just as the mutability of the green screen threatens to undo the integrity of the figure it surrounds.

With Twi-Key, as Estefan suggests, Trecartin reverses the figure–ground hierarchy that dominated art history until modernism, where the figure (i.e. Rembrandt in a self-portrait) was seen in relation to ground (the space behind him), with the figure known as "positive" and the ground seen as "negative" – much like the green screen, waiting to be filled. The two worked in tandem, each dependent on the other, though the figure is naturally privileged. This "natural privilege" is exacerbated in post-internet art, where the green screen suggests a void of nothingness, or the material constituents of zeroes and ones into which any digital depiction might, through a computer glitch, disappear.

Indeed much green-screen work addresses the literal disappearance of the subject. Shana Moulton, for example, uses green-screening and After Effects technology to suggest her literal dissipation into the digital ether. In the video *Swisspering* (2013), her alter ego, the New Age spiritualist Cynthia, approaches a vanity table, applies foundation powder to her face, and then leaves to visit a pottery studio, where she echoes the first sequence by painting a clay vase. Returning home, she uses make-up pads to remove the foundation from her skin, just as Steyerl swipes away her cheeks in *How Not to Be Seen*. The skin of Cynthia's face comes off in each swipe, revealing obviously digitally rendered, modelling clay-like material "beneath" it, until she is simply two eyes peering out of floating red clay. Moulton continues wiping until the free-floating make-up pads remove even the clay, such that Cynthia disappears into the background, with only her eyes remaining, and her body replaced by the pottery vessel she painted earlier in the day. The reference to the tradition of thinking of women as an "empty vessel" is clear (particularly as a mute vessel, as in Keats's "Ode on a Grecian Urn"). Moulton suggests the dissolution of the body into a variety of claims to speak for it: the medical profession, the cosmetics industry, New Age and yoga claims, even the art-historical tradition.

Figure 1.6 Shana Moulton, *Swisspering*, 2013, HD video, 9 minutes, colour, sound.

Courtesy the artist

In Leckey's video *GreenScreenRefrigeratorAction* (2010), the artist literally, and ritualistically, tries to disappear into the green screen. As with the objects in the work *UniAddDumThs* (2014–ongoing), which we will discuss later, Leckey became interested in the intelligent refrigerator – the luxury sort that reportedly texts you when you're out of milk – for its capacities as an object with agency. The video *GreenScreenRefrigeratorAction* shows him speaking against a green-screen background, which also serves as a backdrop for a series of images of brand-new refrigerators, whose specs and advertising material are read out by an automated voice. They suggest not only consumer fetish objects but, particularly in an art context, Minimalist sculpture. *GreenScreenRefrigeratorAction* was first executed as a performance (accomplished twice, at Gavin Brown's enterprise in New York and at the Serpentine in London), and the video that circulates today is made of footage generated by the performances. Leckey inhales refrigerator coolant throughout the work, again attempting to become one with the machine (its gas circulating in his body) as well as to achieve a lack of consciousness: to become an object himself. At one point, he covers himself in a green cloth, such that the original audience, who could see Leckey in front of the actual green screen and in a live feed of the performance on a video screen, watched him disappear into the represented green screen. The work tries to

Figure 1.7 Mark Leckey, *GreenScreenRefrigeratorAction*, 2011, performance at the Serpentine Gallery, London, 12 May 2011.

Photo: Mark Blower. Courtesy the artist and Cabinet, London

ironically synthesise human subject and object, image and object, and artist and commodity, visibility and invisibility – or, rather than flattening out these differences, setting these categories into a cycle of repeated substitution: a churning through of technology's art-historical queries.

Dispossessed of their shadows (if you like)

If these explorations of the green screen frame digitality as marked by contingency, it is also worth underlining the method by which this is done and what is marked out, erased, and left in: the body. Cats aren't green-screened; tables aren't green-screened; flowers aren't green-screened: time and again it is the human body, and more often than not the body of the artist him- or herself. I want to resume the narrative of the increasing immateriality of the image by looking at the work of Leckey, who explores the immateriality and power of the image on the internet, and its migration through spheres virtual and physical, subcultural and mass. His work mostly takes the form of videos and lecture-performances, and one could separate his career into two phases: the first, which has more to do with explorations of class, such as in his history of music and dance subcultures, and the power of music to invoke collectivities, and the second, where he turns towards the internet as a repository of images. His later work often operates as in a register of awed bewilderment, as if he had gone down a rabbit hole and ended in a domain of clickbait and internet folk gold. Primary to his enquiry as it developed is the rhetorical question of whether, if all images are immaterial, how they can be materially and physically affective. The lecture-performance *Cinema-in-the-Round* (2006–2008), for example, investigated the ability of two-dimensional images to represent three dimensionality – or, returning to the terms of our argument, how to understand object within the framework of image.

Cinema-in-the-Round was conceived in response to an invitation by Ian White, a film curator who did much to develop artists' film and video work in London in the 2000s, when the field shifted from being a niche part of the film world to an important strand of critical artistic discourse. White developed a program for the International Short Film Festival Oberhausen of 2007 called Kinomuseum, which looked at the liminal state of artists' moving-image work, poised between the cinema, with its strictures of a fixed audience, fixed duration, and fixed start times, and the gallery or museum format, in which it was increasingly shown, where the audience wandered in and out of the gallery space and in which a community of shared attention was less frequently formed. Leckey's lecture begins with Philip Guston's paintings of cartoonish, globular figures, which he describes as

> paintings that feel like *sculptures* – or as the Campbell's ad at the time said: *They are soup that eats like a meal.*/How can something that is flat and two dimensional and as unnaturalistic and LIGHT as a cartoon suggest something so physical and so HEAVY? How does an image find that presence? And – in turn – channel its effect through MY body?
>
> (Leckey 2008, 61)

Guston's figures are followed by other rotund and corpulent images such as Garfield, Felix the Cat, the ship from James Cameron's *Titanic,* Homer from *The Simpsons* and Hollis Frampton's film of a *Lemon* (1969), a work that is part–film, part-sculpture, showing nothing but a lemon that is projected, object–like, in the gallery space. ("Lemon" is also slang for something that is supposed to do something but doesn't work; the film, without plot or anything actually moving or happening in it, is a "lemon" of a film.) They are all works of exaggerated physicality and thick gloopishness. Later iterations of *Cinema-in the-Round* focus more on Felix the Cat as the first broadcasted televisual image, emphasising the technical make-up of his creation: indeed it is significant to note that *Cinema-in-the-Round* begins in a context of cinematic weightlessness (in a cinema itself) and its exploration of immateriality is only later connected to the digital.

The work queries how the impression of thickness can be created and how this can be perceived viscerally. These are questions of classical art history: how is illusion created? How does the body function as part of spectatorship? And, in a digital realm, what is lost and gained by the transposition of information from object into image? This is a question he addressed by his most significant piece of work, an evolving project that began as a YouTube clip (*Proposal for a Show,* 2010) of images of objects. He then exhibited the material objects and ultimately re-digitised the objects into what may geekily be described as 2D and 3D agglomerations of representational data.

In *Proposal for a Show,* Leckey narrated a discussion of images of things he had been struck by and consequently stored on his hard drive. In 2013, he curated an exhibition, *The Universal Addressability of Dumb Things,* for the Hayward Touring programme. The show sourced many of the objects from his hard drive, which are those understood to contain a certain power, whether of fetish, titillation, or beauty: *Wunderkammer* items such as stuffed animals; sexual objects such as representations of genitalia; quasi-animate objects such as music speakers; objects that advertising and capitalism have rendered into fetishes, such as luxury sports cars; and, of course, art objects – the ultimate in objects with autonomous agency and emotional power wielded over the viewer. He sourced the loans for these objects and installed them in set displays, such that the viewer could only gaze at them as images rather than walk around them. A further stage of the project was the installation *UniAddDumThs,* which replicated the *Universal Addressability* contents and returned them to the digital information he had initially engaged with: 3D scanning the objects, re-photographing the photographs, re-videoing the videos, and making 2D cardboard cut-outs.[15] He wrote to artists whose work he had borrowed for *Universal Addressability,* such as Louise Bourgeois, David Musgrave, Peter Coffin, and John Gerrard, to say he was making replicas of their work, to no complaints – which is itself indicative of a general laissez-faire attitude towards appropriation (and also a measure of collegiate generosity).

Leckey's *UniAddDumThs* project is significant not only for its thematisation of the move from material object to digital information, which we have been arguing for as a narrative of the twentieth century, but also for the weight it gives to participation in the life of the image versus ownership. Leckey has said

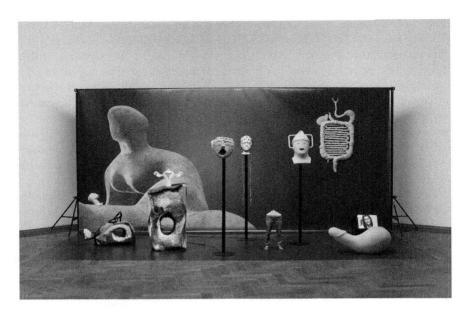

Figure 1.8 Mark Leckey, *UniAddDumThs*, 2014–ongoing, exhibition detail. Installation view, *UniAddDumThs*, Kunsthalle Basel, Switzerland, 2015.

Courtesy the artist and Cabinet, London

that when he received the actual works for *Universal Addressability*, secured at great effort by the Hayward, it felt "a little disappointing to see the real things". They were, he said, "precious and dull" (pers. comm.). This point of view is similar to Laric's confession in the 2010 video of *Versions* that he has an innate preference for the represented subject over the real one. Laric and his collaborators on VVORK.com, an early and influential site for the re-posting of images and texts, addressed the "real thing" in a 2009 exhibition at MU Eindhoven, in which they asserted "the work shown online [to be] an authentic experience, not documentation". Embedded in this notion is that the image comprises not only its visual components but also its unseen, past, and future circulation: VVORK is not an exhibition site but a means of moving along information. The marker of an image's importance is no longer its uniqueness but the number of its replications: the more times it appears, the more significant it is. "Bootlegs and interpretations", VVORK write, "should consequently accelerate the circulation of ideas" (VVORK.com 2009). The real thing is determined in terms of reception rather than ontology.

Leckey's return of the objects to his possession also demonstrates the importance of participation in the post-internet realm. He said he felt "shackled with the real objects". The copy and paste culture of the internet is not about the act of appropriation but about participation, enabled by a sense of freedom and agency in regards to the image, text, or object, in the same way that adding to a meme is a social act, as much about the content produced as about participation. This typifies the *UniAddDumThs* project overall. As with so many other post-internet works, it suggests an ongoing and fluid mode of production, rather than towards one particular and final end. Indeed, *UniAddDumThs*'s thematisation of its mode of production also allows Leckey to include an affective portrayal of his own experience on the internet – from "the gorgeous voluptuousness of YouTube", as he said in *Proposal for a Show* – versus the precious and dull feeling of objects he was legally and ethically barred from manipulating. Like Laric's fore-grounding of *Versions* as a personal poetics, Leckey places his relation to the material at the centre of his enquiry; it should be remembered that *UniAddDumThs* begins on Leckey's own hard drive. "How does an image find that presence? And – in turn – channel its effect through MY body?" In subsequent lecture-performances on engagement with the internet, the body as a visceral perceiving agent is a recurring trope: and not just anybody's, but Leckey's own. The artist himself becomes a privileged point of reception, a means of ascribing subjective meaning to an image whose original signification has been lost or irrelevant. At the end of a hundred years of increasing context collapse spurred on by repro-ductive technologies, performance becomes a means of engaging with an image that is understood to be ever in flux, as it travels through pathways of circulation.

In the next chapter, we will pick up on this question of the body via the discourse of cybernetics, which moves the study from this mainstream art history to a more technologically focused one. Cybernetics can be broadly conceived as the initial workings of information theory, and we will turn our attention from images and forms of visualisation to their material – if immaterial – constitution of informa-tion and data. The body here emerges as a function of information and a socially constituted subject: both and neither, in digitality's odd mode of taking on board illusion. In the third chapter, we will resume the narrative that began with the first mass technologies of image reproduction of photography and film, and look at how its associations – capitalism and its discontents – structure artistic response to it. There, the emphasis on the body and the underlining of immateriality's material substrates work as correctives, puncturing illusions and letting them fade.

Notes

1 See Oscar Masotta, "After Pop, We Dematerialize", written and delivered as a lecture in 1967. Originally published as "Después del Pop: nosotros desmaterializamos", in O. Masotta, *Conciencia y estructura*, Buenos Aires: Editorial Jorge Álvarez, 1969. An English translation can be found in MoMA's research files "Transmissions In Art From East-ern Europe & Latin America, 1960–1980: Research Files 'Total Adventure': Primary Documents from 1960s", at http://post.at.moma.org/sources/8/publications/138 (last accessed on 2 May 2016).

2 Price wrote *Dispersion* for the Ljubljana Biennial of Graphic Arts in 2002 and made it available as a freely downloadable PDF from his website. He published a "finished" ver-sion in 2008, which is now the PDF available from his website.

3 Begun in 1965, the title of each sheet of paper refers to the images' source ("Album photos", "Newspaper photos", "Photographs from Books"), with the images arranged

according to what they show: images of deer antlers, of pornography, of concentration camps, etc. The laconic, anti-aesthetic systematisation trades editorialising on the content or subjectivity for the bare address of history – the horrific residing alongside the banal – in an automated response to a history that exceeds human comprehension. In many ways, it prefigures a search engine's indexing of photographs in its grid-like display, but what is significant here is the glimpse it provides into the gravity of thinking of an image as a pure function of sign exchange value. See the description on Gerhard Richter's website, https://www.gerhard-richter.com/en/art/atlas (last accessed on 12 January 2016).

4 See also Paolo Magagnoli on Steyerl's *Journal No. 1 – An Artist's Impression* (2007), which follows the same conceit of tracking down a lost film reel. P. Magagnoli, *Documents of Utopia: The Politics of Experimental Documentary*, London: Wallflower Press, 2015, pp. 65–67.

5 As an aside, while working as an editorial assistant at *ARTnews* in the early 2000s, I had to call Jeff Koons's studio for an image that would accompany a preview text about a new suite of paintings he was making. The assistant there told me the paintings weren't finished yet, but he could send me the image on the slide that they were using to create them. I demurred; we wanted an image of the real painting. He explained that they projected the slide onto the canvas and copied it from there, what we would get would be just the same as the real thing, if not closer to it. We did in fact run the slide.

6 It should be noted that this pushing forward of the idea of an image is also the project of the journal *October* – as might be evident by the fact that this chapter contains so many texts drawn from it. *October* was highly influential on US academia, but it is not the only story.

7 My thanks to Karl Baker for his comments on this section on Baudrillard. Baker notes, as a codicil, that the 2016 terrorist attacks in Paris and Brussels could be read through Baudrillard as a function of the return of the real (of non-sign-mediated reality, i.e. the "other" of contemporary consciousness) redirected from the margins to the centre of capital itself.

8 See Luc Boltanski and Ève Chiapello, *The New Spirit of Capitalism* (1999; trans. Gregory Elliot), London: Verso, 2007.

9 See, for example, Erika Balsom, 2013, "Original Copies: How Film and Video Became Art Objects", *Cinema Journal* 53.1, 97–118.

10 Sean Cubitt's *Digital Aesthetics*, published in 1999, stands out among many of these early theories in its showing the importance of materiality, the overhangs of colonial mentality, the influence of corporations in developing the internet, and the importance of ethics in analysing digital aesthetics. S. Cubitt, *Digital Aesthetics*, London: Sage Publications, 1999.

11 See Vivian Sobchack, "The Scene of the Screen: Envisioning Cinematic and Electronic 'Presence'", in Hans Ulrich Gumbrecht and K. Ludwig Pfeiffer (eds.), *Materialities of Communication*, Stanford: Stanford University Press, 1994, pp. 83–106.

12 Rosalind Krauss, *A Voyage on the North Sea: Art in the Age of the Post-Medium Condition*, London: Thames & Hudson, 2000.

13 It is also noteworthy to compare this discussion of visuality, which has developed on the left, to the aural metaphors used on the political right, who frame their disenfranchisement as a question of sound: in the US, this is the "silent majority", a term coined in President Nixon's 1969 speech on the Vietnam War, where he averred that the "silent majority" of the nation were actually in favour of the Vietnam War. At the time of writing, the term has been adapted for Republican presidential hopeful Donald Trump's campaign posters: "The silent majority stands with Trump". In Spain, similarly, unionists refer to the "mayoría silenciosa", to enlist all non-protestors to their cause, and in Germany, the "Schweigende Mehrheit", both arrayed on the right of the political spectrum. The formula allows politicians to claim a nebulous and unsubstantiated base of citizens who think alike – a claim that because of their "silence" can remain indefinitely (and conveniently) unproven. Its opposite is the citizenry who "make noise" about an issue, and thus the aural metaphor here suggests an agency – one can choose to make noise about something or stay silent – versus the passivity of being visible, as one's visibility is determined by the

apperception of others. Visibility, particularly in the way that it functions as a political metaphor within internet communities, comprises a state of reduced freedom and agency analogous to the state of passive subjectification that characterises Althusser's process of interpellation. Indeed in Chapter Five, we will look in more detail at the voice as a challenge to visibility as a form of technological surveillance.

14 See James Bridle, *New Aesthetic* [Tumblr feed], May 2011–present, http://new-aesthetic. tumblr.com (last accessed on 3 May 2016).
15 A show in between these two, "Month of Making" (2014) at Gavin Brown's enterprise in New York, displayed the 3D scanning of the objects.

Bibliography

"Anja Kirschner and David Panos: Uncanny Valley" (2013) Part of the Online Series 'Film Interviews'. Institute of Contemporary Arts, London. https://www.ica.org.uk/blog/anja-kirschner-and-david-panos-uncanny-valley (last accessed on 23 April 2016).

"Atlas". *Gerhard Richter* [website], https://www.gerhard-richter.com/en/art/atlas (last accessed on 12 January 2016).

Baudrillard, J. (1981) *Simulacra and Simulations*. Faria Glaser, S. trans. (1981) Ann Arbor: University of Michigan Press.

——— (1991) *The Gulf War Did Not Take Place*. Patton, P. trans. and intro. (2009) Sydney: Power Publications.

Benjamin, W. (1936/1998) "The Work of Art in the Age of Mechanical Reproduction". In: Arendt, H., ed., Zohn, H., trans. *Illuminations*, New York: Random House, 217–51.

Boehm, G. (2008) *Wie Bilder Sinn Erzeugen: Die Macht des Zeigens*, Berlin: Berlin University Press.

Boltanski, L. and Chiapello, È (1999) *The New Spirit of Capitalism*, Elliot, G. (trans., 2007). London: Verso.

Bridle, J. (2011–present) *New Aesthetic* [Tumblr feed], http://new-aesthetic.tumblr.com (last accessed on 3 May 2016).

Buchloh, B. (1999) "Gerhard Richter's Atlas: The Anomic Archive". *October*, 88, 117–45.

Casetti, F. (2012) "The Relocation of Cinema". *NECSUS*, 2, http://www.necsus-ejms.org/the-relocation-of-cinema/ (last accessed on 2 May 2016).

Clark, T. J. (1973/1999) *Image of the People: Gustave Courbet and the 1848 Revolution*, Berkeley: University of California Press.

——— (2002) "Modernism, Postmodernism, and Steam". *October*, 100, 154–174.

Cornell, L. and Halter, E. ed. (2015) *Mass Effect: Art and the Internet in the Twenty-First Century*, Cambridge, MA: MIT Press.

Crimp, D. (1979) "Pictures". *October*, 8, 75–88.

Cubitt, S. (1999) *Digital Aesthetics*, London: Sage Publications.

Debord, G. (1989) "The Use of Stolen Films", manuscript note. In: Knabb, K. ed. and trans. (2003) *Guy Debord Complete Cinematic Works*, Oakland, CA: AK Press, 222–23.

Elkins, J. and Naef, M. ed. (2011) *What Is an Image?* University Park, PA: Pennsylvania State University Press.

Estefan, K. (2014) "A Cute Idea". *The New Inquiry* [online magazine], http://thenewinquiry. com/essays/a-cute-idea/ (last accessed on 23 April 2016).

Gere, C. (2002/2009) *Digital Culture*, London: Reaktion Books.

Harvey, D. (1989) *The Condition of Postmodernity: An Enquiry into the Origins of Cultural Change*, Oxford: Blackwell.

Hassan, R. (2008) *The Information Society*, Cambridge: Polity Press.

Joselit, D. (2013) *After Art*, Princeton: Princeton University Press.

Kholeif, O. ed. (2014) *You Are Here: Art after the Internet*, London: Cornerhouse.

———— ed. (2016) *Electronic Superhighway: 2016–1966*. Exh. cat., London: Whitechapel Gallery.

Kinsey, C. (2013) "From Post-Media to Post-Medium: Re-Thinking Ontology in Art and Technology". In: Apprich, C., Berry Slater, J., Iles, A. and Schultz, O. L. ed. *Provocative Alloys: A Post-Media Anthology*, Lüneberg and London: Post-Media Lab and Mute Books, http://www.metamute.org/sites/www.metamute.org/files/u1/a-post-media-anthology-mute-books-9781906496944-web-fullbook.pdf (last accessed on 4 September 2016).

Kracauer, S. (1927) "Photography". In: Levin, T. Y. ed. and trans. (1995) *The Mass Ornament: Weimar Essays*, Cambridge, MA: Harvard University Press, 47–63.

Krauss, R. (1996) "Welcome to the Cultural Revolution". *October*, 77, 83–96.

———— (1999) "Reinventing the Medium". *Critical Inquiry*, 23 (2), 289–305.

———— (2000) *A Voyage on the North Sea: Art in the Age of the Post-Medium Condition*, London: Thames & Hudson.

Leckey, M. (2008) "Cinema-in-the-Round". In: Sperlinger, M. and White, I. ed. *Kinomuseum: Towards an Artists' Cinema*, Cologne: Walther König, 59–70.

———— (2016) Skype Conversation. 2 February.

Magagnoli, P. (2015) *Documents of Utopia: The Politics of Experimental Documentary*, London: Wallflower Press.

Malraux, A. (1965) *Museum without Walls*. Gilbert, S. and Price, F. trans. (1967) London: Martin Secker and Warburg.

Manovich, L. (1995) "The Paradoxes of Digital Photography". In: Wells, L. ed. (2003) *The Photography Reader*, London: Routledge, 218–40.

Marx, K. and Engels, F. (1848) *The Manifesto of the Communist Party*. Moore, S. trans. Marxists Internet Archive (2010). https://www.marxists.org/archive/marx/works/download/pdf/Manifesto.pdf (last accessed on 16 October 2016).

Masotta, O. (1969) "Después del Pop: nosotros desmaterializamos". In: *Conciencia y estructura*, Buenos Aires: Editorial Jorge Álvarez, 177–92.

Mirzoeff, N. (1999) *An Introduction to Visual Culture*, London: Routledge, 2005.

———— (2011) *The Right to Look: A Counterhistory of Visuality*, Durham, NC: Duke University Press.

———— (2013) "For Critical Visuality Studies". In: Mirzoeff, N. ed. (2013) *The Visual Culture Reader* Third Edition, London: Routledge, xxix–xxxviii.

Mitchell, W. J.T. (1987) *Iconology: Image, Text, Ideology*, Chicago: University of Chicago Press.

———— (1995) *Picture Theory: Essays on Visual and Verbal Representation*, Chicago: University of Chicago Press.

———— (2006) *What Do Pictures Want? The Lives and Loves of Images*, Chicago: University of Chicago Press.

Price, S. (2008) *Dispersion*, New York: 38th Street Publishers (originally published in 2002).

Rancière, J. (2000) *The Politics of Aesthetics: The Distribution of the Sensible*. Rockhill, G. trans. and intro. (2006) New York: Continuum Books.

Sekula, A. (1983) "Reading an Archive: Photography between Labour and Capital". In: Wells, L. ed. (2003) *A Photography Reader*, London: Routledge, 443–52.

Shaviro, S. (2010) "Post-Cinematic Affect: On Grace Jones, *Boarding Gate* and *Southland Tales*". *Film-Philosophy*, 14 (1), http://www.thing.net/~rdom/ucsd/biopolitics/PostCinematic Affect.pdf (last accessed on 4 September 2016).

Sobchack, V. (1994) "The Scene of the Screen: Envisioning Cinematic and Electronic 'Presence'". In: Gumbrecht, H. U. and Pfeiffer, K. L. ed. (1994) *Materialities of Communication*, Stanford: Stanford University Press, 83–106.

Stallabrass, J. (2011) "Negative Dialectics in the Google Era: A Conversation with Trevor Paglen". *October*, 138, 3–14.

Steyerl, H. (2009) "In Defence of the Poor Image". *e-flux journal* [online journal], 10, http://www.e-flux.com/journal/in-defense-of-the-poor-image/ (last accessed on 23 April 2016).

Tomkins, C. (1996) *Duchamp: A Biography*, London: Pimlico.

Vierkant, A. (2010) "The Image Object Post-Internet". *Jstchillin.org* [website], http://jstchillin.org/artie/pdf/The_Image_Object_Post-Internet_a4.pdf (last accessed on 23 April 2016).

VVORK.com (2009) "The Real Thing". *VVORK.com* [website], http://www.vvork.com/?page_id=13441 (last accessed on 23 April 2016).

Wajcman, J. (2004) *Technofeminism*, Cambridge: Polity Press.

2 Cybernetics and the posthuman

The emergence of art systems

The technological basis of art responding to the internet forces a look at technological predecessors. This sounds obvious but its suppositions are worth examining. What do we mean by "technology"? And why would a handheld video performance of the 1970s be intrinsically connected to an experiment conducted on social media? Why would the relation between a self-regulating machine of the Cold War–era and an iPhone be seen as significant, but the connection between an iPhone and a refrigerator be a more surprising one to make? Many histories of "media arts" are organised simply by their common sign of a use of new technologies; under this broad heading, we can find, at times, video art, new media arts, digital arts, net.art, sound art, and even post-internet art.

In this chapter, we will look at the discourse of cybernetics in the 1950s and '60s, which marks the first artistic engagement with early computers. Cybernetics as a discourse develops into information theory, and if in the previous chapter we saw how early film and photography technologies helped create the "image" as we now understand it, cybernetics helps form the user's response to "technologies", as they are now broadly viewed. Technologies has come to mean a self-functioning system, fuelled by the user's input but capable of surpassing him or her in some of its functions. This produces a mode of participation on the part of the viewer: he or she becomes part of the art experiment in the gallery, and the machine is seen not as an object but as a subject like the viewer him- or herself. This also cuts the other way: if the information system is capable of functioning like a human, could a human not be seen as an information system? We will see in the third chapter how this thinking segues into discourses that test the agency of the object, such as object-oriented ontology. Here we will look in detail at the rise of information patterning and the notion of the posthuman, the logical consequence of this man/machine/information elision. At the same time, I also want to complicate the picture that cybernetics is the main mode through which to address early uses of technology. Gender is an important motivation here: one of the goals behind Donna Haraway's figure of the cyborg, for instance, was to navigate between the male-coded domain of technology – cybernetic projects were funded by universities and scientific corporations that were largely staffed by men and oriented to fulfil needs determined by men – and the contrasting cliché of the earth mother, from whose bosom the plentiful milk of procreation descends. Before following Haraway on the cyborgian synthesis of this dialectic, I look at other reactions in the 1960s and 70s to technologies through the work of Martha Rosler and Lee Lozano and their focus on everyday machine items. Their highly gendered universe of technological objects will help set up, in relief, the multiplicitous identities at play in contemporary work responding to digital technologies.

Cybernetics

In a broad sense, cybernetics' ideas of feedback and information patterning provide the basis for information theory, and many of those who worked in the field were later instrumental in developing computer technologies. Crucially, cybernetics also privileges systems and moves away from human subjectivity as the lens through which to see the world – two modes of thinking important to the philosophies of speculative materialism and object-oriented ontology. Throughout the work of Norbert Wiener, the founder of cybernetics, the human emerges as de-essentialised and systems become the reigning heuristic through which to view behaviour.

Cybernetic theory was intended as a universal language that could describe the relations between different actors, doing away with intentionality and thinking instead in terms of what could be predicted from past data and regulated in the future by feedback loops. The term "cybernetics" – from which all future "cyber" prefixes (cyberspace, cybersex, cyberfeminism) are taken – comes from the Greek for "helmsman". It was coined by Wiener, a mathematician at MIT in Cambridge, Massachusetts, to refer to someone who, in order to steer his ship, must both correct the negative consequences of his previous actions – his over-steering of the rudder – and predict the future consequences of his current ones: a metaphor of feedback and control, the two signal elements of the discipline. Wiener's foundational study of the subject, *Cybernetics: Or Control and Communication in the Animal and the Machine* (1948), lays out the potential for the perfection of systems: feedback could be incorporated into the control system of a machine, such that the machine could alter its behaviour in response to changes in the environment and thereby function autonomously and successfully on its own. In this manner, cybernetic systems contained within them the possibility of being scaled upwards to control different contexts, using feedback and communication in areas as varied as traffic flows to the workings of the human brain.

As the historian of science Peter Galison has shown, Wiener's ideas grew out of his work during World War II developing anti-aircraft defences for use by the Allies against German warplanes (Galison 1994). Wiener created an anti-aircraft predictor that would anticipate the enemy pilot's zigzagging flight, in order to locate a future position on the path towards which an anti-aircraft shell could be launched. It was within this endeavour that he elaborated and calibrated the relationship between feedback and systems, particularly negative feedback, and the importance of data. He found that he could not predict pilots' behaviour in general, but he could analyse each individual flight path to provide predictions with reasonable accuracy. The better the individual data for a system, the better was Wiener's mathematical model. In 1941, Wiener enlisted the help of the electrical engineer Julian Bigelow to design the circuits for the machine, though, much to Wiener's disappointment, the statistical analysis offered by their prototype was barely better than that offered by another, simpler one, and his project was abandoned. He wrote ruefully in a letter at the time (1943): "I still wish that I had been able to produce something to kill a few of the enemy instead merely of showing how not to try to kill them" (quoted in Galison 1994, 245).

Galison suggests that Wiener's anti-aircraft predictor was accompanied by a novel theorising of the enemy. Instead of the monstrous, racialised othering seen in the military imaginary, Galison shows that Wiener began to conceive of the enemy as a machine. His was

> a vision in which the enemy pilot was so merged with machinery that (his) human–nonhuman status was blurred. In fighting this cybernetic enemy, Wiener and his team began to conceive of the Allied antiaircraft operators as resembling the foe, and it was a short step from this elision of the human and the nonhuman in the ally to a blurring of the human–machine boundary in general.
>
> (Galison 1994, 233)

The notion of enemy as machine carried over into Wiener's development of cybernetics after the war, when he focused on it less for its practical applications than as a theory of information that could be applied across a number of disciplines. The human being was here thought of not as a psychological or intentional subject but rather a set of behaviours that could be monitored, predicted, and perfected – a black box, whose patterns were solely pertinent. It was behaviourism with a technological inflection.

It is important to remember the atmosphere of intense scientific optimism that followed the war in the US. Wiener's enormous tome of *Cybernetics* was such a popular success that he published a more accessible follow-up just two years later, *The Human Use of Human Beings*. The immense employment and training of engineers and scientists during the war meant there was an audience not only ready to receive his ideas, but who had the expertise to understand them. There was a feeling, with the success of the atom bomb, that science had won the war for the Allies – but also anxiety over mankind's new destructiveness. The perfectibility of society and man offered by cybernetics was a way to kerb this harmful behaviour.

The liberal arts responded to the scientific optimism of the time by trying to systematise the production and reception of meaning as sciences in themselves. This was accomplished chiefly through semiotics, or "the science of signs", which, like cybernetics, was seen as a universal language and was applied equally to art, film, literature, and other creative disciplines. Cybernetics was also taken up by visual art and in an art context has come to refer both to cybernetic theory and to a period of art-making, roughly from the late 1950s to the early 1970s, in which "cybernetic work" explored feedback and information, often, though not exclusively, through the building of new machines that could interact with the viewer via input he or she provided. In the same way that cybernetics segues into information theory, cybernetic art informs a host of subsequent movements, such as media arts, expanded cinema, digital arts, and electronics arts (many of these headings overlap).

Consonant with the idea of cybernetics as a universal language, cybernetics conceived of itself as interdisciplinary. The exhibition "Cybernetic Serendipity", held at the Institute of Contemporary Arts in London in 1968, showed works of kineticism, mobiles, and assorted machines in which input given by the viewer was translated into another medium. An introduction narrated by the show's curator Jasia Reichardt was shown on the BBC2 program "Late Night Line-Up", and in it, Reichardt reflects on how the advent of computers means that people who were previously not considered artists (that is, people who were not involved with creative activities) could now be engaged in the creative field: the engineer who solves a problem "visually", the mathematician who uses his computer to compose music (Reichardt 1968, "Late Night Line-Up"). As Reichardt wrote in the catalogue, "no visitor to the exhibition, unless he reads all the notes relating to all the works, will know whether he is looking at something made by an artist, engineer, mathematician, or architect" (Reichardt 1968, *Cybernetic Serendipity*, 5). These barriers, it was suggested, did not much matter.

Interdisciplinarity also meant cybernetics carried with it a close connection to social praxis, both through the ability to scale cybernetics up towards different systems and in the way that artistic projects resolved themselves. This is important in later theorisations of cybernetics (so-called second- and third-order cybernetics) where the user or the participant was seen as integral to the work.[1] Taken to its furthest extent, this meant the remit of the work was not just a formal proposition but the entire social context it existed within – a categorisation similar to the expansive way art practice is thought of now. The British artist and educator Roy Ascott was key in setting out this social view and in creating projects, long past the heyday of cybernetics proper, that utilised telecommunications technologies to understand social relations as the field of art. In the text "Behaviourist Art and the Cybernetic Vision" (1966–1967), for example, he suggested the political implications of cybernetics' move beyond the autonomous modern art object: feedback allowed "art to switch its role from the private exclusive arena of a rarefied elite to the public, open field of general consciousness" (Ascott 1966–1967, 98). The interactive object would allow for two-way communication that would develop and democratise society.

The clearest expression of a new aesthetics for technological art comes from the writing of Jack Burnham, an *Artforum* critic and lapsed artist. In his writings, as elsewhere, the discourse on cybernetics participates in a weighting that was already sliding towards perceptual and social relations between artists and between art objects and people, which again continues into the twenty-first century in Relational Aesthetics and research-based social projects, among other forms.[2] Burnham was one of the most important and prolific writers on technology and art in the 1960s and '70s, and the curator of the 1970 "Software – Information Technology: Its New Meaning for Art", exhibition at the Jewish Museum in New York. In his book *Beyond Modern Sculpture* and the *Artforum* article "Systems Esthetics" (both 1968), he argued that art has moved beyond Minimalist or specific objects – "craft-fetishism" or formalism – to take in the relation between object and spectator. Drawing on artists such as Hans Haacke, Les Levine, and Dennis Oppenheimer, he showed how the artist initiates the functionings of a system that might or might not be visual in character: "There is no end product that is primarily visual, nor does such an aesthetic rely on a 'visual' syntax. It resists functioning as an applied aesthetic, but is revealed in the principles underlying the progressive reorganisation of the natural environment" (Burnham 1968, "Systems Esthetics", 32). Instead of producing objects, the artist creates an environment, a circuitry of systems. Burnham argues – again, presciently – that the role of the artist has shifted from *Homo Faber* (man as maker

Figure 2.1 Nicholas Negroponte, *SEEK*, 1969–1970, machine, environment, gerbils. Installation view, "Software – Information Technology: Its New Meaning For Art", The Jewish Museum, 1970.

Photo: Harry Shunk and János Kender ©Photo SCALA, Florence, The Jewish Museum 2016.

of tools and objects) to what he called the *Homo Arbiter Formae*, man as maker of aesthetic decisions.

For all its foresight, it cannot be said that Burnham's text is rigourously argued. The text lays out a position, but its reasoning veers from fiat to confusing explanation, and his relation of the emergence of systems aesthetics to the technological character of society is left both enticingly suggested and frustratingly untheorised. (The narrative of art history within *Beyond Modern Sculpture* is likewise problematic and largely over-determined by technology.) Formally, the argument is partially a re-reading of Michael Fried's critique of theatricality, where "theatricality" is replaced by systematicity. Indeed if one thinks of the strange afterlife of Fried's "Art and Objecthood" (1967) essay, where it is regularly cited in order to sympathetically theorise the "theatrical", one can see how perceptive Burnham's move was. But, for all its prescience, the essay has been largely forgotten, and "systems aesthetics" was later disavowed by Burnham himself (Skrebowski 2006). His suggestion at the end of his essay, that "political reality" is not yet for a shift to systems, proved to be correct. Indeed as Conceptualism progressed, the infrastructure of the art world laboured to render any output – rules, words on a wall, puffs of gas – a tradable commodity and specific object. In many ways, we are still in the temporality posed at the end of Burnham's essay: thinking in objects yet living in systems.

Information plasticity

Technological projects of the 1960s deployed feedback to create systems, often initiated or responded to by the viewer. Though cybernetics and Conceptualism overlapped – sharing theoretical bases in the ideas of systems, information, and rules, and, in a US context, logistically through the mediating influence of E.A.T. – they crucially conceived of information differently. (E.A.T., the most famous early technology collective, was co-founded in 1966 by Robert Rauschenberg and the Bell Labs engineer Billy Klüver; it aimed to facilitate collaborations between artists, engineers, and scientists so that artists could learn about and utilise new technologies in their work. It provided means for individuals of the three different professions to network amongst each other and to fundraise for grants in order to use technology for new thinking – whether as art projects or technical experiments – and became the main avenue in the US for engagements between art and technology.) Indeed cybernetics' approach to information plasticity challenges the dematerialisation that is so closely associated with Conceptualism. Information was conceived not only as a semiotic construction but also as sensorially perceived material – haptic and aural registers were as important as the visual and Conceptual. One of E.A.T.'s most ambitious projects, for example, was the Pepsi-Cola Pavilion at Expo '70 in Osaka. The work took the form of a cloud that would react both to visitors and to its own features: an embodiment of a living, responsive environment, devised by the Japanese artist Fujiko Nakaya in collaboration with the physicist Tom Mee. The pavilion itself, which housed the cloud, was a 50-meter diameter geodesic dome that one entered through a tunnel. Once inside, one was given a handset that picked up audio signals from stations positioned throughout the site, while features of the environment sought to alter visual perception. As the art historian María Fernández writes,

> Listening to the sounds of running and gurgling water, the visitor walked to a dark interior referred to as the clam room, where she or he was showered with coloured laser lights. Stairs connected this level with the dome room above, where a hemispherical mirror designed by Robert Whitman and measuring 90 feet in diameter delimited the contours of the space. Here, as is characteristic of spherical mirrors, the mirror produced a three-dimensional inverted image. This inverted image multiplied as the spectator stepped towards the centre of the room, producing the impression of multiple holograms shifting in appearance depending on his or her position in the room.
> (Fernández 2006, 566)

The experimental composer David Tudor provided the sounds: "ducks, turkey gobbling, birds, aviary, frogs, cicadas, lion roaring" (E.A.T. quoted in Fernández

Figure 2.2 E.A.T.'s Pepsi Pavilion at Expo '70, Osaka, Japan, 1970.

Photo: Harry Shunk and János Kender (Shunk-Kender) © J. Paul Getty Trust. Getty Research Institute, Los Angeles

2006, 567). The movement of the visitor through the site triggered not only the aural effects but also the visual effects of light, which in turn affected the fog sculpture that provided the immediate environment.[3] Feedback loops were central to the work and ambitiously conceived – and both performed and visualised in rich terms, going past a simple visualisation of information to try and access the tactile and sensorial feel of nature itself.

The extensiveness (and expense) of the Osaka Expo's visuality and aurality lay outside the capacity of most E.A.T. experiments, but its focus on sensory percepts was not. In looking to materialise invisible flows of energy or information, cybernetic works had what might be called a translational impulse, converting matter from one invisible state into another, sensible one and aiming to make the different constituents of a scientific or electronic process legible. This is information plasticity in a literal form. A prize-winner at E.A.T.'s exhibition "Some M Beginnings" (1968), at the Bronx Museum, was the sculpture *Heart Beats Dust* (1968), made by the artist Jean Dupuy in collaboration with the engineers Harris Hyman and Ralph Martel. The work shows red dust lying on a stretched rubber membrane that is enclosed in a cube, one side of which is encased in glass. Illuminated by light from above, the dust – the material Lithol Rubine, a pigment chosen for its ability to remain suspended in air for long periods – was activated by acoustic vibrations produced by the rhythm of heart beats provided by an acoustic machine. The vitrine where this experiment takes place is shown within a vertical wooden structure, on whose bottom shelf the machine is visible. Rather than overwhelming the viewer in the trick of the illumination of the invisible, *Heart Beats Dust* lays out its constituent elements so that it is clear how the translation is accomplished. Haacke's visually lyrical *Blue Sail* (1964–1965), in which a blue cloth floats above a whirring fan, is another example: the sail is activated by the upward air current, produced by a small machine on the floor – which is both audibly and visibly present. The disjunction in *Blue Sail* between the soaring visual and metaphoric elements (the simultaneous evocation of water and boat, the harnessing of immateriality, the sail's rich, almost Klein-blue colour) versus the prosaicness of the motor labouring on the floor is striking: it elicits pathos as well as representing beauty.

It must be said, though, that cybernetic experiments could be clunky and overly focused on technology. (This is largely how they have come to be read.) Despite Ascott's understanding of the social possibilities for cybernetic systems, many works took a narrow view of the relationship between technology and the social, and there was scant criticism of the way that technological possibilities controlled the type of activity. The project *Composer* (1970), by Allen Razdow and Paul Conly as part of Art & Technology, Boston, shown in "Software" at the Jewish Museum, for example, allowed participants to contribute to a score being generated by a "music composition system" of a digital computer. Visitors could sit in one of four seats in the gallery space and effect changes to the composition by changing the probability that an event would happen. As the blurb in the exhibition catalogue explains, one such change could be "a note will sound on the first beat of a measure – 80% probability" (*Software* 1968, 38). One could

Figure 2.3 E.A.T. exhibition opening, "Some More Beginnings: Experiments in Art and Technology," 1968.

Photo: Harry Shunk and János Kender (Shunk-Kender) © J. Paul Getty Trust. Getty Research Institute, Los Angeles

make a nice reading of this work in terms of the interest in music and chance that was also in the air at the time – in the work of John Cage, most obviously, as well as Rauschenberg – but for me the work, like much else in the exhibition and other mechanical experiments of the time, is over-determined by the role of the computer. What the computer can do is privileged over philosophical or musical notions of noise and pattern, as the key moment of the work is the interactivity enabled between machine and user. Engagement with the viewer becomes increasingly important within contemporary art in that very time frame, but works that relied on computers or machines to create this interactivity sidestepped the important affective and social parameters that determined participation in the Happenings and Fluxus experiments.

Nouvelle Tendance

The visual register was of key importance to the artistic groups allied in Europe under the heading of Nouvelle Tendance, who were among the first to utilise machines as elements of artistic practice. In the 1950s and '60s, a number of groups dedicated to visual research formed in Europe, growing out of concrete and constructivist movements, such as EXAT 51 in Croatia, Gruppo T and Gruppo N in Italy, Equipo 57 in Spain, Nul in the Netherlands, and Zero in Germany. GRAV (Groupe de Recherche d'Art Visuel) was founded in Paris by a number of artists from Argentina, a country that has a strong history of experiments with kineticism and later cybernetics. They were brought together in a loose network in "Nouvelle Tendance, recherche continuelle" ("new tendency, continuous research", now often translated as "New Tendencies" in English), a series of six exhibitions from 1961 to 1973 held at the Gallery of Contemporary Art (today the Museum of Contemporary Art) in Zagreb. Colloquia and publications accompanied the exhibitions, in both Croatian and English, and the works exhibited ranged from kinetic and Op art experiments, often using new materials such as plastics, aluminium, and mirrors, to more direct experiments with mechanistic systems. The writings offered theorisations of art and technology. The 1968 iteration, for example, laid out the theory of a "secret" revolution of automation and artificial thought (Moles 1968) and declared the computer the medium of avant-garde expression.[4] Broadly speaking the groups were interested in scientific technologies as a means of continuing the modernist aesthetic project, particularly in their prescription for visual synthesis.[5] Technology allowed them to create one unified plane of visual expression, bringing optical phenomena, light, and movement under their tools of expression and erasing the categorical distinctions among them, and the works often

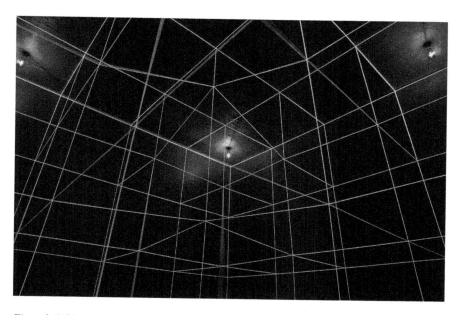

Figure 2.4 Gianni Colombo, *Spazio Elastico* (*Elastic Space*), 1966. Installation view, "Ghosts in the Machine", New Museum, New York, 2012.

Photo: Benoit Pailley. Courtesy New Museum, New York

resolved themselves in operatic forms. Take, for example, the room environment *Spazio Elastico* (*Elastic Space*, 1966–1967), by the Italian artist Gianni Colombo, in which fluorescent elastic string was stretched across a darkened room and illuminated by black lights. The installation has the effect of being both mapped and disoriented in space: an overwhelming and awe-inspiring impact on the viewer.

"Technology" as it developed as a concept within Nouvelle Tendance comprised not only the groups' output but also their mode of production, which mimicked the research teams of experiments[6] – a privileging of collaboration also reflected in other agencies set up in the 1960s that facilitated collaboration between art and technology, such as E.A.T. and Centro de Arte y Comunicación (CAYC) in Buenos Aires (founded 1968). In 1962, for example, in an essay for an exhibition of Gruppo T and Gruppo N in Milan, Umberto Eco noted that "the very nature of the 'research', their aesthetic (or non-aesthetic), and their principle of self-effacement preclude individual expression and display of talent. Personal style, preference, and bias are eliminated. This brings their cooperation close to the anonymous teamwork of scientists" (Eco 1962a). Eco was a profound influence on Nouvelle Tendance, and the groups claimed his idea of the "open work" for technological art. Artwork using machines or computers followed the open work in its course of fluctuating but delimited possibilities. As Eco wrote, in his 1962 book, "The kind of expectation aroused by a message with an open structure is less a *prediction of the expected* than an *expectation of the unpredictable*" (Eco 1962b, 80). (We can see here a crucial distance from Wiener's project: a path not taken for cybernetics.) The idea that the open work was the characteristic work of its time – a feeling of standing with novelty that recalls the privileging of the new inherent in the modernist project – normalised the apparent discontinuity between work of Nouvelle Tendance and Conceptual projects and their conventional predecessors of "traditional" art, allowing the participants to see machine art, though radically different formally, as set within a larger understanding of aesthetics.

Historical context

How much Nouvelle Tendance and US/UK cybernetic work inform the "mainstream" of post-World War II art is debatable. The important historical crossovers between technological artists and those working in Conceptual, Pop, or performative idioms is underplayed by the sequestration of these disciplines into electric and non-electric paths – which also overrides regional differences. In Argentina, for example, artwork of 1960s and '70s freely mixed Happenings, electronic art, and Pop idioms (Spencer 2015). The installation *La Menesunda* (*The Mayhem*, 1965), by Marta Minujín and Rubén Santantonín,[7] became a watershed event in Argentina art circles, mixing new technologies, performative elements, and interaction with the viewers. The work comprised sixteen rooms full of different sensory materials, from a tangled maze of coloured neon lights to a giant dial of numbers (visitors had to dial the correct number to exit the installation). One room had an enormous rotating basket affixed to the ceiling, another a bed with a couple in it, and in another, one could have a beauty session and massage. The work was an "INTENSIFYING EXPERIENCE", as the poster proclaimed, whose different "situations" not only challenged the viewer sensorially but also in his or her sense of propriety in its often awkward and embarrassing situations.

Work in Europe and the US crossed over less with Happenings, and cybernetic experiments were more commonly exhibited alongside Conceptualism, subtended by their shared interest in information.[8] Despite this early curatorial overlap, it is important to note that cybernetics and Conceptualism were distinguished from each other at the time and grew increasingly so as the 1960s drew on. Burnham's rather bitter summation of LACMA's "Art and Technology", which he reviewed for *Artforum*, is revealing about how much far we can push interpretations of Conceptualism's cybernetic concerns:

> In retrospect one could divide the artists participating into three categories: the techno-artists such as Robert Whitman, Rockne Krebs, Newton Harrison, and Boyd Mefferd who were aesthetically allied with the light and kinetic movement; New York 'name' artists such as Claes Oldenburg, Roy Lichtenstein, Richard Serra, Tony Smith, Andy Warhol, and Robert Rauschenberg who were only tangentially connected with art and technology; and finally the oddballs such as James Lee Byars, Ron Kitaj, and Oyvind Falstrom [*sic*] who provided the show's element of serendipity. The 'name' artists tended to do enlarged or elaborate variations of their standard work or to cynically build into their projects hints about the utter futility of technology as a humanistic endeavour.
>
> (Burnham 1980)

Cybernetic artists and "mainstream" Conceptual artists split during the early 1970s. The reasons for this fallout are many, but one is the basic logistical failure of many of the technological projects. The gerbils in Nicholas Negroponte's self-regulating system exhibited in Burnham's "Software", for example, all ate each other. E.A.T.'s "Nine Evenings: Theater and Engineering" (1966), a performance series held at the Armory in New York, fared no better. Writing about it for the *New York Times*, Grace Glueck wrote that it "clanked to an end at the 69th Regiment Armory last Sunday, and there was fallout all over town. 'Boring', 'feeble', 'dull', 'vilely done,' was the opinion of reviewers" (Glueck 1966, D28). The Pepsi-Cola pavilion, of 1970, was luscious in principle and shambolic in practice. There were language difficulties building the structure, Pepsi-Cola intervened at the last minute with a request for their sign to hang over the building, the operating budget went over expectations, and attendance figures suggested that the local audience simply didn't like the structure. Pepsi-Cola pulled its funding from the project just over a month after it opened, and the pavilion proved one of E.A.T.'s last serious projects.[9]

The scientific optimism and spirit of collaboration that surrounded E.A.T. also fell into decline as artists and critics grew sceptical of collaborations with corporations, who funded many of the projects. The "Art and Technology" project at LACMA was the subject of an astonishing screed published in *Artforum*, "The Million–Dollar Art Boondoggle", in which the art historian Max Kozloff alleged the entire project had been a front by the military-industrial complex.[10] The association between cybernetics and the military grew as the military used theories of systems and feedback to create the first system of email exchange, ARPANET, in 1969, and became more acute with the deep unpopularity of the Vietnam War.

It is also worth noting, particularly in regards to Burnham's insights of systems aesthetics, that the technological imaginary of the time cannot be easily mapped on to today's. Later cybernetic projects in the 1970s and '80s addressed networks more specifically – the newfound ability to hook up with others telematically and remotely. But they did not foresee virality: the ability of an image or thought to travel autonomously as content beyond its creator – the email forward function or Twitter's retweet. The concept of feedback, so central to early cybernetic experiments as well as to Conceptual art, is of feedback contained within the system. One of the ironies of the brilliant "Open Systems: Rethinking Art c.1970" (2005) conference, convened at Tate Modern on the occasion of Donna DeSalvo's show of the same name, was that most Conceptual art systems were in effect closed systems, a fact demonstrated by Haacke's condensation cube, which became a leitmotif of the discussions. Indeed Luke Skrebowski, in a paper given at that event, characterised Burnham's "Systems Aesthetics" as standing at a midway point on the transition from "autonomous, closed systems to relational, open systems" (Skrebowski 2006), which were still yet to come.

As cybernetics and electronic art advance, participatory, open-ended systems became increasingly important – almost pushing against the boundaries of what was technologically possible and already anticipating net.art's disjunction between the internet project fully conceived and its gallery exhibition. One well-known example of later cybernetics is Ascott's lyrical *La Plissure du Texte: A Planetary Fairy Tale* (1983), produced for Frank Popper's important exhibition of technological art, "Electra" in Paris.[11] It took the form of an electronic exquisite corpse, in which fourteen different people from around the world added to a shared history, using the IP Sharp computer network and logging in from each of their consoles. Each was ascribed a fairy-tale character. Ascott played the part of the magician and would begin the story with "Once upon a time"; other nodes would contribute to the narrative that evolved online (Ascott 2003, 261). Two years later, Ascott used the Minitel, the French proto-World Wide Web public network of computers, to create a more open-ended version, drawing on the French translation of *Alice in Wonderland* and the scientific treatise *Organe et fonction*, for Lyotard's "Immaterieux" exhibition.[12] The work, *Organe et Fonction d'Alice aux Pays des Merveilles* "existed not in the building as such, but throughout the data space of the Minitel network" (Ascott 2003, 262).

Other artists followed cybernetic concerns away from art itself. Television's potential for invoking and detourning a public became a main focus of technological artists in the 1970s, via decentralised or "guerrilla" television. On the West Coast of the US, in what would become Silicon Valley, technological projects became allied with counterculture and hippie communes. Steve Jobs, of Apple, recalled reading the *Whole Earth Catalog*, the quasi-environmentalist, quasi-computer geek, quasi-cybernetic magazine, that showed how to use technological know-how to fashion better communities and stabilise ecologies (Jobs 2005). The New York-based magazine *Radical Software*, founded in 1968, argued for the political use of video and computer technologies in their capacity for grassroots organisation and mass communication channels. *Radical Software* was published by the Raindance Foundation, an organisation influenced by Marshall McLuhan's analysis that electronic media's supplanting of the medium of print held utopian consequences: readers would cease to be passive consumers of information but could talk back and to each other. This facet had been theorised by Bertolt Brecht, in his idea of the two-way radio from "The Radio as an Apparatus of Communication" (1932). In this early text, which remains a touchstone for emancipatory uses of technological communications, Brecht noted how the decision for radio to be a one-way broadcast – from the broadcaster to the listener and not one allowing the listener to broadcast back – was not taken for reasons of what was technologically possible but because of business concerns.

Raindance itself was one of a number of video art initiatives of the 1970s and '80s that sought to use technology to create an alternative to mainstream media communication and to enable the public to speak back – organising ways for the public to create their own videos or creating activist programs for cable TV. Here, too, the content that was broadcast across the airwaves was seen by consumers, but could not be forwarded on. Again this means that "communications" as figured by cybernetic and radical video art was information traded among two groups of people: a tennis ball lobbed back and forth between producers, who could become consumers, and consumers, who could become producers. It thus followed a model of physical communication rather than one of publication, despite the fact that McLuhan's *Understanding Media* placed new media as within a genealogy of publishing (culture had moved from orality to hand-written manuscripts to print and finally to new media).

The word "meme" did not appear till 1976, coined by the biologist Richard Dawkins in his first book, *The Selfish Gene*. Dawkins delineated the process of the meme as one of imitation (again, rather than the model of an email forward): "Memes propagate themselves in the meme pool by leaping from brain to brain via process which, in the broad sense, can be called imitation" (Dawkins quoted in Gleick 2012, 312). He included as examples ideas, tunes, catchphrases, and images. But the sense of sending an image intact – the thing itself – is absent from this early conception. If we think back to the spirit of Appropriation by the New York artists, who were starting to turn appropriation into both strategy and subject at this time, one can see the radicality of their gesture, which sought not imitate an image but to detourne the image itself to give it new meaning and potentially send it forward on a new path of use – a valence missing from telecommunications projects.

Gender and the post-war body

Thinking through artistic engagement with technology simply through cybernetics or electronic art also risks missing the various ways that non-Conceptual and non-media artists of the 1960s addressed the increasing presence of automation in society. In many ways, these non-direct explorations are more illuminating about a world that was beginning to be changed by electronic technology and foreshadow the way that technology is addressed by post-internet artists – that is, as an everyday object. Pop's ironic celebration of mass-marketed objects explored the changes they effected on domesticity and on what is now theorised as affect. Warhol's Brillo boxes (1964) and screenprint technique, for example, thematise the processes of automation that were able to produce factory-made, mass commodities of identical aspect and perfection. Richard Hamilton's collage *Just What Is It That Makes Today's Homes So Different, So Appealing* (1956) shows a domestic scene littered with new technologies: the biomorphic vacuum cleaner with its extra-long nozzle reaching up the stairs (and the suggestive text that describes it: "ordinary cleaners only reach this far"); the television in front of the coffee table, showing a woman on the phone; the audio-recorder inexplicably sitting open in front of the muscle-man's feet. The background outside the window shows a cinema, while the comic-book raster print on the wall points to another machine-reproduced cultural form. Technology's items of time-saving and desirous consumption are what makes today's homes so different, so appealing.

These new machines – automated washing machines, electric irons, refrigerators, vacuum cleaners, toasters (all of which became mass consumer items in the 1930s) – coincided with other societal shifts by the 1960s to vastly reorganise the structures of family life. They helped accelerate, for example, the decline in the twentieth century of domestic service, which was not only the preserve of the upper classes but of the middle classes as well, allowing the nuclear family to emerge in its dominant form in the West.[13] The architecture of life shifted. The maids' rooms in pre-World War II New York City apartments became repurposed as children's bedrooms. The women who would have been in service – 1.25 million women in the UK in 1901 – looked for jobs elsewhere. Their education levels rose. And for working-class and middle-class women alike, time-saving devices helped birth the modern concept of the housewife, whose freed-up time would be repurposed as homemaking rather than housekeeping. In the popular and cultural imaginary, the depiction of household technology became synonymous with this new role – and with its boredom and confinement. This is a subject often chronicled by Martha Rosler's Pop-inspired photomontages, in which technological objects demonstrate a reinforcement of gender roles and their appropriate forms of labour. Like Hamilton's conflation of modernity and machines, domestic appliances were read both as icons of the "new" and as cementing the particularly oppressive gender roles of the post-World War II era.

We can focus on one appliance in particular to think through how technology was figured in feminist representations of the home: the vacuum cleaner, a kind of bachelorette machine. Hamilton's long-hosed vacuum cleaner reappears in Rosler's photomontage *Vacuuming Pop Art* (1967–1972), a playful skewering of the identity between Pop art and the consumer culture it apparently critiqued. Here it is held in the manicured hand of a well-coiffed housewife, who stands in a corridor lined with Pop artworks: the woman is the worker, as well as the portrayed. The technological object is figured as something at once gendered and important: an item in which power and sexuality reinforce one another. Rosler's vacuum hose snakes around the female figure, encircling her even as she cheerfully grasps the phallic object in her hand. The montage clearly parodies advertising's evocation of desire to sell household objects but also depicts the vacuum cleaner as an object with agency in itself. In the strange composition of the painting, with its narrow field of vision and lowered ceiling,[14] the woman shares the floor with the vacuum cleaner; indeed she is placed slightly to the left so that the mechanism can occupy the middle of the composition.

The metallic object, polished to a sheen, recalls the technophilic representations of new technologies and commodity objects of early photography, which elevated consumer objects to the obsessive, over-aestheticised treatment befitting the commodity fetish. This fetishistic aspect of household goods is made even more explicit in Rosler's series *House Beautiful: Bringing the War Home* (1967–1972), in which she collaged images from the Vietnam War – US soldiers,

Figure 2.5 Martha Rosler, *Cleaning the Drapes*, 1967–1972, photomontage, from the series *House Beautiful: Bringing the War Back Home.*

Courtesy the artist and Mitchell-Innes & Nash, New York

Playboy models, Vietnamese injured and dead – into scenes of the placid domesticity (of women working) that was occurring "home" in the US. The montage *Cleaning the Drapes* (1967–1972), part of that series, shows a woman vacuuming the curtains. Framed by the curtains is a scene of two helmeted soldiers in a sandbagged trench. The woman stands on the edge of the montage, while her right hand and the nozzle of the vacuum cleaner inch closer to the centre of the frame, which is dominated by the image from Vietnam. The curtains on her side billow towards her, as if being pulled back by the vacuum cleaner to reveal the image of warfare heretofore concealed. The image of the soldiers and that of the woman are both in black–and–white, as opposed to the cream colour of the damask curtains, suggesting that, without her knowledge, the vacuum cleaner works to pull the woman out of her state of domestic ignorance and towards a revelation of her contiguity and implication in the country's war, to which her eyes already point in anticipation. The machine is a bridge between two uniformly gendered worlds.

In his perceptive observations on Duchamp's *Fountain* (1917), to bring up another iconic Duchamp work, Calvin Tomkins notes how the readymade displays female characteristics in both its appearance and function: "an object with female attributes that serves as a receptacle for male fluid" (Tomkins 1996, 186). While Tomkins reads this as part of Duchamp's erotic comedy, the set of concerns around the vacuum cleaner skews more threatening. The vacuum cleaner contains entangled male and female signifiers: the phallic hose that sucks up rather than shooting forth; the receptacle of the cleaner body versus the masculine rhetoric of the "powerful" motor. In *Cleaning the Drapes*, the vacuum cleaner closes the gap between the domestic scene of the woman cleaning and the male site of military engagement. Elsewhere, the vacuum cleaner emerges almost as a fiend, a device intended for female convenience that ends up imperilling female subjectivity, in a clear metaphor for the constriction of women's traditional role of labour in the home. In the Catalan Pop artist Eulàlia Grau's composition, *Aspiradora (Etnografia)* (*Vacuum Cleaner [Ethnography]*), a 1973 painting on photography, a bride-like doll lies supine on the floor as the carpet nozzle of a vacuum cleaner hovers over her, already catching the sleeve of her wedding dress in its filter. Its appearance signals woman's upwardly mobile aspirations as well as the caging of the bird – a depiction, that is, that suggests female complicity.

Beyond Pop art, we can see a sexualisation of appliances elsewhere in the 1960s. In the early work of Lee Lozano, for example, comic book-like drawings show toasters, refrigerators, and, yes, vacuum cleaners as sexualised objects. The graphite drawing *Untitled [trumpet penis]* (c.1960s) shows a penis that has seemingly been wedged throughout a trumpet, which a hand grips as if to play. Another drawing, c.1962, shows a vacuum cleaner in three separate parts, the motor, the tube, and the nozzle, the last of which resembles an end of the male member adorned with bristle-like pubic hair. Lozano's carefully drawn text above it reads, "ron k. masturbated with a vacuum cleaner but his cock got too big", comically suggesting the vacuum cleaner as a site of castration, ironically achieved through misplaced desire. Here the merging of the machine and the female sex is taken too far, especially for poor "ron k". The scholar Helena Vilalta notes how Lozano's later work also attests to a "similar epochal fascination with scientific advancements while rebuffing technophilia" (Vilalta 2016, pers. comm.).[15] Lozano's show "Infofiction" (1971), at the Nova Scotia College of Art & Design in Halifax, brought together instructional pieces that dictated how the artist was to lead her life during a specific period of time and noted its effects on her body and behaviour. "If Lozano's paintings from the early 60s", Vilalta writes, "were erotic renderings of the conflation of man and machine, her text works document the process by which she became the very subject of a cybernetic experimentation, testing the increasingly porous boundaries between self and environment". The title itself challenges the idea of pure factual information, hinting at the challenges posed by self-reflexivity within second-order cybernetics.

The vacuum cleaner also demonstrates a connection to the abject in terms of its being a receptacle for waste and dust, as well as in terms of female reproduction. Vacuum suction is a method used for abortion, as well as for emptying the uterus after a miscarriage. It is also, under the name of ventouse, a common means for assisting the delivery of a baby during a difficult labour. If the rotund stomach of the 1960s vacuum cleaners pictured in Hamilton's and Rosler's Pop photomontages suggests a pregnant belly, the suction of the nozzle evokes the opposite: the termination of one (messy) cycle of reproductive labour. The sphere of medicine is an important site of technology, particularly for women in pregnancy and labour and those coping with long-term illness, though medical technologies are a notably minor subject in post-internet art. Rosler's photomontage *Bicillin or Medical Treatment II* (1966) clearly shows the gender dynamics that can be taken as typical of the medical imaginary of the 1960s: a nude woman lying on an examining table who is about to be probed by a phallic medical implement. Rather than a passive subject, however, the image of the woman is clearly pornographic; her head is turned to the camera, meeting the eyes of the doctor, whose canister of Bicillin hovers over her crotch.[16]

The medical, the abject, and this gendered reading, by contrast, are subjects missing in much of post-internet art, particularly post-internet's glossy variant, and I am using this rather counterfactual approach to suggest the enormity of the art-historical shift in post-internet's rendering of technological items: a shift intimately tied to Wiener's "blurring of the human-machine boundary". Within post-internet work, the figuration of everyday technological objects, which mainly takes the form of computers and iPhones, sheds overt signifiers of gender identity. Coming on the back of Pop art, feminist critique, and advertising norms, for example, it is rather significant that Mark Leckey can make a whole work about refrigerators (*GreenScreenRefrigeratorAction*, 2010) without feeling compelled to address, in his performance-lecture, any questions of gender roles or domestic labour. While the body is not an absent subject within post-internet art, the representation of the technological item itself trades gendered characteristics for de-gendered ones; its frame of reference is the cyborg rather than the tangled web of power, penetration, and spheres of influence through which the 1960s saw everyday technological items.

Post-internet work often presents, indeed, sexuality without the abject: a world of online porn, of visual rather than tactile contact, where focus lies on the information that circulates through the network rather than the technological objects (the hardware) itself. The overlap between man and machine suggests an eroticism that is wiped clean and sanitised. Where Lozano's drawings are amateur, with obvious brushwork and clear erotic content, the body in post-internet art replaces markers of human labour and signs of bodily desire in favour of the hygienic, aestheticised visions of stock photography. Cécile B. Evans, for example, exhibited 3D printed sculptures of rows of teeth, each one a perfect model of a perfect tooth, in *Lost, Teeth* (2014). Blood was represented on some of them, in clean, red lines, as if painted in Photoshop. The digital video *My Best Thing* (2011) by Frances Stark is a narrative of sexual intimacy in which Stark and two male partners are represented by blocky avatars against a green screen: a supremely unsexy video despite the frank sex chat. Juliana Huxtable, a transgender artist, frequently evokes a cyborg as a mode of self-representation – glossed to a sheen, and made to be looked at.

It is tempting to read these iterations of female bodies as anti-feminist: deliberately obliterating the abject functions of bodies that feminists laboured to bring under the aegis of proper philosophy. Indeed the degree to which we can consider technological advances as feminist is a frequent area of debate, particularly in regards to Donna Haraway's influential figure of the cyborg.[17] As Judy Wajcman details in the survey *Technofeminism*, the reception of technology ranges from (as her introduction is titled) "feminist utopia to dystopia". On the one hand, the social changes associated with technology are a boon to women: more flexible working hours; greater control over reproduction; the ascendency of a knowledge economy which benefits women's lighter frames; service work that, she writes, privileges communication and social skills; and the internet's enabling of de-gendered identities to emerge online. Most importantly, she notes, the challenge to the autonomous humanist subject by new technologies, particularly the man/machine figure of the cyborg, is such a threat to traditional hierarchies that it cannot but help the position of women.

On the other hand, the move to more flexible working times means everyone works more, rather than less, eating into the time for caring (for children and older parents) that is still largely the area of women; increases in biotechnology mean further control over women; and science and technology are seen as male preserves that are created and developed by men (witness the tiny percentage of women in computer science and technology research fields) and thus can be understood to serve male rather female needs. This is so both because of the intrinsic purposing of the technology – what goals are set and aimed for – but also in the marketing and consumption apparatus that is constructed around each product. Wajcman shows how the microwave, for example, was originally billed as a "brown good", intended for use by busy bachelors who couldn't be bothered (or know how) to cook. It was offered for sale in department stores alongside radios and televisions goods in the entertainment section – other items portrayed as clever, complex technologies that require skill to operate, in contrast to the user-friendly, easy to operate white goods such as washing machines and refrigerators that are marketed towards women. But the microwave ended up being bought by (presumably even busier) mothers who needed to reheat food quickly and literally shifted place from the "leisure" to the "kitchen" section (Wajcman 2004, 37). Technology remains gendered male, and the ascendancy of technology, technosceptics aver, is further means of control over women.

Wajcman posits "technofeminism" as a mediation through these two poles, one in which thoughts on technology and feminism evolve throughout engagement with one another. Wajcman's is not the only use of technology to think through gender binaries: the most famous is the cyborg as popularised by the philosopher of science Haraway, in which Weiner's man/machine hybrid becomes a response to gender and racial concerns. Haraway uses cybernetics to navigate between the stark male/female split between the machine and the artificial-technological imaginary, on the one hand, and Mother Earth and nature on the other. For Haraway, the notion of the posthuman offers a means to imagine a post-gender world.

Haraway theorised her figure in "A Cyborg Manifesto: Science, Technology, and Socialist-Feminism in the Late Twentieth Century" of 1985. Written in a manifesto's urgent tone, she heralds the cyborg, the hybrid that offers a third way in between fixed gender positions: a myth that responds to the "leaky" boundary between animal and man, man and woman, and to wholesale changes in the new information age (Haraway 1985/1991, 152).

> I argue for a politic rooted in claims about fundamental changes in the nature of class, race and gender in an emerging system of world order analogous in its novelty and scope to that created by industrial capitalism; we are living through a movement from an organic, industrial society to a polymorphous, information system – from all work to all play, a deadly game.
>
> (Haraway 1985/1991, 161)

For Haraway, the intelligent mechanisation of industry creates a feminisation and a deskilling of what was once the province of men, dialectically and subversively reordering a host of polarities: cyborg labour replaces human labour; reproductive labour becomes replication and regeneration; the "technological polis" folds the public into the private, with the *oikos* – the Greek term for the household – becoming a site of a revolution of social relations (Haraway 1985/1991, 151). Much of the "Manifesto" is prescient (as is, in fact, so much early writing on technology), but what is most notable about Haraway's insights is her act of reclamation: Haraway claims the Frankenstein-like figure – a longstanding source of anxiety – as a knowing, dissident third way out of gender oppression. Her analysis of deskilling, something that has been treated in more mournful tones of mass lay-offs for industrial workers by artists such as Harun Farocki (as in the video *Workers Leaving the Factory*, 1995), is that of proof of a challenge to gender identity. The loss of integral boundaries between man and animal, or man and machine, again typical sources of fear, becomes a celebration of polymorphous identity, no longer bound by demeaning history (nor entirely forgetting it): "The cyborg is resolution committed to partiality, irony, intimacy, and perversity. It is oppositional, utopian, and completely without innocence" (Haraway 1985/1991, 151). Haraway trained as a historian of science and came to the notion of the cyborg via her studies in primatology, in which she critiqued science's ostensible objectivity as a pale cypher for masculine readings. The cyborg's lack of innocence figures as canny recognition of what history works to suppress. And illegitimate children, as she notes, are disloyal to their origins.

The posthuman

In its imbrication of man/machine, the cyborg is one of a number of figures of the posthuman within the cultural imaginary. It is certainly the best known, not only for net.art and cyberfeminist practice in the 1990s but also for post-internet artists, and little has since matched its tone of creative optimism. It is important to distinguish, however, Haraway's cyborg from the notion of the posthuman more generally. In the final section of this chapter, I want to return to cybernetics to look at its two major and lasting developments: the theory of information as immaterial and the theory of the posthuman.

In her study *How We Became Posthuman* (1999), N. Katherine Hayles analyses the theoretical moves that took place within cultural and philosophical thought in order that the concept of the posthuman could emerge: a series of abstractions in which the actual facts on the ground were blurred in order to fit into an over-arching theory. (This notably parallels the dynamics Horkheimer and Adorno identify in *Negative Dialectics*.) Hayles dates the conception of the "world as an interplay between informational patterns and material objects" to the wake of World War II, specifically in cybernetics, and culminating in the field of virtuality. Crucial to her insights is the conception of information as immaterial patterns, a facet of cybernetics that has proved influential beyond measure. As Hayles writes, "criminals are tied to crime scenes through DNA patterns rather than through eyewitness accounts verifying their presence; access to computer networks rather than physical possession of data determines nine-tenths of computer law" (Hayles 1999, 27–28). Walking is the quantification of steps taken; cash in hand becomes graphs on a screen.

Hayles reads the emergence of information via Claude Shannon, a mathematician at Bell Laboratories, in New Jersey, that was an important site of research and development for early computing technologies (and which also hosted artistic residencies in the 1960s). Shannon's theory of information, developed in the late 1940s, was designed to allow information to remain stable as it passed through different machines and systems. Shannon, Hayles demonstrates, reduced information to a set of probability choices (yes or no, zero or one) that would unfold into actual meaning once they reached their new context. The theory proposed information not as a material but as a pattern, which achieved material form only when embedded for transmission in a medium. Information, that is, became a way of communicating meaning rather than meaning itself (Hayles 1999, 50–57), and it could be received as input by humans and machines alike.

Part of Hayles's strategy in *How We Became Posthuman* is to show how many of the theories generated by computer scientists, as contingent responses to different challenges, were later turned around and taken as immutable laws. Thus, for example, if both humans and robots can interpret the messages given by information patterns, it must follow that there is little material difference between humans and robots. The human body becomes conceptualised not as a body but as a means to receive and react to information. It is, effectively, demoted: "embodiment in a biological substrate is seen as an accident of history rather than an inevitability of life". She continues, "In the posthuman, there are no essential differences or absolute demarcations between bodily existence and computer simulation, cybernetic mechanism and biological organism, robot teleology and human goals" (Hayles 1999, 2–3).

Hayles's discussion of embodiment derives from a critique of Western philosophy's privileging of the mind (coded male) over matter (coded female). This problematic is based in the mind/body split of the Cartesian tradition, which theorises the two as apart rather than enmeshed, with the body as the mere container that houses the mind (Grosz 1994). The omnipotence of the mind in the posthuman thus exacerbates the historical philosophical tendency to de-privilege the body as a theoretical subject. The absence of a proper theorisation of the body is also the territory addressed by corporeal feminism, a discourse that developed in the 1990s (and of which *How We Became Posthuman* is an integral text). Corporeal feminism aims to provide a new construction of the body that takes into account its agency and importance in shaping perception and thought – it seeks, quite basically, to overturn the mind/matter split and to show the categories as mutually imbricated. It challenges, for example, the conception of the body as an appendage to the mind, which shadows the thinking of the female as an appendage to the male. Elizabeth Grosz demonstrates, in her study *Volatile Bodies* (1994), for example, not only the symbiotic functioning of mind and body but also cases of their misaligning, such as in cases of anorexia or phantom limbs. By suggesting a "body image" that coordinates the relation between body and mind, she replaces the gendered Cartesian dualism with a notion of the body that reflects a complex site of engagement.

Hayles draws on *Volatile Bodies* to show how the doctrines leading to the posthuman figure the body as a normalised or even Platonic form rather than a site of sexual, racial, and anatomical difference. Dematerialisation, Hayles writes, emerges as an ideology, buttressed by a specific cultural construct of what a "body" is (Hayles 1999, 193). She presents, in response, a specific reading of embodiment, in which bodily form is related to its instantiation: "In contrast to the body, embodiment is contextual, enmeshed within the specifics of place, time, physiology, and culture, which together compose enactment" (Hayles 1999, 196). Knowledge is reconfigured not as simply a province of the mind but as an "epiphenomenon corresponding to the phenomenal base the body provides" (Hayles 1999, 203).

The fact that the doctrines of immateriality and of the posthuman get at the heart of Cartesian dualism provides one clue as to why the illusion of immateriality proves so tenacious, despite being so often debunked, as we shall see in the next chapter. The discourse of presence and absence is connected not only to the foundations of the modern Western cultural tradition but also to the constitution of the liberal humanist subject. Cybernetics imperils this subject with its substitution of chance and feedback-derived intelligence over autonomous thinking (or over the idea of an omnipotent deity). By dismantling the separation between mind/body – the *cogito, ergo sum* – we are forced to see thought not as transcendental but as embedded in bodily behaviour. By contrast, by continuing to conceive of the body as separate to the mind, the desire to see the internet as an expansion of immateriality suggests a desire to extend the power of thought: a radical deepening of the humanist subject's belief in his omniscience. Physical-effacing gestures, for example, bring real-world effects closer to simple mental causation. One winks, wearing Google Glass, and websites scroll past. New technologies potentially enhance the workings of the brain, which make the possibility of being able to summon physical entities and vast information just by thinking nearer to reality. The potential of the internet is not just being able to know the weather forecast (whoopee) but the vast extension of mental thought, separate from the messy or hassling realities of embodied existence. In virtual reality games, where people control avatars with expansive imagined levels of capacity with minimal physical engagement, this is made even more explicit.

In the imagination of digital culture, the posthuman is this figure who has been so enhanced by new technologies that his or her abilities exceed that of a natural human. Imagine, for example, the man who wears a monitor that is able to re-start his heart if it should stop: what a scenario for immortality! Or the woman who wears glasses that enable her to recognise the names and architects of buildings she passes in the street, and even the names of people she meets at bars, merely by looking at their faces: what a screenplay for omniscience. As might be clear, I want to sound a note of scepticism here. Despite contemporary culture's very real bleeds into posthumanity, it remains an illusion and is treated it as such. The manifestoes heralding the emergence of the posthuman understand it as a utopian (or dystopian) concept, and it works as a fiction both culturally and in everyday thought. Haraway herself called the cyborg a "myth". And no one genuinely thinks people with heart monitors are cyborgs or that someone wearing Google Glass eyewear is omnipotent. But the strategies of disavowal around the posthuman, and the delight people have in declaring it, are not insignificant.

Indeed, I would argue they form one of a number of repeated instances of disavowal with regard to digital culture more generally.[18] Digital culture bifurcates thinking into two untouching paths: a path of immersion within platforms offering incredible access to knowledge, social connections, and rare cultural forms and, on the other hand, a critique of the political and social environment within which these platforms have been built. Critiques of the internet are often disseminated via the very same internet they address. The inability to synthesise these two, or to engage in proper immanent critique, helps engender disavowal. Doctrines exist as straw men to be repeatedly challenged, with neither ever conquering the other: illusion and challenge remain locked in a dead heat. Hangovers from pre-digital ways of thinking migrate into our understanding of the present. This can be seen, for example, in how digital videos are commonly referred to as "films", even by people who should really know better. We must remember this while we are thinking through the idea of the posthuman, and how its influence operates culturally, as well as for the illusion of immateriality later.

In a critique of Haraway's writing and its reception, Wajcman contrasts Haraway the modernist and Haraway the postmodernist. Haraway's celebration of fragmentation and the open-ended nature of her polemical critiques create a performative thrill, but they are difficult to parse without the appropriate cultural capital – that is, they are only legible to an educated readership. Wajcman observes that when Haraway turns to social causes such as black women in the US or women workers in the global economy, Haraway uses the methodologies her own manifesto disavows, such as "official statistics and conventional sociological categories of gender, race and class" (Wajcman 2004, 99). The cyborg is a metaphorical figure, as Haraway acknowledges, even within the work of its progenitor.

Hayles deals with this fantastical element of the posthuman – that is, its liminal state between fiction and reality – by using as her corpus not only information technology and feminist theory, but also science fiction novels and films where the imaginary of the posthuman develops, such as Bernard Wolfe's *Limbo* (1952) and Philip. K. Dick's *Do Androids Dream of Electric Sheep?* (1968). She takes these fictional representations not simply as rhetoric, but as actualising ideologies that help form the theory behind man/machine hybrids. Likewise, Hayles's crucial discussion of how information patterns supplant the binary of presence and absence also takes into account the illusory nature of immateriality: "The pattern/randomness dialectic does not erase the material world; information in fact derives its efficacy from the material infrastructures it appears to obscure". This "illusion of erasure" of the material world is similar to that which so much of post-internet artworks to undermine: the illusion of pure imagehood that Leckey, as we saw in Chapter One, seeks to interrogate by means of his bodily response. "How does an image find three-dimensional presence? And channel its effect through MY body?" The notion of information patterns and the immateriality of digital communications is also picked up – and wonderfully skewered – by Hito Steyerl, as we will see more closely in the following chapter. For Hayles, accepting this obscuring of the material world is what makes the posthuman potentially a dystopian fantasy, exacerbating the worse aspects of the liberal humanist subject's inclination towards a belief in omnipotence: "obtaining through technological mastery the ultimate privilege of humanity" (Hayles

1999, 287). Only embodied, she writes, can the posthuman emerge as a responsible means of negotiating the new reality of intelligent machines.

Cyborgs now

The artistic development of the posthuman sheds this overt embodied dimension and uses instead the cyborg's basis in information as the site of potential challenge to identity binaries. Indeed, though the body is an important element within post-internet practice, as we saw in Leckey's *Cinema-in-the-Round* (2006–2008), post-internet exists in a push-and-pull between fantasies of disembodiment, which allow for non-gendered identities to emerge, and social contextualisation, in which the body is seen as a privileged site of enquiry. The notion of non-gendered identity, for example, masks the fact that gender and its politics still entirely inhere in everyday life, even as this social context motivates projects exploring fungible identities. As the artist Jesse Darling put it, "[I]f we could really negate our bodies and live in the cool matrix of post-gendered networketopia, then abortion rights wouldn't be an issue; transgender kids wouldn't be murdered in small towns" (Darling quoted in Clark and Farkas 2012). Likewise, for works made by black artists, their reshuffling of the terms of racial identity are made in the context of increased violence, state and otherwise, against people of colour. The feedback loop, if you will, between the illusion of the cyborg as a way out and the real situation on the ground is an internal dynamic to the work.

In ways that Hayles, writing her book in 1999, did not fully foresee, post-internet art explores the way the body has become information given bodily form. This ranges from the literal to the allegorised: our profiles online are blocks of information, assembled together to give an impression and constantly mined for profit. A number of recent offline and non-post-internet works also portray identities as an agglomeration of material information: Kader Attia's great *The Repair from Occident to Extra-Occidental Cultures* (2012), which was first exhibited in Documenta 13, and subsequent iterations such as *The Repair's Cosmogony* (2013), is comprised of shelves of African statuary, made in plaster, and European statuary, made in wood. The work is a critique of the conventions of hegemonic and ethnic representational paradigms but also reads as a means of demonstrating the tensions within Attia's own profile as an artist, where, as a French artist of Algerian origin, based in Berlin, Attia must straddle various identities, representing his (parents') native Algeria as well as his own idiom within contemporary art. The shelves of the project mimic the grid-like organisation of the internet, along with the more basic evocation of bookshelves and shelves for cabinets of curiosities. His identity is mapped out as a series of semiotic propositions encapsulated in the legible forms of sculpture and books, pamphlets and images that lie as if research material.

In addition to the notion of a person-as-information, there is also the social-media sense of the person-as-performance, which draws on Judith Butler's idea of the performance of gender. Both enable actions beyond traditional gender

Figure 2.6 Kader Attia, *The Repair's Cosmogony*, 2013, installation, metal shelves, teak wood sculptures (Dakar, Senegal), white marble sculptures (Carrara, Italy), archival documents, newspapers, and photographs. Installation view at Kunst-Werke, Berlin, 2013.

Photo: Simon Vogel. Courtesy the artist, Galerie Nagel Draxler, Cologne and Galleria Continua, San Gimignano

paradigms. Technology has long allowed female artists an outlet to play with or assume different identities – and, of course, for male artists to do the same. Leckey's dandyish persona, with his dangly pearl earring and shoulder-length hair pulled into a ponytail in what we in the 1990s called "half-up, half-down", suggest an adoption of feminine characteristics as playful as Laurie Anderson's adoption of a male voice in her technologically mediated performances. This ludic entanglement of binaries reflects Haraway's prediction of gender identity as a set of characteristics and assumptions that circulate around certain signifiers.

Works within post-internet art are also less focused on the representation of gender binaries but rather on all the subject positions that do not conform to the abstract modern subject (white, male, heterosexual, wealthy, etc.). Huxtable's performances, for example, are as much about her transgender identity as racial politics. Huxtable has frequently referenced the cyborg as a mode of performance, both in works in which she is the author and those in which she is the subject – such as the 3D print-out of a photograph of her in metallic cyborgian garb, an odalisque-like sculpture made by the artist Frank Benson that became a key image of the 2015 New Museum Triennial "Surround Audience". Indeed, though Haraway's cyborg is most famous for its disruption of gender binaries, Haraway's manifesto also addressed race and social class: the task of the cyborg is to "survive in the diaspora" (Haraway 1985/1991, 170). Referring to the work of the postcolonial film scholar Chela Sandoval, the "Cyborg Manifesto" notes how "the category 'woman' negated all non-white woman; 'black' negated all non-black people" (Haraway 1985/1991, 156) – binaries that Sandoval's category of "oppositional consciousness" sought to contest. In an article of 1999, María Fernández notes how this aspect of a "Cyborg Manifesto" is missing in its reputation and queries the absence of postcolonial politics from electronic media arts, in which, she argues, postcolonial identity's move between different frames of Otherness could engender the same possibilities for identity play as in the performance of gender. She suggests a different relation to the social as the cause for this absence:

> [B]oth postcolonial studies and electronic media theory view identity as multiple and open-ended, but they differ drastically in focus. In postcolonial studies theories of identity emphasize the social – identities are historically rooted, open-ended, collective political projects. Electronic media theory gives primacy to the individual as the construction of identity is viewed as an opportunity for self-development and (re)creation.
>
> (Fernández 1999, 65)

This social context, missing in 1999, is here activated by the works through their development over social media and their use of performance and participatory projects in which social and personal histories are now a more present

Figure 2.7 Frank Benson, *Juliana*, 2015, 3D print of Juliana Huxtable. Installation view, "Surround Audience", New Museum Triennial, New York, 2015.

Photo: Benoit Pailley. Courtesy New Museum, New York

subject. In the performance *There Are Certain Facts That Cannot Be Disputed* (2015), for example, Huxtable creates an immersive, electronically mediated lecture-performance on which images of the US's racial past scroll on a screen behind her, while she evokes this past through a flouncy white antebellum dress – actually, more like antebellum underwear – lit purple on the stage. Ryan Trecartin, as we will see in Chapter Five, engages with a number of subject positions, critiquing them on economic grounds. Jacolby Satterwhite points to the history of outsider art practice in his video, *The Matriarch's Rhapsody* (2012), which uses 3D objects made from his drawings of everyday objects done by his mother, who has schizophrenia, while also touching on the representation of gender, queer, and racial identities.

The cyborg has also changed within artistic practice in tandem with the emergence of surrounding theories, in particular that of immaterial labour by Maurizio Lazzarato. The aestheticised, hygienic representations of the posthuman are often used to signal alienation by technology and exploitation in terms of unremunerated immaterial and affective labour. In Marx's theory of alienation, in which the worker is alienated from the product of his or her labour, the labourer makes a product whose form is shaped by the consumer and that is designed to be an item of exchange value. Rather than the sense of accomplishment and self-sufficiency of making a tool for use, the worker makes commodities for others and receives only wages in return. More broadly "alienation from labour" is understood to mean an alienation from working with one's own hands: a mediation via a computer interface in which any real materiality (the sweat of the producer, the tactility of the object produced) is absent. The hygienic figures of post-internet art are reflections of this online world that does not contain the messier aspects of human existence.

"Alienation from labour" likewise signals immaterial labour, or the notion that the work of cultural producers is thought-work (thinking, writing, research and development, designing products) and the managing of affect (as by advertising or the service industry). This type of work is typical to the knowledge economy and is deeply marked by exploitation: the knowledge economy – and its corollary of affective or immaterial labour – is born on the back of labour that is not properly compensated. Work is done in leisure time, performed by unwaged interns, or wages are simply too low. Artists often do not receive a production budget to exhibit in group shows or biennials, meaning they must use their own fees simply to produce the work and to pay others who might help them make it, leaving no money for a salary afterwards. (This lack of proper compensation is increasingly the case in the post-2008 recession and contributes to social regression in the art world.) Thus, in its post-internet art usage, the shiny posthuman also signals the idealised figure of marketing material and the complex of neoliberal economic strictures that subtend it.

*

In a 2013 article in *Artforum*, the art historian Michael Sanchez noted how artworks seemed to be made with their eventual circulation as images in mind: they are made to look good on iPhones or on the popular site Contemporary Art Daily, which aggregates images of different exhibitions without editorial commentary (Sanchez 2013). His analysis frames the body as a machine and suggests a highly cybernetic feedback loop between image and viewer: works, he argues, respond to the pattern-seeking movements of the eye by decreasing information and affect. They want to be clean pictures, and they do so by adopting a minimalist aesthetic: "a reduction of affect to its zero degree, inducing in the viewer a state of relaxation that counters the anxiety fed by the speed of the scroll interface, slowing the eye down and dilating the pupils". In the next chapter, we will pick up on this question of the body as a machine from a different angle: the idea of a body, or human subject, as an object within a system. A number of contemporary critiques suggest an endowing of objects with agency that, not only contravenes the move throughout the twentieth century towards image, but also questions new forms of circulation.

Notes

1 Cybernetics as a science took increasing account of the role that the viewer played in the feedback system of cybernetic enterprises. See N. Katherine Hayles's account of the Macy Conferences, the colloquia in which the scientists associated with cybernetics developed their ideas, for an analysis of how this occurs. N. Katherine Hayles, *How We Became Posthuman: Virtual Bodies in Cybernetics, Literature and Informatics*, Chicago and London: University of Chicago Press, 1999, pp. 50–83.

2 Lucy Lippard, notably, uses a quotation from Burnham as the epigraph for her *Six Years: The Dematerialization of the Art Object 1966–1972* (1973), Berkeley: University of California Press, 1997.

3 One could see the popular installation *Rain Room* (2012), which appeared at the Barbican in London, MoMA in New York, and LACMA in Los Angeles, and is travelling to the Sharjah Art Foundation in the UAE, as a return of this sculpture in a mode of pure spectacle, replacing the pavilion's haptic, aural, and other sensorial registers with the visual display of falling water. In *Rain Room*, the user moves around a raining room, although it is dry wherever the viewer is.

4 For more on Nouvelle Tendance see Monoskop.org's fantastic entry on New Tendencies, which contains a list of participants of each exhibition, as well as PDFs of each year's colloquy: http://monoskop.org/New_Tendencies (last accessed on 16 December 2015).

5 EXAT 51, for example, which was formed in 1951 in Zagreb, aimed to return to the ideal of a modernist synthesis of visual expression, adapted for a technological society, in order to move past the socialist realism then in place as dogma in Yugoslavia. See Ana Dević, "Reception of Modernism within the Context of Croatian art since the 1950s", paper given at the conference "Inside Out: Reassessing International Cultural Influence", Rio de Janeiro, 3–9 July 2001. Organised by Apex Art, New York. Available at http://www.apexart.org/conference/devic.htm (last accessed on 1 May 2016).

6 This motif remained constant even as the actual understanding of the methodologies differed according to the vast number of participants. The introduction to the 1968 iteration, for example, underplays research and explicitly distinguishes Nouvelle Tendance's method from Anglo-American "trial and error"; the speaker emphasised "experimentation", not "trials", a more fluid and instantaneous means of experimenting than simply following through on a set query (Moles 1968).

7 The work was made in collaboration with Pablo Suarez, David Lamelas, Rudolfo Prayon, Floreal Amor, and Leopoldo Maler.

8 Daniel Spoerri, Jean Tinguely, and Pontus Hultén curated "Bewogen Beweging" (1961) at the Stedelijk Museum in Amsterdam, which later travelled to the Moderna Museet in Stockholm and which focused on kinetic work (twenty-eight works by Tinguely), as well as works by Robert Rauschenberg, Roy Ascott, and Victor Pasmore, who would also become allied with cybernetics. Hultén subsequently staged "The Machine as Seen at the End of the Mechanical Age" at MoMA in New York (1968), which ran concurrently with E.A.T.'s "Some More Beginnings" at the Brooklyn Museum. Hultén's exhibition provided a historical background to the new interest in machine art (with works by Vladimir Tatlin [*Monument to the Third International*], Buckminster Fuller, and the Lumière brothers), while "Some More Beginnings" showcased contemporary engineer-and-artist collaborations. Reichardt's "Cybernetic Serendipity" (1968), shown in its most complete iteration at the ICA in London, with scaled-down versions at the Corcoran Gallery in Washington, DC, and at the Exploratorium in San Francisco; Jan van der Marck's "Art by Telephone" (1969) at the MCA Chicago; Maurice Tuchman's "Art and Technology" project at LACMA (1967–1971); Jack Burnham's "Software" (1970, the Jewish Museum, New York); and "Nine Evenings: Theater and Engineering" (1966) at the Armory in New York (organised by Rauschenberg/Klüver) all likewise mixed Conceptualism and technological collaborations.

9 For an account of this, see Calvin Tomkins, "Outside Art", reprinted in Massimiliano Gioni and Gary Carrion-Murayari (ed.), *Ghosts in the Machine* (exh. cat.), New York: Skira Rizolli, 2012, pp. 302–28.

10 See Max Kozloff, "The Multimillion Dollar Art Boondoggle", *Artforum*, vol.10, no.2, October 1971, pp. 72–76.

11 Co-curated with Marie-Odile Briot and staged at the Musée de l'Art Moderne de la Ville de Paris.

12 Lyotard's exhibition, at the Pompidou in Paris in 1985, addressed postmodernism, information, and globalisation and was influential on a younger generation of French artists such as Pierre Huyghe and Philippe Parenno. See John Rajchman, "Les Immatériaux, or How to Construct the History of Exhibitions", *Tate Papers* [online journal], no.12, Autumn 2009, http://www.tate.org.uk/research/publications/tate-papers/12/les-immateriaux-or-how-to-construct-the-history-of-exhibitions (last accessed on 2 May 2016).

13 In the UK, domestic service peaked in 1880–1881 and then fell thereafter, but its decline was not steady. After dropping drastically – by fifty per cent in the 1940s during wartime – domestic service rose slightly again in the affluent 1950s and then resumed its general course downwards, with upward ticks in the 1980s and today. See for example Lucy Delap, *Knowing Their Place: Domestic Service in Twentieth Century Britain*, Oxford: Oxford University Press, 2011.

14 This strange aspect makes it eerily similar to the corridors depicted in Bruce Nauman's *Live-Taped Video Corridors* (1970), also works of anxiety and surveillance. Indeed Kafka, as well as the controlling architecture of German Expressionism, also does not seem far off.

15 Vilalta's research on Lozano forms part of her ongoing doctoral dissertation at UCL.

16 The territory of the relation between technologies and bodies, particularly women's bodies, was richly addressed by the art historian Cadence Kinsey in her doctoral dissertation. Kinsey shows how medical procedures such as endoscopies are also an image-making technology, demonstrating how the representation of the body is indistinguishable from the technology that produces it and on how the medical histories of looking at the bodies of women cross over with those of politics and pornography. See Cadence Kinsey, *Skins \ Screens \ Circuits: How Technology Remade the Body*, dissertation submitted for doctoral degree in the department of History of Art, London: University College London, 2012.

17 This question has, for example, become important to the project called Xenofeminism, which calls itself, following Haraway, "gender abolitionist" and aims to adapt technology and alienation in the service of feminism. See the "Xenofeminism: A

Politics for Alienation" manifesto by the anonymous collective Laboria Cubonika, at the website *Laboria Cubonika*, http://www.laboriacuboniks.net/qx8bq.txt (last accessed on 1 May 2016).

18 Claire Bishop also reads strategies of disavowal towards the digital in her analysis of why the "mainstream" art world remained preoccupied with analogue and craft technologies for so long, even as digitisation and the spread of the internet were well under way. See C. Bishop, "Digital Divide: Contemporary Art and New Media", *Artforum*, September 2012, vol.51, no.2, pp. 434–41.

Bibliography

Alonso, R. (2005) "Art and Technology in Argentina: The Early Years". *Leonardo Electronic Almanac*, 13 (4), 16–23.

Ascott, R. (1966–1967) "Behaviouristic Art and the Cybernetic Vision". In: Packer, R. and Jordan, K. ed. (2001) *Multimedia: From Wagner to Virtual Reality*, New York: W.W. Norton, 95–103.

——— (2003) *The Telematic Embrace: Visionary Theories of Art, Technology and Consciousness* Shanken, E. A. ed., Berkeley and Los Angeles: University of California Press.

Bishop, C. (2012) "Digital Divide: Contemporary Art and New Media". *Artforum*, 51 (2), 434–41.

Burnham, J. (1968a) *Beyond Modern Sculpture*, New York: George Braziller.

——— (1968b) "Systems Esthetics". *Artforum*, 7 (1), 30–35.

——— (1980) "Art and Technology: The Panacea That Failed". In: Woodward, K. ed. *The Myths of Information: Technology and Postindustrial Culture*, London: Routledge.

Clark, T. and Farkas, R. (2012) "Self-Compression: An Interview with Jesse Darling". *Mute* [online magazine]. 20 June. http://www.metamute.org/editorial/articles/self-compression-interview-jesse-darling (last accessed on 26 October 2016).

Delap, L. (2011) *Knowing Their Place: Domestic Service in Twentieth Century Britain*, Oxford: Oxford University Press.

Dević, A. (2001) "Reception of Modernism within the Context of Croatian Art Since the 1950s". Paper given at the conference "Inside Out: Reassessing International Cultural Influence". Rio de Janeiro, 3–9 July. Organised by Apex Art, New York. http://www.apexart.org/conference/devic.htm (last accessed on 1 May 2016).

E.A.T. (1972) *Pavilion*, New York: EP Dutton.

Eco, U. (1962a) "Arte Programmata". In: *Arte Programmata*. Exh. cat., Milan: Galleria Vittorio Emanuele, 98–101. Reprinted in: Carrion-Murayari, G. and Gioni, M. ed. (2012) *Ghosts in the Machine*. Exh. cat., New York: New Museum and Skira Rizzoli, 239–42.

——— (1962b) *The Open Work*. Cancogni, A. trans., Robey, D. intro. (1989) Cambridge, MA: Harvard University Press.

Fernández, M. (1999) "Postcolonial Media Theory". *Art Journal*, 58 (3), 58–73.

——— (2006) "Historizing Process and Responsiveness in Digital Art". In: Jones, A. ed. *A Companion to Contemporary Art Since 1945*, Oxford: Blackwell Publishing, 557–81.

Galison, P. (1994) "The Ontology of the Enemy: Norbert Wiener and the Cybernetic Vision". *Critical Inquiry*, 21 (1), 228–66.

Gleick, J. (2012) *The Information: A History, A Theory, A Flood*, New York: Vintage.

Glueck, G. (1966) "Disharmony at the Armory". *The New York Times*. 30 October, Section Arts & Leisure, Page D28.

Grosz, E. (1994) *Volatile Bodies: Toward a Corporeal Feminism*, Bloomington: Indiana University Press.

Haraway, D. J. (1985/1991) *Simians, Cyborgs, and Women: The Reinvention of Nature*, New York: Routledge.

Hayles, N. K. (1999) *How We Became Posthuman: Virtual Bodies in Cybernetics, Literature and Informatics*, Chicago and London: University of Chicago Press.

Jobs, S. (2005) "Stanford Commencement Address". Stanford: Stanford University, 12 June. Excerpted as "Explore Whole Earth: Share Your Story". *Whole Earth Catalog* [website], http://www.wholeearth.com/share-your-story.php (last accessed on 1 May 2016).

Kinsey, C. (2012) *Skins \ Screens \ Circuits: How Technology Remade the Body*. Ph.D. thesis, London: University College London.

Kozloff, M. (1971) "The Multimillion Dollar Art Boondoggle". *Artforum*, 10 (2), 72–76.

Laboria Cubonika. "Xenofeminism: A Politics for Alienation". *Laboria Cubonika* [website], http://www.laboriacuboniks.net/qx8bq.txt (last accessed on 1 May 2016).

Lippard, L. (1973/1997) *Six Years: The Dematerialization of the Art Object 1966–1972*, Berkeley: University of California Press.

Lovejoy, M. (2004) *Art in the Age of Digital Currents*, London: Routledge.

Moles, A. A. (1968) "Introduction à Colloque". In: Kelemen, B. and Putar, R. ed. *Bit International 3: International Colloquy Computers and Visual Arts Zagreb, August 3–4, 1968*, Zagreb: Galerije grada Zagreba, 5–10.

Rajchman, J. (2009) "Les Immatériaux, or How to Construct the History of Exhibitions". *Tate Papers* [online journal], 12, http://www.tate.org.uk/research/publications/tate-papers/12/les-immateriaux-or-how-to-construct-the-history-of-exhibitions (last accessed on 2 May 2016).

Reichardt, J. (1968) "Cybernetic Serendipity: The Computer and the Arts," *Studio International,* Special Edition, Exh. cat., 5.

Sanchez, M. (2013) "2011: Art and Transmission". *Artforum*, 51 (10), 295–301.

Skrebowski, L. (2006) "All Systems Go: Recovering Jack Burnham's 'Systems Aesthetics'". *Tate Papers* [online journal], 6, http://www.tate.org.uk/download/file/fid/7301 (last accessed on 26 April 2016).

Software – Information Technology: Its New Meaning for Art. Exh. cat. (1968) New York: Jewish Museum.

Spencer, C. (2015) "Performing Pop: Marta Minujín and the 'Argentine Image-Makers'". *Tate Papers* [online journal], 24, http://www.tate.org.uk/research/publications/tate-papers/24/performing-pop-marta-minujin-and-the-argentine-image-makers (last accessed on 26 April 2016).

Tomkins, C. (1972) "Outside Art". Reprinted in: Carrion-Murayari, G. and Gioni, M. ed. (2012) *Ghosts in the Machine*. Exh. cat., New York: New Museum and Skira Rizolli, 302–28.

——— (1996) *Duchamp: A Biography*, London: Pimlico.

Vilalta, H. (2016) Email. 20 April.

Wajcman, J. (2004) *Technofeminism*, Cambridge: Polity Press.

3 Challenges to immateriality
Posthumanist thought and digitality

Chapters One and Two detailed the various moves, from the ascendancy of the image to the rise of information patterning, that have resulted in the understanding of digital culture as a weightless, immaterial sphere, in which interaction with others is governed by the individual at his or her keyboard or on his or her smartphone. It's an imaginary of endless search results, YouTube trawling, and copy-and-pasting as constituent parts of artistic production and the use of software programs in order to create the composites and hyper-stylised videos that are typical of post-internet art. Leisure time on the internet merges into work time on the internet, and both are governed by the same experience of the rectangular screen and its endless cycle of things to look at.

But this picture, either of post-internet art or digital culture, is inaccurate. At what might seem the very height of information patterning, visual culture, and mind-over-matter, materiality returns as a specific and charged site of enquiry, among artists and thinkers alike. This has principally taken the form of increased attention to objects, which are theorised and addressed as agents. The approach returns us to the posthuman, but from the other side: rather than imagining humans as objects, these theories propose an ontological equivalence between humans, objects, and all items of matter, perceiving them as equal interrelated actants within networks. (These philosophies – of the new materialisms, which functions as a header for object-oriented ontology, speculative realism, and speculative materialism – are often labelled posthumanist. This is a moniker that derives from being after humanism [i.e. post + humanist], rather than from the figure of the posthuman [i.e. not posthuman + ist].) The means by which objects take centre stage are manifold, as are the responses to objects-with-agency, these hybrid monsters: they range from being part of an oppositional, politicised framework to being symptoms of anxiety and fear.

The return to objects is not a retroactive move towards authenticity but a way to think of our participation in systems as the structuring mode of our cultural output, without thinking of systems merely virtually, or of the outside world as always mediated through human thinking. In order to displace power and subjectivity onto objects, one has to understand systems as linking humans and objects equally. This mode of thinking draws from actor-network theory, which aims to understand the functioning of different sets of relations – from the workings of a car to social class to maritime engagement – as a network. Within this network, the relations among the constituent parts are always in the process of being formed: a state of continual becoming. A car engine isn't a working engine unless all the parts function with each other. It is not surprising that actor–network theory and Bruno Latour, its most famous exponent, have become so important to artists and thinkers within post-internet art: systems and a mode of continual becoming describe both the literal and affective resonances of the internet.

One of the criticisms of actor–network theory has been its equation between people and things, which does not take into account intentionality nor the obvious differences between, say, a carburettor and a person. Digital and pop culture also wrestle with this question more allegorically, such as in narratives where a machine of artificial intelligence or a posthuman figure achieves the capacity that is most sacred to an emotional life – that of loving intimacy with another – as in Spike Jonze's feature film *Her* (2013). We might also remember that the third order of cybernetics, which posited the observer as a function of the system under observation, was so controversial it stymied the Macy Conferences on Cybernetics in which the idea was being developed (Hayles 1999, 11). These questions, that is to say, are radical and difficult to treat in a visual context. How may a network might be understood materially or visually? And how might an artwork represent such a network while also allowing it to circulate as is? In the last part of this chapter, I try to show the latter questions pose enduring difficulties to post-internet art and suggest that, to understand this complex relationship of post-internet art vis-à-vis its own tools, we might look back to net.art. In this section, I move away from the focus on materiality and begin to lay the groundwork for digitality as a mode that mediates between circulation and representation.

Finally, I speculate here, from a bird's-eye perspective, that the turn to looking at objects and their agency, and the move away from human-centred perception of the world, is a theoretical means of understanding the part objects play in a world of systems. Or, rather, my perspective is not a bird's-eye view but from the perspective of the art world: I am seeking to parse here the reasons for these theories' adoption by and influence on artists, and in this way, I want to argue, perhaps paradoxically, that the focus on objects is a continuation of thinking in systems that cybernetics initiated and which Jack Burnham so presciently recognised in the art of his period.

The immateriality illusion

The pushback against immateriality is also influenced by the perceived close connection, as seen in Chapter One, between immateriality and capitalist or neoliberal economic policies. Indeed, "immateriality" comes to stand in for a host of conditions, from the service economy to immaterial labour to finance capitalism, where endless restructuring of debts means money is not cash under a mattress but figures on a computer screen. It is also linked with the idea that immateriality obscures social relations and "real-life" conditions of violence, poverty, and exploitation: the invisible processes by which the internet is built. The developed world's engagement with digital technologies comes on the back of Third World labour, whose hidden capacity is twice forgotten: they are exploited in the conditions of production and metaphorically excluded in the figuration of digital work as "immaterial". The artist Ed Atkins, whose work has been so closely associated with digitality as an immaterial state, frames the obsession with the immaterial as a binary opposition in which the material is subordinated. This suppression, he argues, is motivated by a desire to not know about the material, in an act of disavowal or bad faith:

> it feels important to shed the "immaterial". It pretty much always feels like a lie – that always we're talking about a deferral rather than a lack, or that it's symptomatic of a productive mystification that keeps matter and material consequence in abeyance, over there, out of sight. The figuration of having server farms as "clouds" is an explicit example. Having said that, when this material elsewhere (so-called immaterial) is inaccessible, irretrievable – as in death – the immaterial rhetoric becomes a way of making the intangible imaginatively tangible. Which I think is what happens with the digital: that it's easier to access an imaginary immaterial of metaphoric somethings than it is to approach, address the sweatshops and mines and wrecked bodies in countries countless miles away.
>
> (pers. comm.)

Or, equally, in the words of the artist Trevor Paglen, whose work visualises classified information:

> Intuitively "the Internet" seems like a liminal space, a kind of abstract nowhere that is everywhere, seemingly, a space of pure culture. But the telecommunications technologies and networks are made out of physical stuff in the same way that everything else is. . . . a lot of the metaphors we use like "the Cloud" or even notions like "Internet Freedom" are highly ideological and deeply misleading.
>
> (Paglen quoted in Cornell 2015, 256)

The illusion of immateriality exacerbates the twentieth century's conflation between capitalism and the reduction of everything to image by further removing the physical substrate on which this image is seen: endless digital files pixelating by. The counterfactual within the various critiques that are mounted against immateriality – principally signalled by the strenuous over-emphasis on the technological device – is thus not simply lanced against the logical illusion of immateriality but against ideology, as Paglen notes, and political and economic subjection.

Hayles's crucial insight of the dominant position held by information patterns is also the target of a particularly political brand of post-internet work, which is related as much to the art world as to activism or hacktivism – Anonymous, the

Occupy groups, and other grassroots political organisations that use the internet's social network capacities and tackle the internet as subject, in particular to raise awareness of NSA and GCHQ surveillance tactics. The artist Zach Blas, whose own work involves an attempt to materialise the assumptions behind racial profiling in the US, has called this kind of work "anti-internet aesthetics" (Blas 2014), underlining its oppositional character to illusory tenets of the internet (and, to a certain extent, pointing to the works' deliberately anti-aesthetic character). He lists among these Ricardo Dominguez, Jemima Wyman, Dan Phiffer, and Hito Steyerl, who has emerged as the dominant theorist on the intersection between the internet, aesthetics, and politics.

I want to focus on Steyerl's work briefly, both because of its relevance to our argument here and because of the importance she has played in critical theorisations of the internet and work responding to it. She repeatedly and consistently challenges the ideology around the internet and shows its embeddedness in political and economic contexts. Her analysis hinges on an exploration of the materiality of the images and apparatuses she works with, particularly in her early work. Steyerl was trained as a documentary filmmaker and really entered the art world with her video *November* (2004). The work takes the form of a cine–essay, which is itself associated with a standpoint of critique, through filmmakers such as Chris Marker, Harun Farocki, and Jean-Luc Godard and Anne-Marie Miéville. Its protagonist is Steyerl's childhood friend, Andrea Wolf, who fought with the Kurdish Workers' Party (PKK) in Turkey and was killed there. *November* tells the story of Andrea's disappearance by moving through various media, beginning with an action film Steyerl and Wolf made when they were sixteen. It re-worked tropes from films such as *Faster Pussy-cat, Kill! Kill!* and created a scenario where women played the lead roles, rather than men, and where only the villains had weapons. Steyerl uses this back story and *November's* own formal collating of different media to present a world of constant interchangeability between representation and reality: the movie she and Wolf shot, on stolen reels of film, in which Wolf survives; its stylistic antecedent, *Faster Pussy-cat, Kill! Kill!*; a poster announcing Wolf's martyrdom; and footage she found of Wolf in northern Iraq, originally filmed on Super-8 but here visibly captured from videocassette. Steyerl signals the videocassette format by showing the images in their striated appearance. She then pulls the camera back to reveal she has been filming the footage as it plays on a television set; later she shows the actual videocassettes. (In the video, she also notes that she learned, during the production of the video, that the director of the footage, which she received from a Kurdish satellite TV station, lived around the corner from her in Berlin: "This was when I realised that Kurdistan was not only there, but also here".) Other images and footage in the video derive from movie posters, demonstrations, Bruce Lee action clips, and a martial-arts battle scene from the detourned Situationist film *La Dialectique peut-elle casser des briques?* (*Can Dialectics Break Bricks?*, 1973) by René Viénet. The final stage in this procession of appearances is that of Steyerl herself, participating in a march for the Kurds in Berlin; she was asked by another documentary-maker to hold a candle and to play the part of a "sensitive, contained, and understanding filmmaker".

Figure 3.1 Hito Steyerl, *November*, 2004, DV, single channel, sound, 25 minutes.

Image CC 4.0 Hito Steyerl. Courtesy the artist and Andrew Kreps Gallery, New York

November is a history of images as much as a history of a relationship; as Steyerl says in the film, displacing her authorship onto the images, "Not I telling the story, but the story tells me". As underlined by her portrayal of the footage of Wolf in Kurdistan, the medial disjunctions between the images remain apparent despite their being transferred to digital video: the footage from the film with Andrea Wolf is grainy; the Bruce Lee footage has the oversaturated colour tone of 1970s film; *La Dialectique*, presumably ripped from a videocassette, flickers. It is a story of images projected onto a screen, images where materiality remains significant.

A reigning mode of Steyerl's work is that of the syllogism. Classical montage, as theorised by Sergei Eisenstein, follows a dialectical structure where one image is followed by a second image to create a third meaning. In Eisenstein's *Battleship Potemkin* (1925), for example, an image of the ship's striking mariners being shot at on the Odessa steps is followed by an image of an infant in a baby carriage to give the synthetical impression of the workers' innocence. A form both less ideological and self-reflexive is that of ironic montage. A well-known example here would be that of the baptismal scene in the *Godfather* (1972), where the baptism of the mafia head Michael Corleone's child, and the child's renunciation of

Satan, is interspersed with scenes of the murders of the other mafia families that Corleone has ordered.

In contrast to these synthetical forms of montage, in Steyerl's videos images are paratactically succeeded by similar images from a different context. That is, she equates different images to show that things that are conceived of as separate – the world of art and the world of neoliberal finance; the world of B-movies and the history of female subjugation – are in fact linked with each other. This happens as well on an auditory level, where a soundtrack will reinforce a visual or a discursive point – the song "When Will I See You Again" from 1973, for instance, rounds up the end of *How Not to Be Seen: A Fucking Didactic Educational .MOV File* (2013). Steyerl shows a web rather than a temporal progression (again we might remember how art of this type puts the idea of progression itself into question). The web is a leitmotif of the video she made after *November, Lovely Andrea* (2007), again appearing in syllogistic form: cartoon images of *Spider-Man* shooting spider webs from his wrists, visualisations of the World Wide Web, and the web-like tangle of ropes from which Japanese bondage artists, the ostensible subject of the film, hang. The relationship she reinforces between the means of documenting history and the kind of history written is likewise symbiotic: her point is neither the materiality of digital images, nor the power relations inscribed into history, but that they are co-determinant and are both at risk of being obscured by the equally linked illusions of the internet's immateriality; of its status as a free, unpoliced *demos*; and of the notion of the individual as non-politically determined.

For example, in a lecture given at the art space OCA in Oslo as part of the program "Film as a Critical Practice" in 2007, she detailed the path of the Yugoslavian blockbuster *The Battle of Neretva* (1969) (Steyerl 2011). The lecture charted the transformations, political and incidental, that films undergo within the channels of recirculation. Steyerl describes her search for a single scene, in which a schoolteacher writes out the acronym for "Anti-Fascist Liberation Councils of Yugoslavia" and her pupils recite it back to her. There is one remaining copy of this incredibly popular film in the Sarajevo film archive, which Steyerl happened to see as she went to their cinema on the day that they were screening the film – to an empty theatre – in order to ventilate the print. Such, she notes, is the standard of preservation of Sarajevo's under-resourced national archive. The archive sought to supplement its funding by, she says, privatising itself, selling or lending out the films as VHS cassettes and accomplished the transfer of the footage to VHS by simply recording the films with a VHS camera. Because the formats of feature film and VHS tape are different (VHS being more square), this method cropped off the sides of the films it was meant to preserve (which is, to say the least, not best archival practice). For Steyerl's purposes, this meant the words themselves "Anti-Fascist Liberation Councils of Yugoslavia", written on the blackboard on the left-hand side of the film, no longer appear.

In trying to find the scene, she discovered the proliferation of copies of the film, which, as of her 2007 lecture, appeared in 10 different languages, and 7 different durations, ranging from the original at 175 minutes to the Russian version at 78 minutes (in that version, she says, all the scenes of violence against Russians were cut – in effect, two-thirds of the film). The story that emerges is one of archives as reflective of politics, funding, and happenstance – images as not infinitely circulating and replicable but material footage that is re-dubbed, re-filmed, re-edited and as liable to being lost as house-keys. (The Sarajevo film archive that contains the one remaining true copy of *The Battle of Neretva* lost most of its films when it was bombed in the Balkan Wars of the 1990s.) The politics of the archive is further developed in Steyerl's text "In Defence of the Poor Image" (2009) (Steyerl 2009), which draws an analogy between the resources of wealthy countries and their ability to archive their histories and those of poor countries, whose television and film archives are being dismantled owing to lack of funds. As she showed with the *Battle of Neretva*, the poor image, ripped from analogue film, emailed and compressed, bears in its very low resolution the marks of poverty of its country: countries can now be poor in terms of information as well as food and monetary wealth.

From material to data

As Steyerl's work progressed through the early 2010s, her works focused more on the internet, and her writings, particularly "In Defence of the Poor Image", "Is the Museum a Factory?" (2009), "Too Much World: Is the Internet Dead?" (2013), all written for the online journal *e-flux*, have become canonical for contemporary artists and thinkers working with the internet. Her videos and lecture–performances have become less formally resolved and more pointed in their critique of the financial and political constituency of the art world. They show with often dizzying complexity how disparate entities are bound together – finance capital, surveillance, drone strikes, tax policies, dictatorships, the Arab Spring, and art itself.

One of Steyerl's most basic contestations is against information as abstract or patterned. In one of her most recent lectures, *Duty Free Art* (2015), for example, she challenges the cybernetic paradigm of information patterning detailed in *How We Became Posthuman*. *Duty Free Art*, realised as a lecture and an article in *e-flux*, looks at Geneva's "freeport", a permanent transit zone. A collector may buy artwork at an art fair and ship to it a freeport (which exist around the world– the one in Geneva is the largest), where, because it has not "landed" in any country, it will not incur import duties – thereby saving the collector thousands of dollars in taxes. As more art is bought as a financial asset, more work ends up awaiting conversion in freeports. Works can remain there indefinitely, so a collector could keep the artwork in non–national storage until he or she deaccessions it, either by selling it (thus likely making a profit on the work and never paying taxes for the commodity) or by donating it to a museum (in which case he or she would likely get a tax deduction). Freeports are massive tax havens and also – in a more romantic vein – contrary to what artworks, however broadly you want to define them, are meant to do: to be seen and engaged with. Steyerl is not an artist given to sentimentality, but something of their unfairly being locked up – even of their animism – hangs in her description of the Geneva freeport, which she calls a "cage without borders". Her treatment of the freeport also emphasises the many other arenas in which information moves invisibly.

> Think of the artworks and their movement. They travel inside a network of tax-free zones and also inside the storage spaces themselves. Perhaps as they do, they do not ever get uncrated. They move from one storage room to the next without being seen. They stay inside boxes and travel outside national territories with a minimum of tracking or registration, like insurgents, drugs, derivative financial products, and other so-called investment vehicles. For all we know, the crates could even be empty. It is a museum of the internet era, but a museum of the dark net, where movement is obscured and data-space is clouded.
>
> (Steyerl 2015)

The freeport reduces art to information patterns, circulating around the port but never fully accounted for. As Steyerl notes, the fantastic rise of the contemporary art sector has been aided by the enormous wealth created by finance capitalism; looking at art in the freeport allows her not only to compare art and financial instruments but also to point to their shared structural basis as information patterns.

The case of art – enough art to rival the best museum, Steyerl notes – as the subject of unseen movements also shows how such patterning exists in a world whose socio-legal structures are in place for a world of objects. Just as art is meant to be seen, legal systems track the material. Thus, as is well known, companies that offer online services often avoid paying taxes by locating themselves in tax havens, rather than being physically sited in a country with higher corporate tax rates. Above-board investment vehicles avoid the scrutiny of national regulations in the same way the drug and illegal arms trades do. Provisions for the public, catered for by government, are eroded by these circumventions of national sovereignty.

A second story line of *Duty Free Art* is about the Assad regime in Syria. (This, as we know from Steyerl's methodology, will be analogised to the Dark Net of the freeport – the unspoken circulation of contemporary art into areas most in the art world would find abhorrent.) Edward Snowden's WikiLeaks file dump unearthed letters between the Assad regime and an unnamed starchitect, presumed to be Rem Koolhaas, who was commissioned to design a National Museum of Syria. The project was interrupted by the start of the Syrian Civil War; street protests just three weeks before the announcement of the winner of the competition caused the high-profile naming ceremony to be cancelled, and the winner was never made public. An email requesting confirmation that Koolhaas won the competition, which Steyerl sent to Koolhaas's studio, was responded to with a polite refusal. Note the tenor of counterexample Steyerl chooses: it is set at the violent and the extreme. The Syria WikiLeaks files, Steyerl writes, are "a collection of online videos – of documents and records of innumerable killings, atrocities, and attacks that remain widely unseen. This is the de facto National Museum of Syria, not a Louvre franchise acquired by an Assad foundation". She sketches out a connection from an area of mild corruption (art as a tax dodge, art that is not seen) into a field of violence and complicity and slides us down this chute. Alongside the examples of the Assad administration buying a starchitect in order to legitimise its regime and the willingness of Koolhaas and his OMA studio – which have no small amount of artistic credibility – to engage with what has been shown to be a brutal dictator, Steyerl also shows her complicity: her own participation in this field of contemporary art and her post-NSA revelations use of the same secure email servers as those that enable tax evasion and money laundering. Art's "conditions of possibility", she says near the conclusion,

> are no longer just the elitist "ivory tower", but also the dictator's contemporary art foundation, the oligarch's or weapons manufacturer's tax-evasion scheme, the hedge fund's trophy, the art student's debt bondage, leaked troves of data, aggregate spam, and the product of huge amounts of unpaid "voluntary" labour – all of which results in art's accumulation in freeport storage spaces and its physical destruction in zones of war or accelerated privatisation.

Art, it almost goes without saying, is one of the luxury goods being bought and "invested in" by the hyper-rich. The connection between the art world and the 1% is not simply that most in the art world tend to be leftist and to believe in more equal distributions of income but rather that one's own artwork, criticism, or curatorial endeavour participates in this system of speculation and patronage and also that everyone has to make money in order to live. The complicity with such systems of unfair income distribution that post-internet art routinely flags up is thus a very literal one. Somewhere, someone down the line with shady dealings is bankrolling your political project.[1]

Significantly, this critique of complicity uses materiality to show information's navigation through its apparently immaterial visualisations and the (political and economic) events of the "real" (physically indexical) world. In Steyerl's video *In Free Fall* (2010), she follows the story of a Boeing 747 that performed rescue missions against the Palestine Liberation Organisation, and, once decommissioned, was blown up in the film *Speed*. The video contains images of floating DVDs, which she notes are made of the same aluminium as the airplane – even alleging the Boeing itself has turned into the material substrate for the DVDs of *Speed* itself. To accompany the exhibition of *In Free Fall* at the Chisenhale Gallery in London, Steyerl convened a panel discussion to specifically address the materiality of internet technologies (with Eyal Weizman and Peter Osborne, moderated by myself) and circulated an essay by the Russian writer Sergei Tretyakov, "The Biography of the Object" (1929), which provided a historical basis for her turn away from the image as the primary mode of articulation and towards the object (Tretyakov 1929/2006). Tretyakov's essay looks at psychological novels to transfer the point of view from their human characters to that of the objects narrated within them, as they move through a series of relations with humans. This is a way to communicate social mores rather than individual psychological perspectives: as Tretyakov writes, "People's individual and distinctive characteristics are no longer relevant here. The tics and epilepsies of the individual go unperceived. Instead, social neuroses and the professional diseases of a given group are foregrounded" (Tretyakov 1929/2006, 61). The object does not simply challenge myths of immateriality and their associated ideologies but also provides a way to access the social.

As much as Steyerl foregrounds the materiality of images, she does so *as* images, and images are her subject. The lecture about the *Battle of Neretva* is the story of a set of images; *Lovely Andrea* is structured like a detective novel around her search for one image of herself, when she posed in bondage as a film student in Japan. Her emphasis on or even simply sympathy for objects allows her to transfer the set of concerns associated with objecthood – a critique of its commodity status and its connection to the social – onto the image: the image-commodity, or the social-image. This leads her to a remarkably haptic reading of images in their economic and social terms, for example, as in "The Poor Image", her analysis of image wealth, which focuses on the degradation and compression of re-circulated files. Images accrue wealth, are possessed and are traded in ways more complicated than like-for-like exchange: their slipperiness and reliance on context – or, as Benjamin put it, captions – does not mean they are infinitely replaceable but rather that they can provide covert testimonies in surprising places, or indeed be so over-exposed as to be shorn of any meaning.[2] "The poor image", the essay begins, "is a copy in motion". The relentless testing of images in different contexts at the hands of Steyerl and other contemporary artists is a way to understand images as inflected by paths of circulation as much as intentionality or form.

Object-oriented ontology

This interest in seeing the world from the perspective of objects also finds a codified and more theoretical expression in what has been variously termed the "new materialisms", a suite of philosophical movements that focus on the object, most notably object-oriented ontology and speculative materialism, which have become important to post-internet art. These too are linked to immateriality, almost in dialectical opposition. In the opening remarks to a 2012 conference on new materialism, for example, the conference convenors Jussi Parikka and Milla Tiainen set digital materialism and media archaeology of Germany in the 1990s and 2000s in reaction to the discourse of immateriality within digital development, as well as to expansions of how "material" could be considered. The analysis is worth quoting at length:

> the recent years of media theory introduced an increasingly differing elaboration of how we should understand the notion of 'medium' in this context. Instead of being only something that in a Kantian manner prevents

access to the world of the real or material, or things, the medium itself becomes a material assemblage in the hands of a wave of German media theorists, who have developed a unique approach to media materialism, and hence new materialist notions of the world. Here the world is not reduced to symbolic, signifying structures, or representations, but is seen for such writers as Friedrich Kittler (and more recent theorists such as Wolfgang Ernst in a differing tone under media archaeology) as a network of concrete, material, physical and physiological apparatuses and their interconnections, that in a Foucauldian manner govern whatever can be uttered and signified.

(Parikka and Tiainen 2010)[3]

In the way that language determines how we think, material determines how we move around the world. Phenomenologically, new materialisms demand an understanding of the world as a field of matter that is differentiated – by being active, full of agency, affected by other objects or humans – and in constant relation with each other, in most theories by being set within a network.

Object-oriented ontology (OOO), which is less a media theory and more situated within philosophy proper, provides a philosophical genealogy for this new conception of the role of the object. Object-oriented ontology is principally associated with the philosopher Graham Harman, who, starting with *Prince of Networks: Bruno Latour and Metaphysics* (2009) and the summary of positions in *The Quadruple Object* (2011), aims to understand a world as perceived by objects and in which objects are self-sufficient and have agency. This is an attempt to move beyond the subject/object dualism that dominates Western philosophy. Harman bases his line of enquiry in the standpoint of Aristotle's deductive interest in the world of things, rather than Plato's understanding of the world of idealist Forms. Harman distinguishes his body of thought from the subject-centred understanding of Kant – understood here as Kant's anthropocentrism – and turns instead to Heidegger's notion of being present-at-hand from *Being and Time*. Harman puts forward the notion of withdrawal, when an object withdraws from the world and from relations with other beings (objects or humans). He uses Husserl's account of the relation between a human subject and a sensual object to further elaborate the withdrawn object, which is for Harman is the only real object and which stands in contradistinction to the sensual object, which can only be perceived by the mind. For Harman, withdrawn objects should be given ontological priority over the human-apperceived world of sensual objects.[4]

OOO builds on the work of Latour's actor-network theory, which provides a model for understanding the way in which actors (or subjects) are symbiotically formed by the networks they exist within.[5] He refers to these as "actants" – any material entity that has agency. Latour's actor-network theory has been influential on artists, but perhaps more so his "anthropology of science", *We Have Never Been Modern* (1991, English trans. 1993), in which Latour argues that Western culture never fully accomplished the cleavage between nature and society, nor human and thing, that is the founding claim of modernity. Rather, looking back at the emergence of the scientific method in the seventeenth century and at the discourse around contemporary scientific subjects, such as deforestation and global warming, he shows how hangovers from what we would think of as pre-modern thought structure science today.

Latour's critique chimes with the denigration of the Enlightenment and humanist thought in leftist philosophical circles of the late twentieth century, spurred on by poststructuralism. Where humanism was once thought to presuppose equality among men, humanism is now read as a colonialist and oppressive discourse; rationalism excludes other races, ethnicities, and gender affiliation beyond that of the Western white male and provides theoretical justification for their regulation. Latour's focus on the history of science places him at the centre of Enlightenment thought: the belief in scientific dogma as one of the Enlightenment's cherished universal values. Its abrogation becomes a threat to the entire project, and Latour thus makes room for the validation of other discourses and behaviours. Likewise in undermining the subject/object dualism at the heart of Western modern philosophy, Latour shows how subjects and objects – and real and fabricated, nature and society – can both assume an equal role in the structuring of political and everyday systems.

Art – as I suggested in Chapter One's reading of Mark Leckey's *Universal Addressability of Dumb Things* – is an autonomous object par excellence: how does a piece of art prick you, move you, make you think (or accumulate value)? Understanding the autonomous signifying potential of art is a particular function of what Latour calls a factish god: the belief in naïve belief, or the paradox whereby modern man denigrates fetishes under "primitive" belief systems – as in his example of the natives of the Côte d'Ivoire who worship as gods crude dolls they themselves have made – but valorises laws made by science, whose experiments are equally created and benighted within the manmade bounds of the scientific laboratory (Latour 2011). The potency of both fetish and fact are established by the network they exist within: neither is ontologically superior or even existent as such. Latour's symmetrical critique here furthers his questioning of the construction of the Enlightenment category of science and connects art to a pre-modern discourse of displaced animist power. This is important because the theoretical construction of aesthetics is itself an Enlightenment project (Kant, Schiller, Novalis), as are the public museums that provide the infrastructure for the art world and the bourgeois audience who consumes it. This helps us understand the critique of David Joselit, in *After Art*, of the end of art, as well as that of others who are less explicitly making the same claim: if art is an Enlightenment object, the sustained challenge of current philosophies to the Enlightenment imperils the category of art. The focus on systems; the imbrication of nature and society; the move away from a unique object; the transmogrification of object into image; and the reconception of the category of the contemporary as not temporal but geographical, as transnational – these are all fundamental categorical shifts that the move to objects and networks are set within.

Animism

Within contemporary art practice, the fetish, factish gods, and animism strikingly return throughout the 2000s, in a number of important exhibitions and in the term "techno-animism", which is closely associated with Leckey's work. Latour's critique of science, again, buttresses the ideas of animation or so-called primitive belief systems as a means to challenge the very drawing of the category of what it means to be modern. Animism was the subject of an exhibition by the curator Anselm Franke at the Haus der Kulturen der Welt in Berlin (2011–2012), having grown out of his show-within-a-show in Manifesta 7 in Bolzano (2008). At Manifesta 7, Franke used the site's proximity to Trento, where the famous Council of Trent met in the mid-sixteenth century to discuss matters of Catholic doctrine, as a stepping stone to the question of a "soul" as represented or augured in contemporary artwork. It was a strikingly anti-rationalist thesis, particularly in the context of art's move throughout the twentieth century from being a means of personal expression or collective belief and towards the role of philosophical or conceptual enquiry on a given subject. The notion of a soul challenged the boundaries of self and other, as did the historical documentation and contemporary works Franke gathered together in the Berlin exhibition. Franke showed how the suppression of animism was constituent to modernity, which presented itself as a rational, technologically progressive, disciplined state (Franke 2012). In this, he recalled Freud's argument, through the idea of the uncanny and his "Totem and Taboo" essay, that the modern subject pathologises animism, which Freud understood as the projection of one's inner feelings onto the outside world.

In returning to animism, Franke sought to bring back "modernism's discontents": "social representations, symbolisations, and projections" by which outer reality is "defined in terms of an objectified nature" as well the colonial or primitive Other, which it is practically synonymous with in ethnography. (Ethnography, itself, is a profoundly modernist discipline.) Franke argues that the West's construction of modernism as a progressive mode was made by marginalising animism as a "primitive" (temporally as well as geographically distant) field and suppressing animist tendencies within its own midst. These, he writes nicely, "led a delirious, symptomatic, and anarchic life in the realm of the fictional, in the works of the Romantics, in the phenomena of the mediumistic and in the pathological" (Franke 2012).

I would also add to this list the cult of authenticity of the late nineteenth century's Arts & Crafts movements and, as Franke also notes, the belief in oneness with nature – all of which prove paradoxically so important to the kind of work produced under the sign of post-internet art. This was made apparent in Massimiliano Gioni's 2013 Venice Biennale, "The Encylopedic Palace", which examined artworks and art objects that were ascribed their own power by incorporating supernatural, spiritual, psychiatric, or electronic elements. Leckey's *Universal Addressability* likewise directly confronted the idea of techno-animism by exhibiting technological objects that act as of their own power and volition, often in intelligent ways – from speaker systems to so-called smart refrigerators – alongside more traditional examples of animistic fetishes, such as geoglyphic hill figures. In the subsequent chapter, we will look more in depth at the ways in which the nineteenth-century response to new technologies has returned in the present. The uncanny, Romanticism, Gothic tropes, fetishised authenticity, and animism pervade the work that is, in name at least, at the very forefront of technological progress.

It is useful to include also the computer itself in this list, as well as the iPhone, the FitBit, Google Glass, smart watches, car operating systems, and the many intelligent devices that comprise the "internet of things". The computer is often figured as a site of trepidation, a factish god, which can easily turn against or overwhelm its user. One of the earliest theorisations of computers, Sherry Turkle's *The Second Self: Computers and the Human Spirit* (1984/2005) showed computers as tools that not only do things *for* us but animate objects that do things *to* us. It presented a psychological reading of the relationship between computer and person, drawing on the anxiety provoked by the household computer object, the relation between artificial intelligence and the uncanny, and the fears of how it would alter categories of "alive" and "machine" for children who grew up with computers.

Post-internet art's explorations of non-thinking responses, autism and neurological spectrums of apperception likewise test the proposition of human as system. In the *Long Tail*, for example, Leckey posits the workings of the long tail – the user-generated torrents and seeds that allow for internet niches – as autistic: it can only relate to its own world. "It can't put itself in your shoes" (Leckey 2015, 209). The autistic subject also appears in alarmist literature as the end-game of too much internet use: the user who retreats into him- or herself and loses all capacity for socialisation. As used by artists, however, the figure attains different shades. Autistic people do not filter information the way that non-autistic people do; for them, the feel of a wooden grain, the feel of the fluidity of running water, the coldness of metal objects, and the background sound of air conditioning are all as stimulating as the expressions on a person's face. Neural diversity and a more immediate sensorial responsiveness is seen as a field of promise, not reduction.

Wiener's man/machine overlap also appears within new research into brain functions that frame reason and emotion as neurological systems. (The attention paid to neurological functioning and disorders is now common territory in middle-to-high-brow circles, such as in the writings of Oliver Sacks, and, I would argue, allows for a de-politicisation of the human subject, occluding the influence of politics and economics on behaviour.) In an internet context, the brain as cybernetic system is often allegorised by the search algorithm, in which interest is based not on the user's emotional state but on the feedback systems of one's search history and the search's parameters. This has the added effect of endowing the object with agency; the image itself becomes the tool for attracting searches. Rather than saying that people have a knack for creating popular Instagram images, we might say that people's images are skilled in attracting attention. In an article in *Dis*, for example, the artist Timur Si-Qin, who investigates stock photography and advertising, writes about the ways in which internet searches generate certain patterns (Si-Qin 2013). He reverse-applies this logic to the human brain, showing how eyes and neurotransmitters have evolved to process certain aspects of the visual world over others: "clearer and in colour in the centre of our vision as opposed to blurry and colour-less at the periphery, contributing to the compositional convention of central placement, which is psychologically linked to importance". For Si-Qin this physiological reading can be applied to the emotions generated by images as well – "when you merely see an image of water being splashed on someone's face, your heart rate slows down . . . the image induces a sensation of relax-ation" – a cybernetic-inspired reading of human behaviour that attempts to codify exactly how images such as stock photography can (consistently and broadly) provoke the same emotions in their viewers: in effect, what enables them to be universally applicable (one can think here of another attempt to systematise this).

The animist power of the computer object is intensified in the internet of things, in which surveillant and intelligent mechanisms now inhere in objects that track and respond to our daily use, and by the new functions of the com-puter itself, whose digital processes increasingly take over activities that they can do faster or better, from looking up word definitions to finding restaurant recommendations. Social-media platforms are run by for-profit corporations who structure their websites in order to keep visitors on their sites, and the internet is devoid of time-keeping mechanisms – in the same way that casinos have neither clocks nor windows, so gamblers cannot sense time passing by – and its patterns of activity do not correspond to any natural rhythms. The internet *sucks you in*. Artists often occupy a standpoint of subordination in relation to internet searches, whether explicitly describing the objects of their searches as something they happened to run across or by framing themselves as unthink-ing, reactive systems. This standpoint is affective in character: a sense of horror or self-annoyance at the time spent in front of a computer screen. We can see this in a rather wonderful description by Jacolby Satterwhite of his working method for his green-screened composites, which show him contorted in all sorts of physical positions (Satterwhite 2013). Here, it is the interaction with the internet that he figures as exhausting, not the activity of performance. He begins by ascribing aerobic activity to the physical part of his work, versus his stationary time in front of the computer:

> Currently my performance sessions in front of the green screen are the most aerobic part of my studio practice. When I transfer and alter that data, my initial desire is to amplify and heighten the intensity of each gesture. This may be a reaction to the ratio of time that I am sitting stationary, animating and editing, versus the time I am moving. I am constantly at work creating multiples of "me" on various scales; shapes, colours and purpose are com-posited in spaces with endless possibilities.

Then, the computer becomes associated with the endlessness of its possibilities, and in comparison his performance activity comes to seem kerbed:

> Because of the endless resources of images, textures, references and sound bites offered on the Internet, the digital atmospheres I choose to perform in restrain themselves with a careful selection of drawings as initial prompts. These prompts are pulled from the Internet. For instance, the video *Reifying Desire 5* references drawings of toiletries and vaginal care products. This immediately sends me to Google, searching for art historical references of female bathers in a salon.

The incorporation of these images then becomes, not only demanding on the artist, but also on the viewer, who is almost physically assailed. Viewers have for centuries handled different layers of art-historical allusion; here they are given a martial metaphor of being phenomenologically overwhelmed.

> Thus the viewer is bombarded with references to Picasso's *Les Demoiselles d'Avignon*. This type of neosurrealist play yields massive digital space and endless possibilities. It keeps me poorly postured at the computer, which actually may be the most physically demanding activity, not performing.

And so by the end, Satterwhite has reversed his earlier statement and decided that sitting in front of a computer is more physically exhausting than his literally aerobic actions. The activity with the computer affects not only his mind but is written onto his body: "it keeps me poorly postured". I am quoting Satterwhite at length, first because I like the account's almost performative quality (it starts somewhere and brings you somewhere else; talking is performance too), and second because his experience appears typical of artistic production methods within digital culture. Though the public only sees the finished product of an artwork, the means of arriving at this – physical and mental – are not irrelevant. In the enormous paintings of the Renaissance, we can read the need for assistants and a corporate working method; the *plein air* paintings of the Impressionists were enabled by the innovation of tubes for transporting oil paints. The experience of sitting at a computer and generating material from inside a rectangular screen must also be questioned as a legible part of the artwork itself. Indeed, the very origins of the term "art after the internet" come from its working methods: the artist Marisa Olson used the term to delineate her work from net.art, which was made *on* the internet, while the work she was making came after surfing the net, looking at images and videos, and emailing and chatting (Cornell et al. 2006). The term, as has endlessly been noted, is both confusing and, by now inaccurate, as no one shuts their computer off but walks around all day attached to a smartphone. As the art and technology writer Michael Conner says, art after the iPhone is now made "during during during" (Conner 2013). And this during-ness, this ubiquity, is part of the subject of post-internet art itself: a radically self-reflexive, even narcissistic line of enquiry.

Net.art and digitality

As Parikka and Tiainen's (2010) introduction to their "New Materialisms" con-ference also makes clear, new materialisms and media theory concerns digitality rather than the internet per se. While net.art is primarily concerned with the internet as medium, post-internet art could be more accurately described as an exploration of digitality; at the end of this chapter, we will explore this state as one comprised of disconnections. The conflation between digital culture and internet culture derives partially from context – whatever is online is digital and, in a modified vice versa, whatever is digital is or could be online. In the excerpt quoted from Satterwhite earlier, his description refers to engagement with the internet, in order to produce his digital collages – fantastical, almost New Age-y images that show his body, often clad in cyborg-like reflective gear, contorted into or framed against geometric forms. They are clearly "digital" in their availing of green-screen effects to make the background, in their cita-tion of futuristic elements, in their flattened perspective, and in their use of the human body as yet another shiny computer effect, unmarked by traces of human labour – and indeed, in their openness to a reading where Satterwhite's body is yet another form of matter in the pictorial frame or within the object as it circulates. That is to say, despite the anti-medial stance we can see within post-internet art, where an artwork's formal resolution in a particular medium matters little, digitality emerges as a particular set of concerns. In a lucid analysis of post-internet art produced in response to the show "Speculations on Anony-mous Materials" (2013–2014) at the Fridericianum in Kassel, the theorist Kerstin Stakemeier frames the digital as its own imaginary: "a structure of production methods, materials, body images, distribution channels, and not least crises that it shares with other branches of production". For her, post-internet art is "meta-mediumistic" in that digitality becomes the sign that unites all others. She shows how even works that draw out haptic presentations of images – such as James Richard's *Rosebud* (2013), which looks at scratched-out censorship to Mapplethorpe photographs – or which point to the human hand as the source of production, as in Josh Kline's series of sculptures of hands (*Creative Hands*, 2011, and *Tastemaker's Choice* 2012), are produced or exhibited digitally. Materiality is always digitally mediated.

One might say, too, that the internet, or representations thereof, is also always digitally mediated. That might seem to be adding another layer of semantics onto something quite self-evident – eventually, I will find myself saying the digital is digitally mediated – but I want to suggest that "digitality" picks up on some of the concerns that fall under "immateriality" in the binary opposition material/immaterial initiated by the discourse of photography and film in the twentieth century and tracked through Chapter One. (Notably, in doing so, I am pivoting this chapter's discussion away from materiality.) Post-internet art, despite its moniker, scrutinises the condition of digitality, or the presence of the set of digital concerns in the material world, where digitality means a grouping of political, labour, economic, and social conditions that impact on the image and the body. This is not to drive a wedge between "internet" and "digital", as they are deeply imbricated with each other and should be discussed in concert, but rather to signal how the "digital" has been promoted into a meta-sign for contemporary computer-inflected culture.

The digital in this way is a point of contrast between post-internet art and its most immediate technological predecessor, net.art, which emerged during the 1990s to explore the potential of the internet as a medium for art-making. Net. art and post-internet art, as we shall see later, have an odd chronology between them. This is true particularly in a US context, where a number of the artists, curators, and platforms associated with net.art have also now become associated with post-internet art, such as Guthrie Lonergan, Petra Cortright, or Lauren Cornell. The concerns of these artists remain focused on internet culture or come out of the standpoint of that arena. Other net.artists are still making work. I will later use the chronology of one such artist, Olia Lialina, to suggest that instead of periodisation we can think about the two types of work as divergent in terms of focus and scope.

I also want to use net.art somewhat in relief. Though closely associated with the internet in terms of production and exhibition, it moved fluidly between online and offline instantiations, with central concerns being the formation of communities and the use of information sharing to do so. Despite the fact that the institutional and commercial art world famously had difficulties exhibiting net.art in conventional gallery settings, net.art itself had no trouble existing "in real life". I underline this to suggest that the emergence into the gallery for post-internet art and art concerned with digital technologies is profoundly fraught, but not due to the technical or aesthetic problems of moving an online experiment into a setting for physical viewership. Instead, I want to point to "digitality" as a complicating concern: a mode of alienation between the producer and the circulating image that he or she has made.

First, second, last, third

The overarching difference between net.art and post-internet art is their purview: post-internet art, and art today concerned more broadly with the internet and digital technologies, looks at the everyday effects of internet and digital technologies, focusing particularly on affect. This is in part technologically determined, as internet and digital technologies become an ever-greater part of everyday life. It also forces a different relation to networks and particularly objecthood, as the offline character of the investigation, either in source or in formal resolution, utilises and struggles with materiality in a way that net.art did not.

There has been a large amount of grumbling about post-internet art's amnesia regarding work with the internet that has been done before. The term "post-internet" art is only unhappily accepted, and many have tried to come up with other definitions and typologies. Lialina, for example, suggests breaking up the chronology into the first generation: "Artists working with the Internet as a new medium"; the second: artists who "studied JODI at university"; the "Last": "Net artists active in between dot.com crash and Web 2.0 rise; and the third: the present (Lialina quoted in Jones 2015). The typology ambiguously separates off contemporary from net.art practice, as "third" comes after the "Last", suggesting both that net.art is authentically over, and that it continues in a third version.

This schematic was cited in an interview with Aleskandra Domanović and Oliver Laric, who worked together on the early contemporary art blog VVORK. com. (Domanović and Laric collaborated alongside Christoph Priglinger and Georg Schnitzer on the website, which ran from 2006 to 2012.) The righteous indignation that post-internet's history is "incomplete and distorted", as Laric put it, is indicative of a general dissatisfaction at the idea that post-internet work came out of nowhere or that it is the first to truly engage with the internet (Laric quoted in Jones 2015). The use of the internet for identity play, as we shall detail in Chapter Four, is also an important strand of net.art, such as in the pranks of the made-up Yugoslavian artist Darko Maver, who played on the audience's predilection to see the Balkans as a site of violence and gore, or in the work of Lynn Hershman Leeson in her fictional persona of Roberta Breitmore. Other critics bristle at the overstatement of the claims made on behalf of the internet and the digital. As Andrew Weiner put it in a review of the 2015 New Museum Triennial curated by Lauren Cornell and Ryan Trecartin, the show's claims of absolute novelty are a "McLuhanite fantasy that The Internet Changed Every-thing", which, he continues, ignores "the ways that digitalisation has reinforced existing socioeconomic divisions" (Weiner 2015).

Much of the work net.artists made regarding networks and the symbiosis between man and machine presages post-internet art: there are a lot of visionary texts that have been forgotten or even works that seem essentially re-made with no mention of their predecessors by artists or critics. The controversy engen-dered by Claire Bishop's claim in *Artforum* that, as of the early 2010s, no artists were reacting to the digital is art-historically imprecise but a faithful reflection of the art world's then fixation on analogue technologies and craft. The tome *Mass Effect: Art and the Internet in the Twenty-First Century* (2015), edited by Cornell and the film curator Ed Halter, seeks to close this gap, mapping out the different moments of artistic engagement with the internet and giving voice to the frus-tration and lack of clarity on how they should be connected ("first", "second", "last", "third"). Part of Lialina's achronological chronology reflects the fact that many of net.artists are still working (such as herself), whether one categorises the work as net.art or post-internet. The unsettled question of a history is also suggested by the ongoing furore over the prefix "post" in post-internet art. The term is often read as suggesting work made after the historical emergence of the internet, which leaves in limbo the status of net.art and media arts, both of which were also made "after" the internet. This is, as I mentioned in the Introduc-tion, part of post-internet art's traumatic self-image: one both of radical novelty but also of no-time, of no progression. This uncertain temporality is similar to postmodernism, which was likewise concerned with the recirculation of signi-fiers rather than their production and with pastiche as a mode of historical representation. In contrast, net.art, as well as the tech industry even today, took novelty as profoundly different: it perceived its moment as a beginning.

This sense of optimism is key. Net.art came about in the 1990s, alongside perestroika and the collapse of the Cold War. Manifestoes abounded, proclaiming the new in the time-honoured manner of the historical avant-garde: Haraway's cyborg manifesto (1983), VNS Matrix's "A Cybermanifesto for the 21st Century" (1991), and Alexei Shulgin and Natalie Bookchin's tongue-in-cheek "Introduction to net.art" manifesto (1997).[6] A number of important net. artists were from Russia and Eastern Europe, such as Lialina, Shulgin, and Vuk Cosic, and for them, net.art provided not only inexpensive channels of communication that had been previously unavailable but also a chance to exercise their own beliefs in anti-commodity approaches to art-making against the Western art world. Feminists took advantage of the internet as a tabula rasa: a territory free of inherited power hierarchies. Various groups, gathered under the term cyberfeminism, worked to exploit the web's capacity for disembodiment and its lack of gender constraints. (The term "cyberfeminism" is said to be coined both by the scholar Sadie Plant and the Australian collective VNS Matrix in the same year, 1991.) Part of the cyberfeminist project was already retrospective: to re-write the history of technologies to show women's crucial contribution, undoing the image of technology as a masculine domain. Plant's influential study *Zeroes and Ones: Digital Women and the New Technoculture* (1997), for instance, showed the historical importance of women, such as Ada Lovelace, Anna Freud, and Mary Shelley, to computing and suggested the very make-up of digital technology – coding – as feminine in origin: the proto-binary system of punch cards was inspired by the Jacquard loom and practices of weaving. (Notably this lineage for coding – the support structure the punch cards were held on – already challenges Claude Shannon's ideal of immaterial information.)

Other cyberfeminists conceived of identity as multiplicitous, drawing from Haraway's cyborg, third-wave feminism, and postmodernism, and sought to understand women and women's sexuality as polyvalenced.[7] They used the internet to create a field of new forms of pleasure and knowledge, where power and sexuality were stripped of patriarchal norms. Multimedia artworks (CD-ROMs, video games, virtual reality modules) stressed interaction with the user where he or she could experience this new reality. In VNS Matrix's video game *All New Gen* (1995), for example, "cybersluts", "guerrillas", and "anarcho cyber-terrorists" hack into the Big Daddy Mainframe, the Oedipal embodiment of patriarchal technological power, to create a new world order.

Net.artists' creation and inhabitation of alternate communities of likeminded people was important both to their thinking and the work produced; they used platforms and mailing lists, such as äda'web, Eyebeam, Rhizome.org, and 7–11, to promote and discuss works and joined "surfer clubs" to share internet folk art – the wild, terrible, and fascinating things on the web. These platforms are as much a part of the net.art project as the artworks they supported. In turn, the "mainstream" art world largely ignored them or didn't know where to put them. Art exhibited on a screen was deemed not aesthetic enough. It was difficult to

Figure 3.2　VNS Matrix, still from *All New Gen*, 1992, interactive installation.

Courtesy VNS Matrix

sell or simply to see on a platform beyond a computer console. Some major institutions considered ways to exhibit the work, such as the San Francisco Museum
of Modern Art in its "010101: Art in Technological Times" exhibition (2001)
and the Whitney with its 2000 biennial, but these were exceptions.

Net.artists intervened directly in the fabric of the world and took advantage
of the internet to both initiate and exhibit their projects; while the "medium"
was generally code, many of the works were realised in the real world. And perhaps because of mutual antipathy with art institutions, instead of aiming after
a gallery public, net.art often directly connected with the general public. The
public and its relationship to distribution is later picked by Seth Price in his text
Dispersion (2002/2008), where he posits the distributed tentacles of the web as a
more potent site for a public than the public "plop art" sculptures that dot city
sidewalks and squares. The internet allowed a number of subcultures to come
into contact with each other, transforming what were individual unique interests
into shared pastimes: this was one of the projects of the surfer clubs, where all the
members shared the same aesthetic, which was reinforced by their interaction
with and accumulation of new examples.

Like cybernetics, net.art was concerned with technological systems and with the prospect of using these systems to link to other people. Because of advances with communications technology, cybernetic projects that worked to create the infrastructure for networked encounters moved towards testing what could be done now that the technology was available. Net.art is often read principally in terms of site specificity – in which the means of production, formal resolution, and reception all aligned: the work was made on computers, about computers, to be seen on computers. This, for example, characterises the work of JODI.org, a collective of the Dutch artists Joan Heemskerk and Dirk Paesmans, which, as Lialina notes, is one of the most influential net.art projects on the generation of the late 1990s. JODI.org modified and reassembled different technological elements, such as video games or screen grabs, creating a sense of operating system chaos rather than order, and ran a popular blog. But this wasn't simply narrow self-reflexivity. They also helped champion the free software movement and the more general ethos that information should be free.

Net.art projects' open-ended nature shifted agency onto the user to complete the work or follow his or her path through it. One of the most famous is Lialina's *My Boyfriend Came Back from the War* (1996), in which various frames showing pictures of a man and a woman and various sentences allow the user to construct his or her narrative of what happens to the couple in question. It was

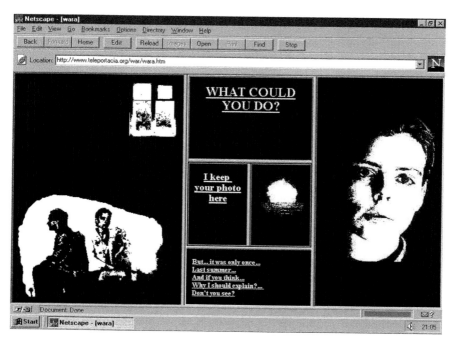

Figure 3.3 Olia Lialina, *My Boyfriend Came Back from the War*, 1996, website.

oriented both away from the typical conception of the artist as producer and worked to activate a specific community who would interact with the work. One of the chief differences between the net.art moment and that of the post-internet moment is the scale of internet usership. By the mid-2000s, the idea of the "mass" audience comes into play, and artists start thinking of virality, audience, and anonymity in wholly different ways. The anonymity of much of the pioneering generation of net.artists, who often chose to represent themselves not as artists but as pure functions of the internet (JODI.org, VVORK.com, 0.10010110101.org), for instance, is different from the attempts at anonymity by artists such as Ann Hirsch or DIS, who attempt to bring themselves into line with the "default" or "mass".

Many net.art works were concerned with the formation of communities, in cyberspace or IRL ("in real life"). In the *King's Cross Phone-In* (1994), Heath Bunting listed the phone numbers of different telephone booths around King's Cross Station in London on newsgroups and email lists and invited all to call the telephone boxes on 5 August 1994. It was an open work, though the group would have been self-selecting according to those who received the information in the first place. Bunting issued instructions for what to say as well as, curiously, what he would say about the work when it was actually over:

(1) call no./nos. and let the phone ring a short while and then hang up
(2) call these nos. in some kind of pattern
    (the nos. are listed as a floor plan of the booth)
(3) call and have a chat with an expectant or unexpectant person
(4) go to Kings X station watch public reaction/answer the phones and chat
(5) do something different

This event will be publicised worldwide

I will write a report stating that:

(1) no body rang
(2) a massive techno crowd assembled and danced to the sound of ringing telephones
(3) something unexpected happened[8]

The documentation of this work is inevitably the email announcement from which this list of instructions is quoted. The locus for the event, that is, is given as the initial, online proposition and not the results that will follow (which in any case seem irrelevant as Bunting had already decided what he would say happened). This focus on the original proposition in the documentation is pronounced but not atypical for net.art projects, which often took the form of a user-generated experiment. In the Barbie Liberation Organization (BLO) campaign of 1993, for example, the group ®TMark transferred $8,000 from a group of military veterans and used this money to switch the voice boxes in GI Joe dolls with those of Barbie dolls, so that when customers bought the GI Joe soldiers they said things like "The beach is the place for summer!" (This followed the introduction of a new Barbie doll who, in reality, said "Math is hard".) ®TMark uploaded a detailed video on how to switch the boxes onto their website so that others could accomplish the same feat. This project is historicised by means of the Barbie Liberation Army poster announcing the event: the moment of proposition rather than the moments of execution. This is no doubt owing to the fact that it would difficult to represent the different realisations of the Barbie or *King's Cross Phone-In* project, but it is also a particular means of representing the history of net.art projects and pranks. The reproduction of these calls to projects is as much a documentation of a history as of artwork. The historicisation of the movement itself, that is, reflects its liminal position between artistic and social experiment.

Other works moved fluidly and consciously between IRL and online communities to deliberately affect offline legislation and norms. Shu Lea Cheang's *Brandon* (1998–1999) used coding as a means to bring in different participants – dispersing the authorship of the work – as well as working with offline communities to dislodge broader social assumptions, in this case about gender, that it read as instantiated in offline thought. Cheang based *Brandon* on the rape and murder of the transgender teen Brandon Teena in Nebraska. (This case later

Figure 3.4 Shu Lea Cheang, *Brandon*, 1998–1999, Interactive networked code (html, Java, Javascript, and server database), dimensions vary with installation.

Courtesy Solomon R. Guggenheim Museum, New York

became the story of the feature film *Boys Don't Cry*, 1999.) Over the course of a year, Cheang used a website to tell a non-linear story of Brandon's identity, collaging together hyperlinked images of bodies, chat-room conversations on crime and punishment, and moving images. She stresses that it is a "multi-artist, multi-site, multi-institution collaboration", with different participants and coding languages within the work (Cheang quoted in Ho 2012). Other dimensions of the work took place offline, in performances such as "Would the Jurors Please Stand Up? Crime and Punishment as Net Spectacle" (1999), in conjunction with the Institute on Arts and Civic Dialogue at Harvard University, which used a virtual court system to preside over a net-public trial of sexual assaults in real life and cyberspace. *Brandon* challenged the very vocabulary of bodily representations as well as fixed and stable identities, offering instead a multi-user, non-linear, hyperlinked array of images and text to create a composite picture whose totality could never be viewed. The visualising tool of the camera is here seen to be as inadequate as the legal frameworks in place for trying sexual assault cases.

Private/public

The world "online" was conceived of as a place of radically free information, in which the desire to make information visible and able to circulate trumped conventional notions of private/public. It is worth remembering the enormity of the shift of making our private lives public: the architecture of many of our homes still contains the split between the public rooms (the living room and dining room, for example) and the private ones (the bedrooms, kitchen, and playroom). This is also at times a gendered split, as is borne out by the headscarves and *abayas* worn by Muslim women, which serve as an extension of privacy while out in public. In 2000–2003, Eva and Franco Mattes, the artists behind the net.art project 0.10010110101.org, created *Life Sharing* (2000–2003), where they allowed others complete access into their computer files – images, emails, word documents – making their lives publicly accessible. Though the only ones who could access their shared files – they are a couple – were those with the technical nous to access the server they set up for the project, it tested the dispersion of boundaries of private life to other people and also created the impression of the life of the Mattes couple as reflective of, or reducible to, data: the autobiography reflected in their files was tantamount to a portrait of the couple themselves.

In my focus on border-crossing between online and offline behaviour, I don't want to mischaracterise the importance of the online world to net.art but rather to give further nuance to its portrayal. The online world was often seen as a refuge from offline existence. In *Life Sharing*, the Mattes were in a sense attempting to live their lives online, as circulating information. This online/offline split does not map onto the material/immaterial, or material/digitality, split of post-internet. The online world was not a "deferral" of real-world concerns but rather a new reality that artists worked to create from nothing: their aesthetic decisions were in this sense deeply politicised and ethical, which can also be seen in the hacktivist strain of net.art producers and more explicitly political artists. A comparison to the post-internet projects' staging performances of identity on the internet reveals the sophistication by which earlier net.art projects approached the means of internet production. Whereas most of these use existing platforms of YouTube, Instagram, Gmail, or Tumblr, net.art's commitment to open-source technology was explicitly to counteract the monopoly of internet browsers such as Netscape or Internet Explorer – a sense of political understanding that has subsided.[9]

The idea of "jamming" the medium connects net.art to a number of new media projects, such as the video art projects of the Raindance Foundation and of Nam June Paik, and their interference in corporate structures of information. If these publics weren't always formed in the traditional sense of a group of people convoked in the same space, what identified them as a community was their possession of shared information. The knowledge of insider information, much like in the art world at large, distinguished the group from the larger public. The Mattes, for example, were also behind the gambit of Darko Maver (1998–1999). Maver was a Yugoslavian artist they made up, who created gruesome sculptures of murder victims, a subject matter many in the art world connected to the larger context of the Balkan wars of the time. The Matteses then killed him off – and the images "Maver" created were revealed to be actual photographs from the Balkan conflict, re-positioned in an art context. Like *Life Sharing*, Darko Maver began online as a project that was open-ended: it was not clear how the work would resolve itself, and it ended up being more successful than I believe they imagined, as Maver was eventually invited to participate in the Yugoslavian pavilion at the Venice Biennale in 1999.

Figure 3.5 Eva and Franco Mattes, *Darko Maver Resurrected*, 1999, photograph.

Courtesy the artists and Carroll / Fletcher, London

Representation in post-internet work

Though the role of the art market in forcing a difference between these two movements can be overstated – post-internet art is more market-aligned – post-internet art's emergence into the "mainstream" institutional setting of the art world has resulted in some obvious tensions. At its most basic, this is the contradictory desire to make work *about* circulation for a gallery setting in which images are returned to unique objects. One response to this is a shift from direct usage to representation. In 2010, for example, the Mattes made a work called *No Fun* where Franco Mattes staged a suicide on the then-popular site Chatroulette.com. When the Mattes's video feed came up, users would see the artist hanging from the ceiling but, obviously distanced by the internet, were unable to do anything about this or reach him in real life. The work itself is a video reel showing, on the one side, users' responses and the static feed of the hanged Franco Mattes on the other. The responses are quite extraordinary – most people laugh or think it is a joke, and only a few seem genuinely horrified or seek to help. The work itself is morally questionable, as it doesn't acknowledge the scale of its own shock tactics; rather, its hyper-laconic title – *No Fun* – deliberately underplays the affective register of both the represented act and the spectatorial response. *No Fun* consists of a direct intervention via the computer into the lives of anonymous others but also resolves this in a formal, exhibitory setting. None of the respondents can do anything but watch. Indeed, it pays close attention to its conditions of exhibition and is made to be shown in a gallery that has been mocked up to mimic the domestic environment in which one would log onto Chatroulette.com. The conditions it creates are not ones of participation but of spectatorship.

In *The Language of New Media* (2001), writing about the early art of the internet, Lev Manovich held that the internet lends itself to being conceived of as a database rather than something with narrative potential. However the hallmark of database technology – that is, information – is absent qua information in the work of the post-internet artists. Rather, it finds itself dramatically "visualised", and narrative, or more specifically allegory, digitally and visually represented, is paramount. One might call post-internet the "Pictures of" generation. The work is trying to create reflections of what life is like when saturated with digital technology. Exhibition in a gallery setting forces artists to work in a realist idiom that is opposed to the interventionary spirit of net.art – but also of post-internet methodologies itself. Thus, while net.art used the internet for its projects, post-internet often finds itself forced to make pictures about the internet. Camille Henrot's video about the archive of the National Science Library in Washington, DC (*Grosse Fatigue*, 2013) suggests the internet as archive by picturing the opening and closing of browser windows, each of which gives a view onto the kind of arcane and wondrous information that can be found on the internet. That she relates this to the physical shelves in which specimens of the Science Library are kept is symptomatic: these are archives of preservation, not circulation or even technical reiteration. An installation made by Kline that responds

Figure 3.6 Eva and Franco Mattes, still from *No Fun*, 2010, online performance HD video, 15 minutes, 46 seconds.

Courtesy the artists and Carroll / Fletcher, London

to the Occupy protests in Lower Manhattan's Zuccotti Park (*Freedom*, 2015) shows dummy policemen with iPads in their stomachs that display monologues taken from social media. It uses effectively snapshots of Facebook testimonies, illustrating the level of debate on social media rather than enabling one to occur around his project. These are images of invisible processes of communication in a digital medium: a transposition of concerns from one dynamic technological setting to a static technological one.

Importantly, this tendency to fix representations of connectivity stands in tension with the mode itself of working in post-internet art, where possession of images is inadequate and participation is key: think of Leckey and the "precious and dull" objects of *The Universal Addressability of Dumb Things* that he returns to a more plastic, manipulable site of iteration in *UniAddDmbThs*; Laric's privileging of the copy over the real thing; and the widespread tendency to exhibit ongoing versions of a work, instead of delineating one as final. As Joselit argues in *After Art*, and Laric, in *Versions*, an image becomes significant due to its circulation; the more it appears, the more connections to it are made, the more powerful it is. Ownership and dislocation from this network of circulation decreases an image's importance, even as post-internet artists make work designed for possession. Joselit framed art's current crisis as a function of an infrastructure made for the unique (fundamentalist) image, in an era when the reiterable (neoliberal) image, which accrues value through circulation, is ascendant. A museum's acquisition of an image drains it of its actual potency; a museum's collection, ultimately, will become worth less and less (and so, he argues, it should) (Joselit 2013, 85–96). Much social-media activity by post-internet artists, for example, is seen problematically as liminal to their "real" work (we will explore this further in Chapter Six) – this is the same set of activities of blogging, posting, and commenting that have been easily and mellifluously theorised, as we have seen, as part of the larger project of net.art, in which images were less often removed from circulation. This spirit of alienation from one's own labour and one's own image is mediated by digitality, the mode of presentation of an image formally in flux but en route to reification. The interest in sculpture as a formal mode of articulation for post-internet works, as in the work of Helen Marten, in which digital processes informs 3D production, further shows how digitality can be seen at an obverse to circulation, even while signalling participation in a network of exchange of ideas, images, and idioms.

Indeed, the presentation of work under the sign of the digital ostensibly keeps the artwork within the medium of exchange, *renouvellement*, and circulation though it has entered a pathway of acquisition and sequestration. Digitality suggests an image still in flux, rather than the finality associated with indexical or analogue production, but also an image that denies temporal progression in its very technological make-up. Digital coding seeks to replicate, to reiterate exactly what came before, as wholly and as faithfully as possible, with no data loss or corruption. This is part of what Stakemeier calls the crisis character of post-internet art, which she reads as a perversion of science fiction and digital futurology, in which teleological progression falters:

> Digitality is now a link between media and times, a structural feature of a present that is composed of the digital recoding of its past – without offering a future beyond the technological updating of these drifting repetitions.
>
> (Stakemeier 2014, 172)

This again reflects economic and social context. The late Marxist understanding of art as a function of capital, she shows, is beset by its own discordances:

post-internet work is concerned with post-2008 disconnection and the credit crunch as much as with seamless connection. Accelerationism, one of its key modes of connection to economic factors, welcomes mass economic destabilisation on its warped course towards social justice.

The understanding of the current moment as one of radical upheaval plays into post-internet art's uncertain genealogy as well as its understanding of hybridised practice not as a utopian beginning, but as a forced-hand response. In the following chapters, we will look more closely at the work itself to see how it has developed alongside geopolitical upheaval as much as financial crisis, how embodiment emerges within post-internet work, and how identity is framed as a mode of ironic inhabitation. Rather than trying to resolve these disjunctions, I speculate that they are symptomatic: the problems here are the thing, which contemporary work concerned with digital technologies seeks to pry open and investigate, rather than celebrate or recoup. Indeed, digitality can be read for its primary non-metaphorical function: it enables circulation on new networks. This trades the network the artist points to – the circulation of the Mattes's image on Chatroulette – for one of various internet-enabled forking paths of visibility and capital. This question of circulation and the image being "everywhere" – and the affective resonances that have emerged in response – will be taken up in the next chapter.

Notes

1 Notably, Steyerl, who is represented by the Andrew Kreps Gallery in New York, has taken all of her lectures off the regular art market and is now selling *Duty Free Art* as well as *I Dreamed a Dream: Politics in the Age of Mass Art Production* (2013) and *Is the Museum a Battlefield?* (2013) to donate funds to Kurdish areas. The first sale of the lecture went to aid the reconstruction in Kobane, and forthcoming sales will support refugee relief as well as local art production.
2 Weizman's understanding of the forensic object is notable in this context: he looks at objects as a means of providing a testimony, rather than human rights investigations' primary methodology of oral histories. See Thomas Keenan and E. Weizman, *Mengele's Skull: The Advent of Forensic Aesthetics*, Berlin: Sternberg Press, 2011.
3 Opening remarks to the conference "New Materialism and Digital Culture", co-organised by Milla Tiainen and Jussi Parikka, Angela Ruskin University, Cambridge, 21–22 June 2010. This quotation is taken from the transcription on Parikka's blog: http://jussiparikka. net/2010/06/23/what-is-new-materialism-opening-words-from-the-event/ (last accessed on 23 April 2016). See also the *New Materialisms: Ontology, Agency, and Politics*, ed. Diana Coole and Samantha Frost, Durham, NC: Duke University Press, 2010.
4 The theories have not been without their detractors: object-oriented ontology was the subject of a rollicking critique in *Artforum*, in which Andrew Cole memorably described it as "commodity fetishism in academic form". A. Cole, "These Obscure Objects of Desire", *Artforum*, vol. 53, no. 10, Summer 2015. Cole questions the novelty of OOO's privileging of objects and indeed OOO's claim to counter Kantian philosophy, as for Cole the categories of real and sensual object simply parallel phenomena and noumena. Whether these theories are really new is a challenge frequently put to new materialism as well. As this overview suggests, it is beyond the scope of this book to do justice to these theories, nor to the varying ways that post-internet artists interact with them – whether as general research, a means to understand their own ideas, or, more problematically, to supply in advance a theorisation of

their work. My focus is artistic production itself, set into the context of its related theories, and the scholarship on new materialisms is so vast and in flux that only a book-length treatment could adequately respond to it. I am thus here identifying key references rather than fully engaging with its debates.

5 My thanks to Mike Cooter for sharing with me his doctoral work at Goldsmiths University, London, "MacGuffin", which focuses on the structural agency of objects, on this subject.

6 A number of these have recently been collected in the book *Manifestos for the Internet Age*, Paris: Greyscale Press, 2015.

7 See for example María Fernández, Faith Wilding, and Michelle M. Wright (ed.), *Domain Errors! Cyberfeminist Practices*, New York: Autonomedia, 2002, and Jessie Daniels, "Rethinking Cyberfeminism(s): Race, Gender, and Embodiment", *Women's Studies Quarterly*, vol.37, nos.1 & 2, Spring/Summer 2009, 101–24.

8 From "King's Cross Phone-In", *Art and Electronic Media* [website], 23 February 2012, http://www.artelectronicmedia.com/artwork/kings-cross-phone-in (last accessed on 23 April 2016). See also Rachel Greene, *Internet Art*, London: Thames & Hudson, 2004, pp. 34–36.

9 As Pauline van Mourik Broekman, who was part of the magazine *Mute*, points out, open-source technology should also be distinguished from free software, which regarded open-source systems as transitional to corporate platforms. As she notes, the fact that free software and its politics are by and large absent in the common narrative of net.art is testament to the fact that the "mainstream" art world's knowledge (and historiography) of the period remains only partial.

Bibliography

Atkins, E. (2014) Email. 24 June.

Blas, Z. (2014) "Contra-Internet Aesthetics". In: Kholeif, O. ed. *You Are Here: Art after the Internet*, London: Cornerhouse, 86–97.

Cole, A. (2015) "These Obscure Objects of Desire", *Artforum*, 53 (10), 319–23.

Conner, M. (2013) "What's Postinternet Got to Do with Net Art?" *Rhizome* [blog], 1 November, http://rhizome.org/editorial/2013/nov/1/postinternet/ (last accessed on 23 April 2016).

Cornell, L. (2015) "Trevor Paglen in Conversation with Lauren Cornell". In: Cornell, L. and Halter, E. ed. (2015) *Mass Effect: Art and the Internet in the Twenty-First Century*, Cambridge, MA: MIT Press. 255–66.

Cornell, L. Olson, M., Arcangel, C., Bell-Smith, M., Staehle, W., Connor, M. and Jones, C. (2006) "Net Results: Closing the Gap between Art and Life Online". *Time Out New York*. 9 February, https://www.timeout.com/newyork/art/net-results (last accessed on 16 October 2016).

Daniels, J. (2009) "Rethinking Cyberfeminism(s): Race, Gender, and Embodiment". *Women's Studies Quarterly*, 37 (1/2), 101–24.

Fernández, M., Wilding, F. and Wright, M. M. ed. (2002) *Domain Errors! Cyberfeminist Practices*, New York: Autonomedia.

Franke, A. (2012) "Animism: Notes on an Exhibition". *e-flux journal* [online journal], 36, http://www.e-flux.com/journal/animism-notes-on-an-exhibition/ (last accessed on 23 April 2016).

Greene, R. (2004) *Internet Art*, London: Thames & Hudson.

Harman, G. (2009) *Prince of Networks: Bruno Latour and Metaphysics*, Melbourne: Re.press.
——— (2011) *The Quadruple Object*, London: Zero Books.

Hayles, N. K. (1999) *How We Became Posthuman: Virtual Bodies in Cybernetics, Literature and Informatics*, Chicago and London: University of Chicago Press.

Ho, Y. (2012) "Shu Lea Cheang on *Brandon*". *Rhizome* [blog], 10 May, http://rhizome.org/editorial/2012/may/10/shu-lea-cheang-on-brandon/ (last accessed on 23 April 2016).

Jones. C. (2015) "Aleskandra Domanović and Oliver Laric in Conversation with Caitlin Jones". In: Cornell, L. and Halter, E. ed. (2015) *Mass Effect: Art and the Internet in the Twenty-First Century*, Cambridge, MA: MIT Press, 107–22.

Joselit, D. (2013) *After Art*, Princeton: Princeton University Press.

Keenan, T. and Weizman, E. (2011) *Mengele's Skull: The Advent of Forensic Aesthetics*, Berlin: Sternberg Press.

"King's Cross Phone-In" (2012) *Art and Electronic Media* [website], 23 February, http://www.artelectronicmedia.com/artwork/kings-cross-phone-in (last accessed on 23 April 2016).

Latour, L. (1993) *We Have Never Been Modern*. Porter, C. trans. Cambridge, MA: Harvard University Press.

——— (2011) *On the Modern Cult of the Factish Gods*. MacLean, H. and Porter, C. trans. Durham, NC: Duke University Press.

Leckey, M. (2009) "In the Long Tail". In: Cornell, L. and Halter, E. ed. (2015) *Mass Effect: Art and the Internet in the Twenty-First Century*, Cambridge, MA: MIT Press, 199–212.

Parikka, J. and Tiainen, M. (2010) "New Materialism and Digital Culture". Angela Ruskin University, Cambridge, 21–22 June. Quoted from the transcription on *Jussi Parikka* [blog], http://jussiparikka.net/2010/06/23/what-is-new-materialism-opening-words-from-the-event/

Plant, S. (1997) *Zeroes and Ones: Digital Women and the New Technoculture*, London: Fourth Estate.

Satterwhite, J. (2013) quoted in Cornell, L. (2013) "Techno-Animism". *Mousse*, 37, http://moussemagazine.it/articolo.mm?id=941 (last accessed on 23 April 2016).

Si-Qin, T. (2013) "Stock Photography as Evolutionary Attractor". *Dis Magazine* [online magazine], http://dismagazine.com/dystopia/42017/stock-photography-as-evolutionary-attractor/ (last accessed on 3 May 2016).

Stakemeier, K. (2014) "Prosthetic Productions: The Art of Digital Bodies on 'Speculations on Anonymous Materials' at Fridericianum, Kassel". *Texte zur Kunst*, 93, 166–82.

Steyerl, H. (2009) "In Defence of the Poor Image". *e-flux journal* [online journal], 10, http://www.e-flux.com/journal/in-defense-of-the-poor-image/ (last accessed on 23 April 2016).

——— (2011) "The Politics of the Archive: Lecture Given as Part of 'Film as a Critical Practice'". OCA, Oslo, 16 May, http://www.oca.no/programme/audiovisual/film-as-a-critical-practice-hito-steyerl (last accessed on 23 April 2016).

——— (2015) "Duty Free Art". *e-flux journal* [online journal], 63, 2015, http://www.e-flux.com/journal/duty-free-art/ (last accessed on 23 April 2016).

Tretyakov, S. (1929) "The Biography of the Object". *October* (2006), 118, 57–62.

Turkle, S. (1984/2005) *The Second Self: Computers and the Human Spirit*, Cambridge, MA: MIT Press.

Weiner, A. S. (2015) "Surround Audience: New Museum Triennial 2015". *Art-Agenda* [online magazine], http://www.art-agenda.com/reviews/"surround-audience-new-museum-triennial-2015"/ (last accessed on 23 April 2016).

4 Violence and the surveilled internet

In Rabih Mroué's *The Pixelated Revolution* (2012) a Syrian protester records a sniper in the act of shooting him. To the sniper's raised gun, the protester raises his camera phone. There is the sound of a gunshot, and the man falls. The video shows the sky. Is the man wounded or dead? Mroué's work, which takes the form of a "non-academic lecture" in a narrated digital video, looks at the practice of Syrian protesters who capture their own deaths on camera, with these videos being later uploaded to YouTube. He pits this specific phenomenon against the long-standing relationship between the camera and death, where taking a photographic image is seen as akin to stealing one's soul. Mroué recalls another nineteenth-century belief, that the last image one sees before dying is imprinted on the retina of one's eyes. If you could only peel away and develop this film, you could see the last moment of a murdered man's or woman's life.

The folk belief suggests an identity between the retina and the photograph: the retina acts like a photograph, with the image somehow burnt onto its celluloid film. But Mroué turns the analogy around: for the Syrian protestor, the eye acts not as a photograph but as a lens, and the camera, an integral part of the body– an optical prosthesis. Can we learn, he asks, the murderer's identity from this new eye? And why does the protestor not run away from the raised gun? Mroué speculates that the mediation of the mobile phone isolates the event from reality: the protester thinks what he sees is happening in a movie and that he won't die. Mroué, too, believes that the cameraman hasn't died, because we see his images. But what, he asks in the end, about the images we have not seen?

The posited relationship here between the camera phone and the Syrian Civil War is symptomatic of the treatment of networked images in art concerned with the internet and digital technologies: it taps into an undercurrent of violence while attempting to understand how new technologies mediate and communicate the relationship between "here" and "elsewhere" in the context of the internet. Who watches the YouTube videos that show the protestors' deaths? The camera phone in this case is not simply a mode of recording technology but a means of circulation: the images are asked to perform in a mode of virality as well as testimony.

The first waves of understanding the internet as affecting cultural production and consumption more generally – how the internet affects culture

Figure 4.1 Rabih Mroué, *The Pixelated Revolution*, 2012, video, colour, sound, 21 minutes, 58 seconds, video still composite.

Courtesy the artist and Sfeir-Semler Gallery, Beirut & Hamburg

offline – focused on the internet primarily as a mode of circulation. Again, in Seth Price's 2002 text *Dispersion*, the artist argued that the internet transforms the notion of the public from one of a mass audience to one of dispersed strands of interest. Mark Leckey's *In the Long Tail* (2009) performance similarly analysed the way circulation on the internet privileges subcultures rather than mainstream pop culture, building off a 2004 article by *Wired* editor Chris Anderson in which he coined the term "the long tail".

In the following, I want to argue that post-internet art and art responding to digital technologies have moved beyond these site-specific and internet-related readings, firstly, towards a more affective and demotic portrayal of the internet's circulation and, second, in a move to undermine the myth of cyberspace as a non-physical, purely mental space. The idea of circulation is pictured in a narrative, even sociological way, in works that suggest a conflict between offline modes of existence and the pressing need (or desire) to be online all the time, testing what this can mean for the self. Politically, the effects of the internet as a circulatory mechanism and its memes are seen as exemplary of globalisation and feed into the anxieties it provokes. In the second half of the chapter, I focus on a more obvious challenge to the virtuality of the internet: the "War on Terror" and its associated conflicts.[1] The years of the Web 2.0 and the internet's emergence as a mass medium coincide with the conflicts of the war on terrorism, which has itself utilised networks as military tools, in what is known as network-centric warfare. The practice of warfare has also become more visual: it is conducted through targets in cross-hairs, by networked drone operations, and through intelligence-gathering via satellite imagery.[2] Operating a drone means operating computer consoles, an identity exploited by video games. The military origins of the internet, via ARPANET, which was the first network of computers, is also a factor here, though I suspect the influence of this association is waning. As important is the feel of the war on terrorism – the notion of the West being continually at war against an enemy who is both an a-territorial network, and one who keeps shifting. Since 2001, the US and its coalition partners have waged war against the Taliban in Afghanistan; the Baathists in Iraq; the Ghaddafi regime in Libya; and Al Qaeda, IS, and other Islamist non-state armed groups globally. This is the historical context for the Web 2.0, and I argue that it is reflected both in art's preoccupation with violence and its presentation of the conflict as shadowing the form of the network, supplanting the here/there binary of classic ethnographical film with a here/everywhere.

Finally, before we turn in earnest to these discussions, I want to pick up on one last element from the Mroué lecture-performance with which we began this chapter: that of the camera as an optical prosthesis. Mroué's protester, whose body has been extended by technology, mistakes the mediation of life for reality. But how gross an error really is this? Much actual life takes place online, and its virtuality does not invalidate what happens there. A large part of post-internet art is devoted to understanding how online life can be understood as part of "material" life (this indeed is part of Marisa Olson's very term), and one important means of doing so is to understand the normalisation of technology as it impacts upon the body. To complete our reading of the posthuman, we will have to turn to its once opposing figure – the uncanny – in order to understand the way in which this polarity has been adapted for a discourse of circulation and hyper-visibility.

The uncanny valley

One recurring trope of post-internet art is that of the overly lifelike digital representation (see, for example, the work of Josh Kline, Ed Atkins, Magali Reus, Gil Leung, or Hannah Sawtell) – fetishistic in its slick appearance, whether of clean, globular raindrops running down a preternaturally shiny surface or a face of unsurpassingly flawless skin. This is figured equally as a celebration of the capacities of digital representation, a semi-ironic embrace of advertising norms, and an anxiety over critical co-option. I want to look at this slickness from a historical precedent: that of the initial apparitions of the posthuman in an art context versus the response it engendered in the form of Mike Kelley's ode to angst and low taste, the exhibition "The Uncanny" (1993).

In the 1970s, the Japanese robotics professor Masahiro Mori identified the concept of the "uncanny valley" to describe a valley-shaped curve of affective response to human likeness such as robots, animation, stuffed animals, or puppets. If the likenesses were too amateurish or wonky, Mori found, the audience would not believe in their reality: they would fail to elicit any empathy. On the other hand, if they were too realistic, they would provoke strong feelings of aversion from the observers. (Jasia Reichardt, the curator of "Cybernetic Serendipity", helped bring the term to the attention of the West in her book *Robots: Fact, Fiction and Prediction* in 1978.) The fear or disgust elicited by these too realistic likenesses, the hypothesis holds, makes the robot fall into the "uncanny", the concept of something being both familiar and strange, that Freud identified in his 1919 essay of the same name. "What is *heimlich* [secret, concealed] thus comes to be *unheimlich*", he famously writes (Freud 1919/1959, 375). The "unheimlich" (uncanny) allows for the revealing of what has previously been kept hidden. As we face the public airing of our own repressed impulses, we are unnerved and even disgusted by what we see. The robot or the digital avatar, so realistic as to appear human, becomes not just surprising upon discovery of its mechanistic or digital origins, but horrific.

One guiding spirit for thinking through the return of this figure is the late Kelley. The California artist, who mined his own history as fodder for artistic production, crossed over between art, film, music, and writing and waged a deliberate and knowing assault on taste as a classist signifier. He was keenly interested in the suppression of memories signalled by the uncanny as well as the uncanny's formal resolution in the mode of literaless, collecting lifelike sculptures, under-stylised reproductions, totemic fetish items, mannequins, and dolls. In 1993, he curated a major exhibition looking at these objects alongside works of contemporary art, "The Uncanny".[3] The exhibition posed the figure in mode of anxiety and unrest. Valerie Smith, the organiser of the Sonsbeeck festival, which commissioned the project, wrote later:

> It began, in part, with a profound fascination with the human figure, followed by a more reflective view on this fascination. To a certain extent, it was a response to recent shows at the time, such as Jeffrey Deitch's 'Post Human' (1992–93), which dealt with technological evolution and genetic engineering to improve the construction of our bodies and personalities with the aim of creating superhumans – promoting the 'Me generation' on a global scale. Despite (or perhaps because of) the fact that Mike was included in 'Post Human', he reacted against Deitch's concept of body commodification as the zeitgeist. 'The Uncanny' offered a more demanding psychological perspective – a critique sited at the intersection of metaphysics,

ontology and the belief systems that surround the relations between objects and human beings.

(Smith 2013, 19)

As Smith writes, Kelley's "Uncanny" exhibition sought to look at repressed memory syndrome, or the ways in which repressed events, being denied expression, appear in other, strange forms. Kelley noted, in his catalogue essay, how struck he was by Freud's and others' enumerations of items that provoke the uncanny and what he was seeing in the art world at large (Kelley 1993/2003).[4] He sought to contest, as Smith shows, the "new" figuration of the body that Deitch alleged in his show of the posthuman, as well its relationship to contemporary developments in technology, to reveal instead its historical and primary, subconscious roots.

Deitch's "Post Human", the counterpoint to "Uncanny", took an optimistic, technology-infused look at figurative sculpture, in which the body appeared powerful, shiny, sublime, and anatomically inimitable. Visuality is key throughout. The catalogue to the exhibition mimics the high-production values aesthetics of a glossy magazine, collating images of works by Duane Hanson, Gilbert & George, Joseph Beuys, and Katharina Fritsch alongside advertisement-like photographs showing the body as an emblem of glamour and power: Ivana Trump before and after plastic surgery, a still dark-skinned Michael Jackson, and virtual sex simulations. Like the work of DIS, it converged the languages of advertising and branding with those of artistic image-making and, together with the show, explored the notion that technology could create better humans – figured as better bodies. Technology would become physically and visually legible, writ on the body itself. Bodies could become commodities, circulated and sold, the magazine-like catalogue implied – even fetish objects, glossed to a shine. The overlap between this presentation of the body and that of the contemporary shiny, hygienic, posthuman bodies discussed in Chapter Two is not incidental.

Though it explicitly espoused an idea of the body-commodity, "Post Human" appears tinged by its association with the market in ways it did not intend, and which may have hurt its art-historical reputation. All of the work within it was eminently collectible and expensive, and the premise itself, as Smith indicates that Kelley noted, in line with the aspirational culture and conspicuous consumerism of the 1980s. Perhaps we also now know Deitch goes on to become an art dealer with Deitch Projects, in the exaggerated persona of a canny businessman.[5] But its market alignment appears most striking because "Post Human" is at odds with the history of the 1990s as it has been written, in which art's powerful reaction to AIDS and its exploration of the abject are dominant. A number of the artists associated with this thematising of a loss of control over the body were in "Post Human", such as Robert Gober or Kiki Smith. Yet, for Deitch, the unmooring of the human body as a stable reference point, beset by plastic surgery, chemical enhancement, and mechanistic improvement, was a step towards newfound freedoms and enhanced humanity (Deitch 1992).

It is easy to understand why someone with a modicum of criticality and investment in a psychological relationship to the body would want to counter Deitch's glossy exhibition. Kelley dismissed Deitch's hook of technological progression and indeed all his claims of newness for these representations of the body, and instead put forward representations of the body as psychological provocations of feelings of unease. Within the *Wunderkammer*-like sections of the "Uncanny", we begin to see the exhibition as forming a B-side to "Post Human", a history of weirdness, repression, animism, and idolatry in mass-produced copies and superfluous number. Kelley went after kitsch as well as the uncanny – a "cheap and false version of the true" (Kelley 1993/2003, 82). The "Uncanny", with this mix of motivations, thus sought not to look at a history of representations of the animate body, such as classical sculpture, that "timeless" phenomenon, but its kitsch counterpart, representations of inanimate bodies.

Reviewing the show after its 2004 partial reprisal at Tate Liverpool and MMK Vienna, the scholar Margaret Iverson notes how Adorno called the copy the very counterpoint to autonomous art (Iverson 2005). The superfluous number, the idea that the object on show is one of an untold number, deepens the sense of the uncanny, not only in its link to the repetition compulsion, but for the patheticness of its attempt to stave off death. At issue in the "Uncanny", as in the uncanny valley, is the similitude to life without reaching life itself: not a question of the immortality of Deitch's "Post Human" body but of the idolatrous attempts to come to terms with or deflect thoughts about the possibility of death.

Looking back, one can see that a further point of contrast between Kelley's "Uncanny" and Deitch's "Post Human" is not simply its treatment of the body but the two exhibitions' differing relation to site specificity and circulation. The inclusion of Kelley's exhibition as a work within the Sonsbeeck festival was predicated on its site specificity, which was Sonsbeeck's theme at the time.[6] The superfluity and excess contained within the show made it an exhibition if not antithetical to travelling, not one light on its feet either. "Post Human", by contrast, which travelled to four sites,[7] took the motif of circulation on board, figuring its catalogue as a magazine, thus facilitating the transition of the exhibition's sculptures to circulating image. That is, if the uncanny is concerned with the repressed made visible, the posthuman understands visibility as a mode of circulation.

This is notable also because the two exhibitions' relation to the number of objects might seem to point the other way: Deitch's show's investment in the saleable, unique object and Kelley's embrace of the numerous, which for theories of information mean increased importance. But Deitch's circuit was explicitly that of capital: he linked these works to a chain of exhibition, consumption, and commodification that made their lifelike statues into powerful financial propositions, not just collected dolls. It is this conversion that Kelley contested with his call for kitsch and superfluous number as much as anything else.

Both these positions vis-à-vis commodity critique structure the field of post-internet art. Kitsch and lo-fi or DIY aesthetics signal criticality as a function of indexicality and an aversion to iteration, even while made in digital form, while glossier works point to Deitch's network, whether in the formal exhibition parameters of the white cube or in circulation on the internet where attractability helps move an image along. But there is a crucial difference with regard to the structuring of the uncanny. The notion of something repressed has been traded for a strategy of hyper-visibility: nothing is hidden. In this, we can see the radical undermining of privacy as a sphere of human engagement as well as an internalisation of the reality of surveillance. The question becomes not a fear of the repressed, but a fear of not being able to repress or keep anything from public view. The uncanny becomes desired. We might look here to a moment in the video *Happy Christmas!!* (2015) by Ed Atkins – foremost among artists in exploring the field of the uncanny and its relationship to death – when a digitally rendered gorilla stretches his mouth into an unnaturally wide grin, lifts his hand, and gives an anatomically impossible thumbs-up.

Privacy and the Gothic

The uncanny, of course, has always been thrilling. As we saw in the previous chapter, digital technologies have rekindled fascination with ideas of the animate–inanimate, magic, and the effigies of factish gods. People are predisposed to making meaning out of things, and the inscrutable workings (for most) of smartphones and computers prompt a desire to ascribe significance to their chance effects. Mark Leckey, for example, has noted the occultist tinge of the words used to describe 3D scanning: the "wand" that one passes over the object to be scanned and the stipulation that the object should not be too "occluded" or "specular". I would even hazard that the popular meme of funny auto-corrects to texts on iPhones can be placed in this category: the phone talking back to us, the insubordinate supernatural *eiron* to our stories. The feeling of magic and the animate is also a means of making sense of new technologies, and periods that feel so stylistically distant as the 1800s crop up in tropes and plot points in post-internet work and work responding to digital technologies, adapted for a discourse of immateriality.

Like the latter half of the twentieth century and the twenty-first century so far, the nineteenth century negotiated the widespread adoption of new telecommunication technologies, such as the telegraph and the telephone, and later the recording technologies of the photograph and the film strip.[8] These all took on uncanny resonances. When telegraph lines were first installed in the US and Europe in the mid-1800s, people complained of sightings of ghosts travelling along the wires. In 1848, two sisters in upstate New York claimed that rapping coming from the floorboards of their bedroom were Morse-code messages from the dead. Photographs and films were regarded as sites of ghostly exchange, in a view that remained prevalent well into the twentieth century. André Bazin famously commented that film is "time mummified" – a notion that harkens back to both the idea of necromancy and the Victorian fascination with Egyptian preservation techniques but which was made as late as 1958. Anselm

Franke, in his discussion of animism, turns too to the photograph as picturing the dead, as a meridian line between life and non-life: "Cinema, from its outset, is populated by zombies, Frankensteins and man-machine hybrids, and mummies deserting their graves" (Franke 2010, 33–34). Nineteenth-century popular lore held that photographs would steal your soul and that – as Mroué recalled – the eye was itself a strip of celluloid on which the last image before death could be exposed. Thinking back to this initial response to photography, indeed, one can only imagine what an eerie and extraordinary experience it must have been to look for the first time at the face of someone missing or dead.

In an article on early reproduced images, "Phantom Images and Modern Manifestations: Spirit Photography, Magic Theater, Trick Films and Photography's Uncanny", Tom Gunning looks at the genre of trick photography, which showed ghosts within pictures of real persons to suggest the interest in the spectral as a conscious part of early use of the technology. Work responding to digital technologies partakes in this Frankensteinian paradigm, but where Frankenstein and early cinema betrayed ontological fright at the mimicry of life, in practice this fear was abetted by delight: audiences thrilled to spirit photography and trick film. The uncanny was an element of new technologies to be excitedly afraid of.

This delight in fear also shows itself in the genre of the Gothic, which navigated through a clash of the old and the new, weighted toward the former as it struggles with its own obsolescence. The domestic home was the primary site of this negotiation, both in terms of reception (one of its principal forms was the novel, whose audience was mainly women) and as a means of thematisation. Old, creaky, labyrinthine houses were mainstays of the genre, serving as metaphors for both the constraints on women's lives and the suddenly outdated lifestyles they contained. The architectural elements of these sites became characters in themselves, aiding and abetting the horrors that went on within. By focusing on the domestic sphere, authors of Gothic novels could reflect on or directly channel changes to the orbit of women's rights and roles, as well as the nineteenth century's broader political and economic changes. The sheer unknowable "otherness" of Gothic villains – their monstrosity, vampirity, non-humanity – reflects not only the scale of these great social alterations, but also the difficulty in making sense of them. A similar substrate of anxiety, located around the appearance of the domestic and concerning the physicality of the works' instantiations, characterises a number of moving-image works made during the late 2000s and early 2010s, and I want to focus on these to challenge the notion of the digital imaginary as a clean, green-screened space of limitless representational possibility. While works of this latter type form the popular image of post-internet art, and are indisputably part of the genre, the posthuman unmooring from time and space is also repeatedly challenged.[9] The recurrence of the site of the domestic, furthermore, also augurs a shifting role and importance of the sphere of privacy, with which domestic space becomes increasingly aligned.

We have seen in the last chapter how Leckey has addressed techno-animism, or as he put it, the fact that we are surrounded by "devices that bring non-living things to life" (Leckey 2010). Again his exhibition *The Universal Addressability of*

Dumb Things (2013), which was organised by the Hayward Touring programme in London and toured around the UK, brought together stereo systems, talismanic objects, fossils, 3D models, "spirit creatures", and a number of "prop-relics", or props from TV shows and films that have achieved the status of both sculpture and documentation. The term was used by Alexandra Keller and McKenzie Ward to discuss the exhibition (and sale) of props and paraphernalia from Matthew Barney's (art) blockbuster, *The Cremaster Cycle* (1994–2002) (Keller and Ward 2006). In post-internet art, the prop-relic becomes a powerful hybrid, freely mixing elements from videos in sculptural effects, and creating installations that determine the site of spectatorship.

Other works of Leckey's suggest the kind of intrusion into the domestic home that is a mainstay of Gothic literature. His film *Made in 'Eaven* (2004), for example, shows a digital re-creation of Jeff Koons's *Rabbit* (1986) in the middle of an antiquated front room, complete with a fireplace and draughty sash windows. (*Made in 'Eaven* is most commonly shown on 16mm transferred to video, on a television monitor mounted within a box: a means of display that phenomenologically ramps up its physicality, rather than hiding it within a projection, say.) The space is Leckey's studio, recognisable from earlier videos that take the place as subject. This sense of familiarity is reflected materially in the 16mm stock on which the film is shown, with a warm graininess that contrasts

Figure 4.2 Mark Leckey, *Made in 'Eaven*, 2004, DVD, 20 minutes (looped).

Courtesy the artist and Cabinet, London

with the cold digital representation of the silver rabbit. The "camera", or the point of view represented as such, circulates around the rabbit, but is never itself reflected. Indeed, the rabbit only ever shows its surroundings, not the artist who films it. As a symbol captured in a place of creation (the studio), the rabbit can be read in various ways: as a representation of the anxiety of artistic influence; as a product of immaterial labour; as the pressure to produce something as cold, hard, and cash-generating as the Koons rabbit; or as a figure of postmodernity, with its deliberate banality and consumerism.

A similar intrusion occurs in the weird and wonderful world of Shana Moulton's videos, in which she plays a tall, pattern-clad woman called Cynthia whose subjectivity is dispersed among New Age crystals and cures, infomercial creams, and strange apparatuses. Moulton's work follows Cynthia through her various activities – pottery-making, labyrinth-walking, massage therapy – as she appears with different ailments, real or imagined, she must attend to. (The film curator Thomas Beard memorably called her a "one-woman *Twin Peaks*", underlining the videos' cosy relationship with fantasy [Beard 2010].) Cynthia reflects the way that American female subjectivity is in a symbiotic financial relationship with beauty and self-help products, as if femininity is in an endless state of emergency. It also speaks, in a non-ironic sense, of a need for spirituality and a genuine questioning of how to constitute and represent the self. This note of earnestness is echoed by Moulton's "digicraft" DIY aesthetics, where Moulton uses After Effects technology to hammy rather than seamless effect. Her visage and body often float like Chagall figures across the screen, which is conspicuously separated into different digital layers. She presents the digital landscape as (literally) porous, and the domestic environment that Cynthia dwells within is repeatedly challenged: holes are digitally carved in the wall in which natural vistas emerge, sculptures begin talking in clumsily overlaid mouths. In *Restless Leg Saga* (2012), pharmaceutical logos appear off a television screen and dance over Moulton's prone body. The digital world is alive, a displaced autonomy underscored thematically by Cynthia's obsession with New Age wellness, which similarly ascribes agency to inanimate objects such as crystals or patterns.

Television sets often return in work of this type, not as agents of circulation but as their opposite: a material means of exhibition or a prop-relic connected to an affective register. As opposed to the rampant circulation of images of the internet, the use of material elements in installations or viewing platforms serves to ground the works, contrasting the circulation of images with the specific conditions of spectatorship. The ontological priority given to installation or video varies from work to work – that is, whether the prop is a relic of the video or whether the video is a prop for the installation, but their relationship is generally mutual. Ryan Trecartin and Lizzie Fitch, for example, complemented their seven-part video cycle, *Any Ever* (2011), with installations they call "sculptural theatres".[10] The videos portray a suite of characters in various reality TV-like sites (and equally sites of screen spectatorship), such as bedrooms, rec rooms, and airplane cabins, each of which was extended into the space of spectatorship by the sculptural theatre in which the viewer could sit to watch the video.

Figure 4.3 Lizzie Fitch/Ryan Trecartin, *Equal Plaza*, 2011. Sculptural theater exhibiting: *KCorealNC.K (section a)*, 2009, HD video. Installation view, *Any Ever*, MoMA PS1, New York, curated by Klaus Biesenbach, 19 June – 3 September, 2011.

These sculptural theatres are at times works in their own right, while in other presentations Trecartin asks for seating elements and treatments to accompany his movies; there is a consistent focus, that is, on the conditions of spectatorship as much as the video itself. The items from the video extend the haptic space of the onscreen work into the literal playing field of the viewer, bringing him or her further into the affective and bodily resonances of the work.

The push and pull between the material and immaterial functions both in Trecartin's work and its dissemination; he posts his work online while at the same time thematising this setup in exhibition contexts. One could even speculate that the fetish of the film strip or projector, typical to the gallery display of work in early 2000s, has been replaced by the prop–relic object: it contains the talismanic potential and material grounding previously associated with cinema as film (and is, like the film strip, easier to sell). The elaborate sculptural theatres also under-line the resistance to circulation embedded in post–internet work: Trecartin's work is a viewing experience rather than images viewed.

Moreover, as the domestic sites of Leckey's studio, Cynthia's bedroom, or Trecartin's YouTube "glass bedrooms" suggest, the personal home is often figured as the site under threat of invasion – a porousness of the walls of the family home familiar from Gothic literature. For his installation *Modern Family*

(2014) at the Chisenhale Gallery in London, for instance, Ed Fornieles created a riotous imagined site of family relations. He announced the exhibition with a kitsch image of himself and his former girlfriend, the actor Felicity Jones, and the three children they would never have. In the gallery, he created a family bed, a barbecue, and other sites of family togetherness, executed in makeshift form with cheap materials. The bed's mattress, for example, was stuffed with laughing vibrating toys (in a move Kelley would have liked). Screens were positioned on the wall as in waiting rooms, angled downwards, or casually affixed to garden trellises. These showed news feeds aggregated under whatever hashtags were popular on sites such as Tumblr, Instagram, or Twitter. Instead of the stable referents of family photographs, in *Modern Family* these hashtagged posts scrolled by in real time, contrasting the family as what Fornieles calls "a mechanism for identity creation"[11] – we can again look back to Buchloh's formulation here – and its connection to mnemonic images with the constantly refreshing feed in which people perform these identities now.

As the frequent use of television monitors suggests, post-internet art often espouses a more positive attitude towards television than the stereotype of TV as a mind-sucking "boob tube". (I suppose if you really want to see mind-sucking behaviour, wait for YouTube.) Television, when it emerged in the 1950s, was lambasted for much the same effects as the internet is today: of taking families away from a shared togetherness and towards individual consumption of effects, with canned laughter replacing the real laughter of others in the room. The scholar Maeve Connolly has been instrumental in parsing this changed attitude towards television among artists, looking at the use of televisual props in art installations to suggest "the important historical relationship that exists between broadcasting and domesticity" (Connolly 2013, 77), and, in her book *TV Museum: Contemporary Art and the Age of Television* (2014), at television as an emblematic element, alongside the museum, of the public sphere. Television's relation to communality is being appreciated in other ways as well: domestic space, especially the living room, was re-organised around the television set, instead of the fireplace. While this substitution was read as replacing conversation with viewership, it today emerges as a (now lost) fixed point of attention. The internet and its viewing platforms of YouTube and on-demand TV create a shift from one of collective spectatorship to one of atomised individual viewing. Instead of a rhetoric of bringing the family together, advertisements for internet providers boast that they provide enough bandwidth for everyone to access his or her own devices in different rooms of the home. The attention economy is one of attention pulled apart.

The threats to the domestic sphere also symbolise the larger sense of social media's incursion into the domestic sphere, which is not simply portrayed as a site for family activity but as an arena of privacy. Post-internet art coincides with the Web 2.0, and more generally smartphones as an extension of the self – always by one's side, even while sleeping. Privacy is often coded as analogue or physical, whereas virality appears as a part of digitality and connected to violence. Indeed, one way we can read the meeting point between violence and circulation is via privacy, a factor that reflects how privacy has been changed from being part of a binary with "the public" into a circumscribed and privileged place that safe-guards a number of individual rights, from abortion and homosexuality in the US, to – particularly in terms of rights on the internet – freedom, as the activist Jacob Appelbaum makes clear in Laura Poitras's documentary *Citizenfour* (2014):

> What people used to call liberty and freedom, we now call privacy. And we say, in the same breath, that privacy is dead. This is something that really concerns me about my generation, especially when we talk about how we're not surprised by anything. I think that we should consider that when we lose privacy, we lose agency, we lose liberty itself, because we no longer feel free to express what we think.[12]

In one remarkable scene in Atkins's video *Hisser* (2015), a solitary digital figure is seen masturbating in his bedroom, turned away from the viewer and facing the corner, as if to shamefully hide his activity from our eyes. Domestic space in other works betrays a similar invasion of privacy; the bedrooms portrayed by the work of Trecartin/Fitch, which is more affirmative of digital culture, are seen as always already invaded by a host of loquacious characters, as if one's Facebook feed had come alive in one's bedroom (the horror). Moulton shows characters literally stepping off the TV screen into her private space, to be ingested by her body. I want to suggest this incursion into private space as not simply an issue of changing social mores, but of biopolitics and free speech. In the following discussion of the representation of violence in post-internet work, we will move away from the prism of the uncanny through which we began and back towards the posthuman and the questions of circulation that it evokes and suggest that digitality is itself framed in connection to violence.

The violence inherent in the system

This link between digitality and violence inheres, to a certain extent (that is, taking into account medium's downgraded position), in the medium of the digital itself, as is suggested by the fact that much of the work treating violence betrays the high-production values and slick effects associated with commercial digital production instead of the messy, even homespun aesthetics of Trecartin or Fornieles. Phenomenologically, the non-analogue nature of digital technologies suggests that when the representation onscreen disappears, there is nothing left: no film strip, no external proof of the life of the work on screen. This participates in the feeling of radical substitution of the green screen, and work of this type often thematises this contingency, picturing it as a force acting upon a figure. Importantly, as we shall see later, the mimicry of digital representations also allies it to a mode of complicit critique.

In Atkins's work, for example, both violence and digitality are keyed up and made an explicit feature of the work. Uncannily lifelike figures are shown in states of reflection, on subjects from the nature of digitality to vague admissions of past wrongdoings. In the video installation *Ribbons* (2014), for example, virtual characters sit alone, drinking hard liquor and smoking cigarettes right down to their ends. The men, good-looking and only half-clothed, are tinged with eroticism: these are James Dean-like figures of the American masculine ideal, hiding their feelings in a glass of whisky. Atkins scrutinises the masochism inherent in this male stereotype: the violence is figured as self-inflicted as well as, formally, by the technologies themselves. At one point in *Ribbons*, a man lays his head on the table, and it slowly deflates: a digital puncturing of realist illusion. In *Hisser*, the first – and only – words spoken by Atkins's figure, a rugged, pockmarked dude, are "I'm sorry. I didn't know", repeated again and again as he sits on the edge of his bed. It's not clear what he's sorry about, nor what he doesn't know; the work contains no narrative frame nor even a gesture towards one. Instead, the video performs as an iteration of affect. *Hisser* begins with a nude male figure walking across a white screen, tracing, in his straight lines and right angle turns, the mathematical notion of space that is often taken as the representation of the "reality" of cyberspace. This figure is then portrayed in the bedroom, still clearly digitally rendered, in which popular posters and vaguely tasteful furnishings mark the room as both personal and excessively normal – a bedroom stylised to look like a bedroom. Fake analogue effects, such as the focusing of a zoom, or the moving of a camera up and down, highlight in relief the video's digital construction while also positing analogue representation as the mode connected to bedroom or private space: analogue as the uncanny of digital technologies, privacy as the uncanny to viral mediation. In the evocation of a digital everywhereness, the private bedroom is simply an analogue effect, as fake and as comforting as the iPhone's shutter sound.

Figure 4.4 Ed Atkins, *Ribbons*, 2014, three channel 4:3 in 16:9 HD video with three 4.1 channel surround soundtracks.

Courtesy the artist and Cabinet, London

Early on, both in titles (*Us Dead Talk Love*, 2012) and in interviews about his work (Obrist, 2012), Atkins referred to the digital figures of his videos as dead or as cadavers, pointing to their ontological state as animate–inanimate and their almost spectral immateriality. His means of creation of these works also underlines the masochism they thematically represent: he often uses data captured from his own facial expressions to animate his figures, and, summoning the uncanny valley, they appear too human-like. In their vague evocations of culpability, they seem to almost return the revulsion or discomfort their likenesses might conjure on themselves, as another form of remorse or self-hatred. They welcome our disgust. The interpretation that Atkins is in some way symbolically killing himself in these cadaverous renderings is perhaps a literal one but, I would argue, not totally off the mark. Indeed the willingness of many artists to play the characters themselves that undergo violence is significant: Trecartin, for example, plays the ghoulish boy Skippy whose death is the central plot point of his early video *A Family Finds Entertainment* (2004).

Other works look at video games, both as a site of creative expression and as a conspicuously digital medium charged with violence. In Morag Keil's sound installation *Civil War* (2012), speakers within Tupperware containers, suspended from the ceiling, blast a collage of noise: sounds taken from around South London's Peckham Rye train station, snippets of online advertisements that precede YouTube clips (here in French), and the screams and sounds of violence from video games. Its martial tones clearly expressed by its title, *Civil War* is a soundtrack of life on- and offline. Ian Cheng's algorithmic video work explores the aesthetics of video games, with simulations that take place in an unplaceable, desiccated landscape. (Cheng uses the term "simulations" to refer to these works as they are not animations but code that creates new representations, unfolding, notionally, forever – a performance of changeability rather than a representation of it.) In the video *Thousand Islands Thousand Laws* (2013), a video-game gunman patrols the environment, looking left and right for a threat that never materialises. Eventually, he too disappears among the skeletal representations of birds and swamp creatures of the mise-en-scène. In *Metis Suns* (2014), cartoon figures appear like thrown dice on the screen; they scramble and twist helplessly and recede into drawn lines that just as quickly fade from view.

Cheng's work plays with the radical flux of the internet, which is performed by the algorithms for his simulations as well as pictured in the constant movement of his works. In *Something Thinking of You* (2015), a thing that can be best described as a bird-like collection of debris flits and rolls about on the ground, losing folds and spawning others. The video follows this figure, keeping him at the centre of the screen. At one point in the recording of the simulation that I saw (the work changes every time the work is shown but "recordings" of the simulation are available to view on Vimeo; the work debuted in 2015 as a livestream on Cheng's YouTube channel) the vegetation and debris that constituted the ground dropped away, revealing a site of pure white – the digital substrate – which was just as quickly populated and moved on from. Like the figure itself, the surrounding matter is in a state of constant flux. Even

Figure 4.5 Ian Cheng, *Someone Thinking of You*, 2015, live simulation.
Courtesy the artist

without the obvious signs of violence of *Thousand Islands Thousand Laws*, this is territory that feels cataclysmic: on the edge of or after ecological disaster or in the state-of-nature fantasies of the popular films *The Road* (2009) or *The Revenant* (2015).

Other works use the beheadings and violence of YouTube clips as source material or, echoing the military origins of internet technology, point to the fact that the military uses the same new technologies of reproduction as artists do. Harun Farocki's video *Immersion* (2009), for example, shows how virtual reality is used as a means of therapy by US soldiers with PTSD, where military psychologists ask returning soldiers to act out traumatic memories, which they relive via the virtual reality (VR) headsets that stage their memories. (Farocki's film is more complex than this treatment allows; the VR scene that the psychologists prompt, seen on one side of the two-channel installation, as well as the entire conceit of the psychologists and the soldiers, is at the end of the video shown to be fake. We, ourselves, are immersed in the illusion of Farocki's representation and take its depiction for reality.) In Atkins's *Counting 1* and *Counting 2* (both 2014), one can see the digital after-effects of a decapitation; with rather marvellous black humour, a head bounces down some stairs, with correspondent sound effects for when the forehead meets a step (thud) and when the severed neck does (squelch). Seth Price used footage of the 2002 massacre in the Jenin refugee camp in the West Bank and images of random street violence and accidents in the video *Digital Video Effect: "Holes"* (2003), as well as footage of jihadist beheadings for a series of works titled *Hostage Video Still with Time Stamp* (2005). In *Hostage Video Still*, he printed images from online videos, often of a jihadist – his own head cropped off – holding aloft the decapitated head of his victim. These images are printed onto transparent sheets of Mylar, forcing a binary contrast between visible/invisible, in which the gruesome after-effects of violence – the image in the video one might look away from – is the only thing pictured. At the same time, the Mylar is itself exhibited in a way as to compromise its visibility, either crumpled, as a jacket hung on a hook on the wall, or furled, the image spinning back on itself. Price's usage frames visibility as liminal, visualising obstruction as much as lurid graphicness, while also – self-consciously and horribly – moving this source material from one network to a second of capital and luxury consumption.

Paul Chan, in *Now Promise Now Threat* (2005), the third video of what became known as *The Tin Drum Trilogy* (2002–2005), included YouTube footage of recent beheadings from that time period at three signal points. *Now Promise Now Threat* is structured as a conventional documentary, with interviews with residents in Omaha, Nebraska, on the mingling of politics and religion, the contradictions of a pro-life stance vis-à-vis support for the war, and the economic conditions of the Midwest. The YouTube footage is abstracted and only recognisable through the movement of colours associated with videos of beheadings: two figures in black flanking a figure in bright orange, and then red seeping across the screen – a powerful invocation of the abject in the war on terrorism.[13] *Now Promise Now Threat* utilises what Laura Marks has called the "skin" of the screen: the notion that the screen becomes the barrier between viewed subject and viewer, engendering a haptic, not just optical, response, particularly by images that contain some kind of texture – images which are, for example, grainy, lo-fi, decayed, or unclear.[14] Chan's overlaying of a scrim on the profoundly disturbing footage emphasises bodily response, while also performing, as an occluding mechanism, its both proximity and remoteness to the rural Nebraskan community.

Chan's *Tin Drum Trilogy* addressed the Iraq War in three videos that were after-the-fact corralled into a trilogy: *RE: The_Operation* (2002), *Baghdad in No Particular Order* (2003), and *Now Promise Now Threat*. His subject is the war as well as how it impacted upon, related to, and was received by citizens in the US. *RE: The_Operation* is structured as a series of emails written by various figures involved in the conflict on the US side, such as George W. Bush or Donald Rumsfeld, and is ostensibly sited in Iraq. This epistolary conceit focuses on the distance between the over there, where the war is happening and the authors are writing from, and the US, where they are writing to (and presumably where Chan's work will most frequently be shown). *Baghdad in No Particular Order* was made after the US artist, as part of the activist group Voices in the Wilderness, travelled to Baghdad to survey the damage there, and comprises images shot while on the trip – everyday scenes such as children laughing, young girls dancing, booksellers in the street. The third, *Now Promise Now Threat*, resumes *RE: The Operation*'s focus on the US perpetrators of the conflict, looking at the reaction back in the US, specifically through the perspective of the people of Omaha.

Throughout these three different approaches to the relation between an invading country (Chan's own) and a country under invasion (Iraq), the

Tin Drum Trilogy tests the ethnographic paradigm of "here" and "there". In this model, an audience "here" (in a developed country) watches violence or images of primitivism "there" (in the undeveloped country) – a geographical displacement that mimics the power relations between the two fields, of the Western cameraman and the "other" captured by his lens. *The Tin Drum Trilogy*, instead, locates its works in "here", "there", and "in between".[15] The "there" video, *Baghdad in No Particular Order*, is the least authored (it is a collection of clips of images, following the genre of observational film) and the one whose formal coherence is explicitly disavowed by the title ("in no particular order"). "Here", in *Now Promise*, is repeatedly and traumatically assaulted by the intrusion of the YouTube videos of executions, and in *RE: The_Operation*, the epistolary thematisation of the ethnographic paradigm of "here"/"there" is so suffused with violence, sexual and otherwise, that the template itself appears corrupted. This is a rather schematic reading of the three films, but I think suggests how technologies that bring the "there" back home, such as email and the circulation of videos on YouTube, have affected the US's sense of culpability towards a geographically distant war. (The title, notably, draws from Günter Grass's allegory about German guilt after World War II.)

The scholar Paolo Magagnoli has argued that instead of a strategy of opposition, contemporary artwork takes on a "homoeopathic dosage" of its object of critique. He draws this notion from two sources for two different applications: first taken from Hal Foster, about violence in relation to Chan's work and second from Fredric Jameson, of consumer capitalism in relation to the work of Hito Steyerl. Foster delineated the concept of the homoeopathic dose in the essay "Dada Mime", which looks back to Dada and its signature techniques of montage and disjunction. Foster reads the Dada artists' use of these methods both as signalling opposition to World War I, in whose shadow the work developed, and as bringing its disintegration upon themselves. "A key persona of Dada", Foster writes,

> is the traumatic mime, and a key strategy of this traumatist is mimetic adaptation, whereby the Dadaist assumes the dire conditions of his time – the armouring of the military body, the fragmenting of the industrial worker, the commodifying of the capitalist subject – and inflates them.
>
> (Foster 2003, 169)

The pandemonium of Dada nonsense performances mimicked the pandemonium of the war, the rise of urban capitalism around the artists, and the psychological violence both of these effected. Dada internalised these disruptions, inhabiting them in the way that a shaman might inhabit an evil spirit – give physical form to it – and thus dispel it. For Magagnoli, this helps explain why Chan's *Tin Drum Trilogy* appears to both critique and celebrate the very violence of its subject (Magagnoli 2012). For Steyerl, Chan uses Jameson's glossing of the term, which appears as the same method (imitation) but in Jameson's different context of an economic critique of the possibilities for post-Marxism, to analyse

Steyerl's frequent use of pop and commodity imagery within a filmmaking practice that is critical of contemporary capitalism: a "kaleidoscopic mimicry", he writes, "of popular culture" (Magagnoli 2015).

I want to suggest that this technique of a homoeopathic dosage is important to work that responds to digital technologies in its representation of violence and that it is connected both to context and to the set of affective relations put into play by the medium itself. Mimicry is integral to the mode of digital representation: this is in production, where digital representations are made by affixing sensors to a face or object or by scanning them with a wand; in style, which privileges naturalism and lifelikeness over expressionist or abstract stylisations; and in reception. The revulsion within the uncanny valley turns on lifelikeness, and the posthuman fears of the Pygmalion myth turn on artificial intelligence fully aping the capacity of humans. The idea of the traumatic mime also helps us understand the genre of personation, which we will look at in the next chapter, and the espousal of high-production values and cosiness to commodities that also mark post-internet work. Mimicry, as a representational paradigm, allies its subject with the object of critique, here executing violence on both.

Within the orbit of works that use violence as a subject of representation, the homoeopathic dosage could also be speculatively related to a contemporary feeling of helplessness or disavowal: remember that the consortium of countries in the Iraq War, arguably the founding event in the chain of recent Middle Eastern crises, went to war over the objections of the majority of their citizens. President George W. Bush lost the popular vote in the 2000 election, and the day after Britain joined the Iraq invasion, one million people marched against it in London – to this day the largest protest in the UK's history. In the same way that the televising of the Vietnam War played a decisive role in turning the American public against the conflict, the means of mediatising the conflicts of the last fifteen years is also significant: the Iraq War, the Arab Spring, terrorist bombings, and operations against IS have unfolded on social media, which carries with it a rhetoric of participation or an active response on the part of the viewer, even if it is only as incommensurate and ineffective as a thumbs-up or sad-face emoticon. The feeling of participation is compounded by the awareness of globalisation patterns, in which culpability is both known and repressed, a new uncanny: one buys products from companies who do business in illegal Israeli-occupied settlements in Palestine or from those that employ workers under deeply unethical conditions in Bangladesh or Zimbabwe. The tendency towards online activism and information sharing means life online has violence at its margins – or to use a more appropriate metaphor, in its feed – which helps fuel the slippage between everyday activity and symbolic violence that the characters, as in works by Atkins or Cheng, undergo.

The interconnectedness of violence and our lives back "home", to call up Martha Rosler's response to the Vietnam War, is most explicitly argued by Steyerl, who, in both her videos and her writings, has repeatedly pressed the connection between the experience of digital media and the physical violence of the world. Suggesting the culpability between the passive internet user, consumer, or spectator and the violence wrought by political and economic inequities, her critique of artistic production joins it together with the economy and political situations that support it. *In Free Fall* (2010), for example, demonstrates how sites of apparent digital illusion are tied to the real world. As discussed above, she traces a specific Boeing passenger plane that had been sold to the Israeli air force in the 1970s, where it took part in hostage rescue missions against the PLO, to a junkyard where it was bought by a special effects team. It is, in fact, the plane in *Speed* that the character played by Keanu Reeves blows up. (So it alleges: fact and fiction are mixed in this video.) What was left of the plane after the movie's filming, Steyerl asserts, was then sold to China to make counterfeit DVDs sold on the black market. The spectacular violence of *Speed*, which viewers can revel in as consequence-free entertainment, thus is shown to be part of a wider material network of real violence and the precarisation of labour. Images, their material substrate, and their means of production and of circulation are all bound tightly together in a network that means engagement with one facet – watching the film – entails culpability in all: the undocumented migrants hawking DVDs on the street, the Israel–Palestine conflict (and the colonial West's role in creating that), and the consumption of violence as fiction.

The relation of everywhereness to the digital and internet imaginary, forces of economic globalisation, and to the networked status of internet work arguably challenges the here/there binary that is foundational to conventional representations of warfare and violence, in documentary, ethnographic, feature, and artistic film alike. As I mentioned in the discussion of Paul Chan, in these, a filmmaker goes "there" (i.e. a war-torn country, most often a developing country) to film

Figure 4.6 Hito Steyerl, *In Free Fall*, 2010, Video HDV, single channel, sound, colour, 33 minutes, 43 seconds.

Image CC 4.0 Hito Steyerl. Courtesy the artist and Andrew Kreps Gallery, New York a situation of violence and returns "here" (i.e. to a developed country) to edit and exhibit the film. Critical documentary and artist's film often attempts to jam or lay bare this device: think of Chris Marker's structuring of *Sans Soleil* (1983), his film about Japan and the Japanese people, as a series of letters written from an unnamed "he" to the film's female French narrator, taking the "he" as the omnipotent but never geographically located subject. Works such as Steyerl's investigation of the circulation of images in globalisation, and the use of affect rather than documentary as a means of approaching violence "elsewhere", are arguably the roots of a new attempt to understand violence as imbricated and everywhere, though in practice most of post-internet art is still accomplished in a Western "here" treating a violence "there".

We could also look to the geographical displacement of populations them-selves as a more credible challenge to this ethnographic paradigm, via migration's effect on claims to cultural representation. As Kracauer foresaw, geographic locations are no longer pertinent to identity, or rather, they are confusingly pertinent. Chan's *Tin Drum Trilogy*, for example, has the exceptional codicil of being re-made by the artist Urok Shirhan, who was born in exile in the Middle East to Iraqi parents but raised in Amsterdam. She saw Chan's *Baghdad in No Particular Order* and realised that the footage he shot was remarkably similar to images taken by her father when he also visited Baghdad after the war. In *Remake of 'Baghdad in No Particular Order'* (2012), she supplanted Chan's images with those of her father's. The work exists both as a two-channel projection showing her video and Chan's side-by-side and as a video of her father's footage exhib-ited with a booklet she made of Chan's video with timestamps alongside the images. *Remake of 'Baghdad in No Particular Order'* is less a refutation of Chan's right to create a film about Iraq but an uncanny doubling, a questioning of the notion of possession and rights to images more generally. As she explained in an interview about the project:

> my father is Iraqi and was forced to leave and has been living in exile since; Paul Chan is an American who has been to Iraq and been in Baghdad; and I'm an Iraqi child of the diaspora who has never been to Iraq. In terms of the question of authority, who has the most? Looking at my position with the other two, I wonder: do I have more of a right to speak of and for Iraq? Does it mean something else when I speak about Iraq as opposed to an American speaking about Iraq, when I've actually never been there? Is authority about being there and seeing it with your own eyes, having the ability to go, having the audacity to speak? Or is it that I have some sort of bloodline that gives me more power or authenticity to speak about a place?
>
> (Shirhan quoted in Bailey 2015)

In Shirhan's work, the images become, not performative illustrations of life in Iraq, but indexical placeholders – signifiers of a loss, both the loss of Iraq for her father and the loss of certainty about background felt by children of the diaspora and long-term migrants. How is identity conceived in migration? Here, the importance of images returns: Iraq exists only in image form for Shirhan, as for the great majority of the world who has never been there, and the authorship of images is lost within their circulation. It is less accurate to say that Iraq exists "here" or "there" than that it exists as mediatised, and, in echoes of postmodernism, the creation of a story about Iraq is only playing with the layers of this representation.

Plot points

Violence as a particular feature of life online is also explored with regard to surveillance and data mining – in this sense the internet user is not only affectively connected to violence but literally participates in the same network that organises surveillance, arrests, and extraordinary renditions. Both the NSA and the US drone program were expanded under the Obama Administration. The NSA has leaned on telecommunications companies in the US and abroad to provide it with reams of data on individuals – for US citizens, this is metadata (whom you called, for how long you spoke, etc.) as a matter of course, and the content of email messages and phone calls, on request. For non-US citizens, this is the content of any messages the NSA might be interested in. These revelations came thanks to Edward Snowden, as did information on the logistics and operational command of drone strikes under the Obama Administration. Art concerned with the internet has variously wrestled with the visibility and invisibility of data – coming to terms with the effects of its invisibility and trying, conversely, to visualise it – and in terms of the NSA revelations this impetus became politically charged, particularly in the work of artists such as Steyerl, Trevor Paglen, James Bridle, Adam Harvey, Jill Magid, Laura Poitras, Constant Dullaart, and others, in ways such as looking at drone strikes and drawing explicitly on the history of the war on terrorism; using encrypted servers to carve out or simply signal resistance to forms of surveillance and data mining; and referencing the role that social-media and smart-phone communication technology played in the Arab Spring and associated crises. As Mroué's *Pixelated Revolution* shows, digital recording technologies and social-media platforms have become part of military and insurgent conflicts as well as their opposition, used as tools of consciousness-raising precisely because of their viral capacities.

Here, the notion of privacy that is treated with regard to private space, personal activity, and psychological freedom becomes political and hinges on visuality: what can be seen? This is not simply a question of visibility and invisibility but of structures and methodologies that allow the visual to emerge: the cybernetic paradigm of information as patterned means that one needs to be able to read data for its patterns, find appropriate algorithms, and have clean enough data to generate a statistically significant result. Even with images, it is not always clear what we are seeing: we have talked about this earlier in terms of context collapse, and here many of these works labour to show that the inscrutability of networks of surveillance and the power structures of conflict mean that the content of what we are seeing is itself occluded from the public's awareness. Visuality is a resource, as unevenly distributed as money and power.

Paglen's photographs of surveillance sites, for example, mimic landscape photography renderings of the countryside. They are high-production value, bucolic, and often intensely *beautiful* images (which isn't always a register sought after by critically credible work). What they depict, however, is not some unbroken, innocent vista of land but depictions of nodes in surveillance networks or drones in the night sky, information that is given solely contextually – that is to say, non-visually – via the work's titles (such as *Untitled [Reaper Drone]*, *Untitled [Predator Drone]*, both 2010) or by press release or wall text. Other photographs show secret military sites in the US, classified American satellites, networks of secret prisons in Afghanistan, or the underwater sea cables that information travels along. Though the subject of depiction is flagged up in the titles, these subjects often remain invisible nonetheless. For Paglen, this invisibility is at once a reflection of the obliteration of different moments of violence within history and a tactical weapon; similar to the work of Price, his visualisation works to submit these moments to the public with their visuality compromised almost as an indexical marker of the processes of forgetting or occlusion. *The Last Pictures (The Narbona Panel; Humans Seen Through a Predator Drone)* (2012), for example, shows an image of Canyon de Chelly in Arizona, a narrow canyon where members of the Navajo Nation were slaughtered by Spanish soldiers in 1805. The image, like the site, bears no trace of this history. Paglen juxtaposes this with an image of migrants in the same area crossing the US border, captured by a drone as part of the US's domestic surveillance program. Besides the more obvious parallel between the Spanish massacre and the conditions of migrant routes in the US today, the work suggests knowledge as structurally invisible, both in a romantic sense (history is illegible in a landscape) and in the government's espousal of secrecy around their overseas military actions and domestic law enforcement.[16] Paglen uses the network of the art world as a means to circulate

Figure 4.7 Trevor Paglen, *The Last Pictures (The Narbona Panel; Humans Seen Through a Predator Drone)*, 2012, two gelatin-silver prints, 61 × 81.3 cm.

Courtesy the artist and Metro Pictures, New York

information, occupying a parallel vector of money and power: circulation is a political strategy.

Paglen has described himself as an artist–activist, and much work in this vein sits astride the worlds of contemporary art and activism. Revelation is a primary mode, figured as information sharing. Bridle, for example, began a Dronesta-gram project, where users could share images of drone targets, sourced from the London-based non-profit organisation, the Bureau of Investigative Journalism. In his *Citizen Ex* (2015) project, he conceived of an extension for web browsers that maps the physical infrastructure for the internet and creates an "algorithmic citizenship" of where the internet thinks you are, based on your browsing history that day. Similarly, in the installation *The Censored Internet* (2014), Dullaart, using the work of Reporters without Borders, a French non-profit organisation that defends freedom of information and freedom of the press, made an installation of all the flags of the countries that Reporters without Borders had designated as "enemies of the internet". A Wi-Fi station available in the room reflects the restricted access of the local customs where the work is installed.

The frequent use of cartography also serves to make visible the points of data collection and to thematise, in the image of a network, the contiguity between "ordinary" users and "extraordinary" tactics and states of exception. Mapping also exposes in an apparently objective register the unseen and mar-ginalised journeys that comprise globalisation: of information, commodities, power, and people. In the video *The Mapping Journey Project* (2008–2011), for example, Bouchra Khalili interviewed eight migrants in order to create maps of the Mediterranean based on oral retellings of their clandestine journeys, from Marseilles to Ramallah, Ramallah to Bari, Bari to Rome, Rome to Barcelona, and Barcelona to Istanbul. The map became not a visualisation of Europe but of the precarious and dangerous routes by which to enter it illegally. Other works also take advantage of crowd-sourcing to bring to light information that could be useful to citizenry. (Here, we can also think about the changes for refugees with WhatsApp messaging and Google Maps, which allow them to pass information on to each other or to locate themselves geographically, rather than having to wholly rely on people smugglers.) Mülksüzleştirme Ağları uses data-compiling software to map the overlaps of power and geography in Turkey, in the ongoing project *Networks of Dispossession* (2013–). Using the free software Graph Com-mons, the project collates together different maps to expose the relationship between private corporations and the Turkish government. The map, as form of data visualisation, brings to light controversial projects that displace those without political power (whose geography is also mapped by the project), such as a planned third airport in Istanbul or a hydroelectric power plant that will inundate a reservoir in eastern Turkey.

Our willingness to hand over data in so many ways – to social-media plat-forms like Facebook, most famously, but also to any website where we purchase something and indeed just by being present on the web – also questions how notional complicity on the internet is. There is a sense that we are being naïve to the point of Stockholm Syndrome, or simply that we know very well we might be monitored, but we aren't doing anything wrong so we might as well continue. Partly owing to the compromised position of visibility and partly to the insecure and downgraded status of the documentary image, I want to argue that the voice as a symbol of embodiment has become a key strategy for political articulation. We will pick up this argument at the end of the next chapter, when we will look specifically at the construction of the self. Discourses of visibility, as I have suggested, often leave out the body as the perceiving object or ignore the way that power is distributed equally through space across objects and subjects alike, even while attempting to understand how bodies and objects are regulated. This has been one of the contributions of speculative materialism, as well as of feminist spectatorship theory in the 1970s. Laura Mulvey's now canonical theory of the male gaze understood the gaze to be sexual, desiring, and coming from an instantiated body. Violence on the internet shows itself not simply in images of warfare, but in hard-core pornography and soft-core misogyny – a subject also widely treated by artists, such as Ann Hirsch's images of her vagina or Sidsel Meineche Hansen's explorations of pornography and the body. (We will also look at some of these in the next chapter.) Here – to round out the discussion of the visualisation of violence and to open one up of language and embodiment – I want to turn to the artist Jesse Darling, whose work is exemplary of these concerns. For as Barbara Kruger's posters indelibly show, visibility is also linked to sexual violence.

The body as a battleground

Darling is a prolific writer and speaker on subjects of precarity and their relation to a post-internet context, particularly with an understanding of how visibility and audience affect the performing body. (Darling uses the third-person plural pronoun [they/them] as a refusal of binary gender.) They built up a strong online presence through their blog, Tumblr, and Twitter posts and in this way reflect a type of post-internet practice that we have so far not focused on: the uncertain overlap between discrete exhibited artworks and a fluid, ongoing performative practice of activity online, whether in blogs, participation in threads, a Tumblr feed, or other forms of social-media engagement. In their art practice more traditionally conceived, Darling makes sculpture, composites, and performance that, in contrast to the high-production values of much of post-internet art, utilises poor materials. Their sculptures – thin, spindly, made of reused material, or just barely representational – imply a violence to or reduction of the human form, undertones that are also perceptible in their titles: a tea towel with two burnt eyes suggests a face (*Domestic Terror 1*, 2016); in *Material Girl* (2014), a hanging figure is formed out of a ripped-open Sainsbury's carrier bag and orange ropes. This choice of material can be traced to *Arte Povera*'s allegorical valorisation of low materials and underscores a major theme of their writings: the economic precarity of the artist today and the hopelessness and urgency of the attempts to fight it. The poverty of their forms can here be read literally, as a move to force back attention away from discourse over circulation and visuality to the actual conditions of working life. The use of lo-fi material also relates to Steyerl's reading of the poor image, which is here used to suggest a challenge to the normalised body. A crucial insight of Steyerl's "Poor Image" essay (2009) is its understanding of the image as embedded within context – if you want a terrible pun, it's not the pure image, but the poor image. The legibility of the context is related both to its evocation of a haptic response and to the notion of embodiment as developed by N. Katherine Hayles and Elizabeth Grosz: "embodiment is contextual, enmeshed with the specifics of time, place, physiology and culture"

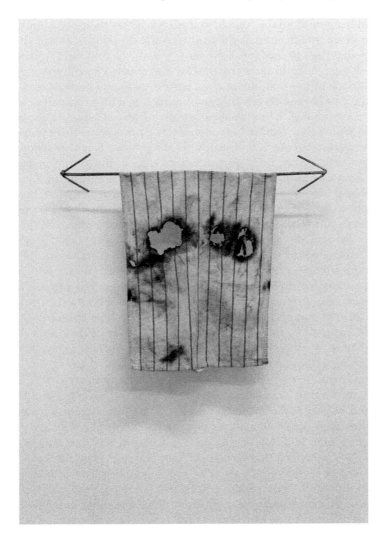

Figure 4.8 Jesse Darling, *Domestic Terror 1*, 2016, steel, cloth, 89 × 64 × 40 cm.

Courtesy the artist and Arcadia Missa, London

(Hayles 1999, 196). The poor image, as for Darling, signals the socioeconomics that surround the image, the materiality of its production and reception, and the multiplicity of bodily and sexual identity.

Other works of Darling's picture a body bound up, with evocations of sexual violence, S&M bondage, and a desire to complicate biological markers of gender – compressing some body parts, adding prosthetics for others. The photographs *Photoshop 1 (Healing Brush, Clone Stamp, Paint Bucket)* and *Photoshop 2: (Free Transform, Difference/Exclusion, Tolerance: 60)* (both 2012) show Darling standing in a kitchen, partially blocked off by painted and roughly cut cardboard hanging from the ceiling, so that one can see their body but not face, in a kind of makeshift internalised analogue crop. In the first image, duct tape binds together their breasts, torso, and crotch; in the second Darling stands hips askew, holding a dildo to their crotch. Darling renders Photoshop's crop effect here as a mode of messy, dismembering representation, in contrast to the more common use of Photoshop as a process of rendering it more palatable. Visibility is also the leitmotif of the lecture-performance *Habeas Corpus Ad Subjiciendum* (2012), in which they pictured the internet as a panopticon that renders them unable to speak: a paradigm of visuality abutting one of language whose site of conflict is Darling's own body. *Habeas Corpus* suggests the lecture-performance as a literal process of interpellation, accomplished by the words of PowerPoint slides being projected across their body. This reading is not mine but of the work itself, which uses its own interpretation as a means itself of interpellation, as Althusser's famous example, "Hey! You there!", streams across Darling's face and torso. (Kruger also appears with the classic: "Your gaze hits the side of my face".) Critical theory, that is, becomes both a means of critique and a form of subjectification in itself: *Habeas Corpus* scrolls through a variety of ways of attempting to situate oneself in the world, all of which generate a feeling of being boxed in without any move to manoeuvre. That is, rather than a critique of visuality as a form of violence, the performance signals the same mutual dependency that was thematised by the use of tape to bind and reshape their body. Darling, recalling the mode of complicity discussed already, needs the audience to exist: "I am nothing without you".

The performance is ostensibly an ironic manifestation of what life is like online: a portrayal of the addictiveness of social-media visibility and the cannibalisation of positions of genuine resistance. This again occurs not simply in the theoretical co-option of critique but as a function of how images circulate online: the context collapse of the internet means that a feminist critique of sexuality – a woman in a "powerful pose", for example – circulates as an image to-be-looked-at by desirous gazes. This is compounded by the pressure to be attractive – not at all unique to the web, but a guiding prescription of selfies and other forms of internet self-representation: "Like all young-girls I saw myself fucked and fucking as a glowing bright-eyed simulacrum called beauty", Darling notes. In suggesting a state of mutual dependency, *Habeas Corpus* transforms visuality on the web into a discourse that turns not on visibility and invisibility but on the mediation of the body: a slide musing on the uncomfortability of the silence in the room segues into a discussion of how awkward it would be if the viewer encountered Darling in the flesh, and not just their image, even while Darling stands in front of the audience. Embodiment is disallowed as anything but a visual phenomenon, and Darling themselves become a 2D image flattened by the interpellation not just of the slides but of the viewers' gazes; this 2Dness is how they and the lecture-performance travel. Embodiment becomes, problematically, contradictorily, circulable – something also tested by works focusing on oral articulation, which we will look at in the next chapter.

The elision *Habeas Corpus* suggests between person and image returns us to VVORK.com's preference for the representation over the real thing but with another inflection: here, the desire to see images of women rather than to engage with a real woman herself. Meineche Hansen also approached this notion in the exhibition "SECOND SEX WAR" (2016) at Gasworks in London, which brought together different representations of CGI models used in adult entertainment, framing the posthuman as both a slave and commodity within technology. (Her query also focused on immaterial labour: what are the rights of images in their labour of the accumulation of capital?) Darling's attempts to get ahead of this dynamic – to reclaim pornographic representations of women as feminist – and her recognition of the failure of this endeavour suggests the non-notional and specific threats to women that the normalisation of images of sexual violence and the control of men over sexual Pygmalions imply. In the next chapter, we will look at another response of a group of women to representations of femininity online; I find these compromised, though in some ways reflective of the sexual politics of visuality on the internet as sketched out here.

This rather bleak portrait, of an online world of anxiety, violence, and political ambivalence, is perhaps in contrast to the subject of identity online, where the internet appears as a limitless horizon of anonymous presentation and where we chronicle artists' cheerful shift from a countercultural to a normcore stance. If I try to tamp that perspective by showing how identity online by and large replicates identity offline, I also want to underscore here the delight in digital representations and the capacities of the network I mentioned at the beginning of this text. The powers of connection and virality can be positive social forces; the so-called anti-internet aesthetics artists are in some ways in their exploitations of visuality and circulation, the most optimistic of the lot we have surveyed.

Notes

1 The "War on Terror" was President George W. Bush's term for the pursuit of terrorists after the attacks of 11 September 2001, which "ended" in 2013 when President Barack Obama announced a redefinition of the term. President Obama's interference in semantics here reflects a larger dissatisfaction with the phrase "War on Terror", despite its widespread adoption by the media, as in declaring a war on an abstract term Bush was theoretically legitimising force against any enemy anywhere. The term "war on terrorism" more accurately describes the US and NATO's targeting of terrorist networks since 2001.

2 For a thorough exploration of the visual dimension of warfare, I suggest the third edition of the *Visual Culture Reader* (2013), edited by Nicholas Mirzoeff, as well as Mirzoeff's

TheRight to Look: A Counterhistory of Visuality (2011) and *Watching Babylon: The War in Iraq and Global Visual Culture* (2004).

3 It included, among others, Hans Bellmer, Nayland Blake, Jonathan Borofsky, Jacques Charlier, John De Andrea, Robert Gober, Duane Hanson, Martin Kippenberger, Jeff Koons, Tetsumi Kudo, Dorothea Lange, Paul McCarthy, John Miller, Matt Mullican, Bruce Nauman, Dennis Oppenheim, Tony Oursler, Nam June Paik, Thom Puckey, Charles Ray, Karl Schenker, Cindy Sherman, Laurie Simmons, Kiki Smith, and Paul Thek. An interesting project would be to compare Kelley's "Uncanny" with the show-within-a-show of representations of the body and the uncanny curated by Cindy Sherman for Massimilioni Gioni's Venice Biennial of 2015, which included works by Bellmer, Gober, Hanson, Ray, and others.

4 This essay has been reproduced in a modified version in Mike Kelley, "Playing with Dead Things: On the Uncanny", in John C. Welchman (ed.), *Foul Perfection: Essays and Criticism*, Cambridge, MA: MIT Press, 2003, 70–99. All quotations are from this later version.

5 Deitch's business dealings were in fact already discussed at the time in relation to the artists he chose, according to a contemporary account of the show. Dan Cameron, "Before and After: Entering the World of Post Human", *Frieze*, no.6, September–October 1992, https://frieze.com/article/and-after (last accessed on 7 September 2016).

6 Smith admits this was also partly a dodge that allowed them to accomplish the work (Smith 2013).

7 'Post-Human' began at the FAE Musée d'Art Contemporain, Pully, Lausanne, from 14 June–13 September 1992, and travelled to the Castello di Rivoli, Museo d'Arte Contemporanea, Rivoli, Turin, 1 October–22 November 1992; the Deste Foundation for Contemporary Art, Athens, 3 December 1992–14 February 1993; and the Deichtorhallen Hamburg, 12 March–9 May 1993.

8 The media theorist Robert Hassan calls these changes of "social acceleration" and points out that, compared to the changes ushered in by information technology, the changes to the speed of life of the nineteenth century, such as the telegraph and trains, would have become only gradually part of life: "these technologies were powerfully *constrained by time and space*. Railways took years to plan and to lay down; telegraphs and telephones similarly relied on infrastructures that took time to build". In contrast, the "social acceleration" of information technologies has happened over a period of just fifty years, rendering the experience of technology – and the anxiety and neuroses he argues it has engendered – more acute (Hassan 2008, 187).

9 This discussion develops ideas first worked through in my article "Return of the Gothic: Digital Anxiety in the Domestic Sphere", *e-flux journal* [online journal], no.51, January 2014, available at http://www.e-flux.com/journal/return-of-the-gothic-digital-anxiety-in-the-domestic-sphere/ (last accessed on 28 April 2016).

10 *Any Ever* refers to the seven interrelated movies produced in 2009–2010, but the artists also use it to refer to the different sculptural theatres created to present those movies, as well as the body of sculptures they made together from 2009 to 2012 that revolve around related aesthetics and concerns. Email from the artist, 12 May 2016.

11 Email to the author, 25 January 16.

12 Jacob Appelbaum, quoted in Laura Poitras, *Citizenfour* [film]. HBO Films, Participant Media, Praxis Films, 2014.

13 The first beheading video was that of Daniel Pearl in 2002, the *Wall Street Journal* writer who was executed by Pakistani extremists. Beheading videos became a regular propaganda and recruitment tool for Al Qaeda in Iraq during the US operation there, particularly under Abu Musab Al Zarqawi, who was renowned for his brutal tactics – to such an extent that he was criticised by members of Al Qaeda's central command. (Al Qaeda in Iraq was initially Tawhid and Jihad, or the Organisation of Monotheism and Jihad, and subsequently became the Islamic State of Iraq, the Islamic State of Iraq and Syria, and, finally, the Islamic State.) These videos ran from 2004, the date of the first Zarqawi video (showing the beheading of the American radio tower repairman Nick Berg), and, after

his death in 2006, the videos continued in the pattern he instituted. Most beheading videos undertaken by Zarqawi, who often did the cutting himself, had a similar format: the victim would be kneeling in an orange jumpsuit, designed to reference the prisoners in Guantánamo Bay and Abu Ghraib. He or she would give his or her name and identity and would sometimes read a statement denouncing US foreign policy. The militants would usually be dressed in black, with their faces obscured, and they sometimes wore suicide vests. They would often hang a banner, particularly later as more groups adopted this tactic, with the name of their group behind them. After the victim finished his or her statement, the militants would normally read out a prepared statement. They would then behead the victim with a knife.

Early videos were shot by a single camera on a tripod and would not be edited, usually running to around five minutes. Later videos vary: IS, for example, has released videos that are half an hour long and include multiple beheadings. IS now often use multiple camera angles, edited together into one narrative; this sophistication is indicative of their broader media savviness. On several occasions, they have also edited out the actual moment of the beheading, fading to black just before it. One speculative reason for this is that their message is oriented to the West as well as to potential Muslim recruits, and they do not wish to scare any away with excessive brutality. They also apparently stage dry runs before the actual execution, which is believed to be a way to both rehearse the action and to confuse the victims, who might refuse to read a statement if they know they are about to be executed, but would do so if they believed they were in a propaganda video. IS have also pictured different forms of execution, such as victims being burnt alive, drowned (filmed with underwater cameras), or blown up with rocket-propelled grenades. They have also varied the location and background of the videos, whereas early videos largely took place in small, poorly lit rooms. In 2015, for example, they issued a video of a beheading of 21 Egyptian Coptics on a Mediterranean beach in Libya, with the sea and the European shores behind them.

My thanks to Christian Le Mière for this gruesome information. Personal communication, 1 May 2016.

14 See Laura Marks, *The Skin of the Film: Intercultural Film, Embodiment, and the Senses*, Durham, NC: Duke University Press, 2002.

15 For a discussion of this paradigm and challenges to it, see Catherine Russell, *Experimental Ethnography: The Work of Film in the Age of Video*, Durham, NC: Duke University Press, 1999.

16 The work is part of a Creative Time project called *The Last Pictures* (2012), where Paglen created images that would be launched into space and, thus, potentially represent our civilisation should these images ever meet future or alien civilisations. The images are stored on a micro-etched disc that Paglen developed with MIT scientists. The irony of this project is not the far-fetched, almost mid-twentieth-century focus on space and aliens, but the idea that should Paglen's disc ever make it into the hands of another civilisation, they would have developed the exact same technology that would enable them to transfer the images from their current informational form into a visual one. The project has also been published as a book. See Trevor Paglen, *The Last Pictures*, Berkeley: University of California Press, 2012.

Bibliography

Bailey, S. (2015) "Image Appropriation: Urok Shirhan in Conversation with Stephanie Bailey". *Ibraaz* [online magazine], http://www.ibraaz.org/interviews/177 (last accessed on 29 April 2016).

Beard, T. (2010) "Now That I'm a Woman, Everything Is Strange". In: Gygax, R. ed. *Deterioration, They Said*, Zurich: JRP Ringier, http://www.incite-online.net/beard3.html (last accessed on 7 September 2016).

Cameron, D. (1992) "Before and After: Entering the World of Post Human". *Frieze*, 6, https://frieze.com/article/and-after (last accessed on 7 September 2016).

Connolly, M. (2013) "Televisual Objects: Props, Relics and Prosthetics". *Afterall*, 33, 67–80.

———— (2014) *TV Museum: Contemporary Art and the Age of Television*, Bristol: Intellect Books.

Deitch, J. (1992) *Post-Human*. Exh. cat., Lausanne: FAE Musée d'Art Contemporain.

Foster, H. (2003) "Dada Mime". *October*, 105, 166–76.

Franke, A. (2010) "Much Trouble in the Transportation of Souls, or: The Sudden Disorganization of Boundaries". In: Franke, A. ed. *Animism: Volume I*. Berlin: Sternberg Press, 11–53.

Freud, S. (1919/1959) "The Uncanny". In: Riviere, J. trans. (1959) *Collected Papers*, Vol. 4, New York: Basic Books, 368–407.

Gronlund, M. (2014) "Return of the Gothic: Digital Anxiety in the Domestic Sphere". *e-flux journal* [online journal], 51, http://www.e-flux.com/journal/return-of-the-gothic-digital-anxiety-in-the-domestic-sphere/ (last accessed on 28 April 2016).

Gunning, T. (1995) "Phantom Images and Modern Manifestations: Spirit Photography, Magic Theater, Trick Films and Photography's Uncanny". In: Petro, P. ed. *Fugitive Images: From Photography to Video*, Bloomington: Indiana University Press, 42–71.

Hassan, R. (2008) *The Information Society*, Cambridge: Polity Press.

Hayles, N. K. (1999) *How We Became Posthuman: Virtual Bodies in Cybernetics, Literature and Informatics*, Chicago and London: University of Chicago Press.

Iverson, M. (2005) "The Uncanny". *Papers of Surrealism* [online journal], 3, http://www.surrealismcentre.ac.uk/papersofsurrealism/journal3/acrobat_files/iversen_review.pdf (last accessed on 28 April 2016).

Keller, A. and Ward, F. (2006) "Matthew Barney and the Paradox of the Neo-Avant-Garde Blockbuster". *Cinema Journal*, 45 (2), 3–16.

Kelley, M. (1993/2003) "Playing with Dead Things: On the Uncanny". In: Welchman, J. C. ed. (2003) *Foul Perfection: Essays and Criticism*, Cambridge, MA: MIT Press, 70–99.

Leckey, M. (2010) "Proposal for a Show". *YouTube Video*. 17 December, https://www.youtube.com/watch?v=c8QWrLt2ePI (last accessed on 2 May 2016).

Magagnoli, P. (2012) "The Pull of Violence: Paul Chan's Trilogy of War". *Afterall*, 31, 26–35.

———— (2015) *Documents of Utopia: The Politics of Experimental Documentary*, London: Wallflower Press.

Marks, L. (2002) *The Skin of the Film: Intercultural Film, Embodiment, and the Senses*, Durham, NC: Duke University Press.

Obrist, H. O. (2012) "Ed Atkins: Interview by Hans Ulrich Obrist". *Kaleidoscope*, 13.

Paglen, T. (2012) *The Last Pictures*, Berkeley: University of California Press.

Poitras, L. (2014) *Citizenfour* [film]. HBO Films, Participant Media, Praxis Films.

Reichardt, J. (1978) *Robots: Fact, Fiction, and Prediction*, New York: Penguin Books.

Russell, C. (1999) *Experimental Ethnography: The Work of Film in the Age of Video*, Durham, NC: Duke University Press.

Smith, V. (2013) "Something I've Wanted to Do But Nobody Would Let Me: Mike Kelley's 'The Uncanny'". *Afterall*, 34, 17–28.

Steyerl, H. (2009) "In Defence of the Poor Image". *e-flux journal* [online journal], 10, http://www.e-flux.com/journal/in-defense-of-the-poor-image/ (last accessed on 23 April 2016).

Trecartin, R. (2016) Email from the Trecartin studio. 12 May.

5 Identity, language, and the body online

Who are we online? The internet's capacity for identity shifting is tremendous and forms a substantial part of what we might term the "internet imaginary", or the set of beliefs that internet users subscribe to about the web. I defy you to go a day – a morning! – reading about the internet without coming across a reference to the *New Yorker* cartoon with the caption, "On the Internet, nobody knows you're a dog". This was published in 1993, aeons ago in internet years, and its central supposition – the ability to entirely pass as someone else – has been repeatedly debunked in sociological studies. This has not stopped it from seeming to hold true, then or now. Indeed, the way in which it has persisted as a myth is in itself significant.

Identity play was a central concern in early usage of the web, particularly in chat rooms and MUDs (multi-user domains), as users online chose and discarded different traits and characteristics, such as gender, age, location, or profession. The internet was seen as an incredible forum of exchange with others, free of the visible signifiers of one's identity – a notion of play consonant with the then-contemporary postmodern constitution of identity as a site of multiplicity and fragmentation. It is important to note that even at the time this was illusory. Empirical research into chat rooms of the 1990s showed that the educated white male was still seen as the norm versus people who were other to that specification – women, blacks, and minority ethnicities. In an important article on MUDs in 1998, the scholar Lori Kendall looked at "roll calls", where users were asked IRL ("in real-life") questions about themselves – how much money they made, what ethnicity they were – to show how the sites, despite the rhetoric of a hidden and fungible identity, simply confirmed hierarchies of identity that existed offline (Kendall 1998). As the internet has evolved, particularly with social media, research has shown that users tend now to perform themselves, rather than assuming other identities. "Authenticity" is a goal on sites such as Facebook, or dating sites such as Match.com or Grindr, where users attempt to create the closest possible match between the online presentation of their persona and what they believe to be their true personhood. Emoticons and new codes of online communication allow for more nuanced and efficient modes of interaction. Users tend now to use their own names on user-groups, which is mandated by such dominant sites as Facebook, rather than the styled monikers of the 1990s (rockstagrl@ . . .). Identity on the web remains in a mode of performance, although at present the performance – perhaps more anxiously – comes as an attempt to perform one's real self.

One can see this movement from passing to authenticity reflected also in culture at large. The late 1990s and early 2000s were keenly interested in the notion of fake personhood and anonymous creation, such as the teenage rent-boy "JT Leroy", whose memoir *Sarah* (1999) was exposed as having been authored by a forty-something female writer in Brooklyn; the collectively created persona of Annlee, in the project inaugurated in 1999 by Philippe Parreno and Pierre Huyghe; Eva and Franco Mattes's Darko Maver project (1998–1999); and the imaginary persona of Reena Spaulings, whose story was collectively authored in the eponymous novel by the Bernadette Corporation (2005), to cite only a few examples that touched on the art world. The present moment's fascination with the performance of identity now touches on the autobiographical, such as the fictionalised first-person narrative of Karl Ove Knausgaard, which closely follows Knausgaard's own biography, or – bridging these two moments – the Proustian recountings of Elena Ferrante, a pseudonym whose real identity has not been revealed. Like that of Proust, Knausgaard and Ferrante's novels begin in childhood and chart their own becoming as writers: their stories preside over multiple selves arrayed over a series of episodes, and their identities emerge as changing and contingent. Similarly, within contemporary artworks responding to the internet, one of the most salient features is a return of the first-person point of view. The "I" becomes the guiding figure – the Beatrice – amidst representations of labyrinthine web searches, pseudo-academic arguments, or apparently confessional divulgements. How this "I" might be understood as autobiographical is intricately related to the performance of identity on the internet, particularly in its later instantiation where the performance of identity does not aim for impersonation but for selfhood.

Any inkling of the "performance of identity" also necessarily brings to mind Judith Butler's theorisation of gender. In *Gender Trouble: Feminism and the Subversion of Identity* (1990/2006), Butler famously demonstrates that gender is always in the midst of being performed; it is never a priori or essentially existent. In contemporary usage of the internet, "performance" not only retains the sense of acting or pretence but also of repeated action and activity – a corporeal and temporal dimension. The artist Brad Troemel has termed the participation of a number of so-called social-media artists "aesthletes", conjoining the words athletics and aesthetics to suggest the physical exertion involved in the constant performance of identity that the creation of an online persona entails (Troemel 2013). This is similar to the writer Gene McHugh's identification of an artistic stance that sees meaning "accrued through the on-going performance of an artist making individual works through time – less the individual work and more the on-going exhibition of multiple instances of work" (McHugh 2011, 220). (This also describes McHugh's own activity; he kept a blog for the course of a year, from 2009 to 2010, which is now published as *Post Internet: Notes on the Internet and Art*, from which the earlier quote was taken.) Another way to think of social-media activity on the web would be that of serious play: a term used initially in Plato to characterise Socratic dialogues, which suggests an experience that is designed not to arrive at an end but to open the door for different possibilities and outcomes. (Serious play's contestation of purposiveness also suggests a way to think about an artist's social-media activity vis-à-vis their "actual" work.)

Finally, the performance of identity also allows identity to be multiplicitous, both in its online iteration (capable of being separated into different fora such as Twitter for professional work, Facebook for friends, Instagram for travel, etc.) and more fundamentally as fluid and shifting. Popular notions of identity in the West have changed enormously in the past twenty years: there has been further acceptance of homosexuality and greater visibility given to transgender people and mixed-race couples and children. The binaries that structure thinking about identity (women/man, hetero/homo, black/white, Us/Other) are increasingly pushed back against, certainly in liberal enclaves such as the art world. The question of identity, thus, is incredibly rich – one of those tantalising fields, like the ontologies of fiction and documentary, whose analysis will always seem to fall short of the desire we have in asking about them: who am I, when I am being someone else? One way to start thinking about identity, then, is to think of how we are asking that very question.

Linguistic explorations

In the entirety of Proust's six-volume *The Remembrance of Things Past*, the narrator and main protagonist – the very subject of the book – only divulges a name twice ("Marcel"). He is more often known in scholarship as *un monsieur qui raconte et qui dit « je »* ("a man who speaks and who says 'I'"), from Proust's description of his narrator in a 1913 letter. At the same time, few novels are so popularly associated with their author as *The Remembrance of Things Past*. The Proust imaginary is full of its writer and his creative process: the reclusion, the cork-lined room, the mining of his own memories. And indeed part of the joy of the novel is the inseparable relation between the emergence of the young man and the emergence of the writer; *Remembrance of Things Past* is the story of a man learning to use language to recount stories, specifically the story of *Remembrance of Things Past* itself. The project is deeply performative and rests on the premise that the emergence of the self is the emergence of the ability to use language.

Proust is in many ways an odd choice for thinking through the unfolding of identity online. One gets the sense he would have hated (but might have used) Facebook. Memes would have made him retch. Twitter's 140-character count clearly would have bested him. But Proust's opus touches on so many aspects of identity online it is difficult to ignore: the confusion between the "I" and the narrator; the ambiguous terrain of sexuality in his work and his use of nomenclature to allow gender fluidity; the confessional impulse; and, most importantly, the performance of the self through language. The sociologist Erving Goffman analysed the public performance of identity in terms of a "front stage", which is what people present to others, and the "back stage", where one relaxes and is oneself (Goffman 1959). Social-media sites such as Facebook and Instagram are commonly assumed to collapse these two: thus the anxiety over the appearance of embarrassing images from the weekend in colleagues' feeds or, conversely, the staging of "real-life" activities such as cooking or children's birthday parties as part of the "front stage" of management of identities for celebrities. The implication of this on one's subjectivity itself is less known and is the source of numerous studies on wired teenagers. What happens when everyone sees everything and there is no private place to explore a new part of a personality?

This is where Proust's performance of the self through language remains such a helpful guide, as by switching the focus to language one is able to understand how existing power structures determine subjectivity. This is, of course, the key insight of poststructuralism. Butler showed how discursive apparatuses reinforcing gender and class hierarchies structure the way one speaks; the very idea of "gender trouble" is a means to get away from phallocentric language – from the prison-house of language, to use another well-known formulation. In thinking linguistically, our thoughts are limited to what we are able to express using the analytical expressions of our language and to the way it determines both thinking (for Nietzsche) and reflects and enforces class, race, and gender privileges in its pronouns and word choices. Goffman's front stage and back stage are equally determined by the language we speak: however we are presenting the self, we are presenting a self inflected by social and historical forces that are beyond our control.

Language also chimes with the actual engagement of life on the web, which takes place as much (if not more) on a keyboard as by posting or re-circulating images or choosing icons. One is typed into being. The fact that this deployment of language is written rather than oral underscores the way in which representations of internet identity understand identity as operating autonomously from oneself.[1] Written words are what one uses to speak to someone when the person (or oneself) is not there. Likewise, language is crucial for artists in considering the performances of themselves online: this is apparent in the importance of dialogue as a motif; the emergence of the lecture-performance as a significant genre; the collaging of texts from different sources; and the representation of the clash between centre and margin as a linguistic one. In the final part of this chapter, we will look at the strong link that emerges between speech and embodiment, and at how this is used in a context of deterritorialisation and the state of exception, specifically as theorised by Giorgio Agamben. Language becomes, ambivalently, a function of embodiment and a means to participate in and contest government power structures.

The dialogic

In an article from 2014, I discussed the tendency for digital work and work that is loosely associated with the post-internet art generation to use dialogue as a format (Gronlund 2014). I compared this to the desire for "narcissism" that Rosalind Krauss identified at the heart of video work of the 1970s, when artists such as Joan Jonas and Bruce Nauman used the camera to explore themselves, literally using it to trace their bodies or exploiting video's capacity for instantaneous feedback to try to close the gap between self and representation (Krauss 1976). This inward-gazing focus on the body and the self is opposed to the way the artist's body and character appear in work of the 2000s and 2010s. Where in the 1970s the focus was inward into one's own psychology, now the artist appears as an externally constituted character. He or she literally lives on autonomously on YouTube or Vimeo, blogs or Twitter, and his or her thoughts circulate beyond the control of the maker, picked up and moved on and virally circulated through the copying and pasting of everyday internet readership – a "readership" in which response and recirculation are implicit.

Audience is of utmost importance to interaction online: since the Web 2.0, nearly any linguistic utterance online is conversational. People feed back in comments and recirculate posts, and one's online behaviour is shaped not as writing for an abstract audience but as two-way communication. This shift in thinking about the representation of oneself online – as part of a conversation rather than a performance on a proscenium stage – also dovetails with shifts in the thinking of subjectivity. Rather than the Freudian or psychoanalytic models that were so influential on art in the twentieth century, since the 1970s, art has been changed by major debates in identity politics, feminism, and postcolonialism, and the "self" is now less often conceived as a psychologically coherent whole and more as a number of subject positions represented in a public field. This notion of identity as constructed through a social field, and the specific conditions of interacting on the internet, is thematised by the tendency towards pictured dialogue. (By contrast Krauss's theorisation of video art in 1976 focused on the tendency of video works to feature monologues delivered directly to the camera. Her typology of this aesthetics, of narcissism, was derived from the Freudian analytic model I am claiming art has moved away from.) My argument in this text was that the high incidence of such a form suggested a mode of extreme publicity – the spectre of a respondent always on the horizon. The social field or audience of the internet is symbolised in the works in the figure of the interlocutor with whom characters speak.

As a corpus for this hypothesis, I looked at videos that mimic existing dialogue formats, such as that of TV interviews in Josh Kline's videos *Forever 27* and *Forever 28* (both 2013), which feature Q&As between dead celebrities and entertainment reporters, or Alex Israel's series of interviews in *As It Lays* (2012). Frances Stark's *My Best Thing* (2011) re-creates a dialogue in an online sex chat room. Others stage scenes, such as Ed Atkins's two-screen *Us Dead Talk Love* (2012), which represents a conversation between two cadavers. Others actively generate a back-and-forth with either the internet user or the internet itself, such as Cécile B. Evans's *AGNES* (2013) project for the Serpentine Galleries in London, in which the bot Agnes interacts with users of the Serpentine website, or Erica Scourti's conversation with herself via Google algorithms for *Life in AdWords* (2012–2013). Liz Magic Laser's performance *I Feel Your Pain* (2011) re-staged conversations originally held among politicians, while *Stand Behind*

Figure 5.1 Frances Stark, *My Best Thing*, 2011, digital video on flash-drive, 1 hour, 40 minutes.

Courtesy the artist; greengrassi, London, Marc Foxx, Los Angeles; Gavin Brown's Enterprise, New York and Daniel Buchholz, Berlin

Me (2013) imagined vox pops between TV producers and the typical man or woman on the street. Many of the characters in these dialogues are played by the artists themselves or their stylised avatars (Israel, Stark, Scourti). That these partially autobiographical characters are developed via the formal device of a dialogue has important consequences. Rather than being set out through positive statements, the use of the dialogue means these characters' identities emerge through the self-correcting and dialectical process of conversation: identity is given in concert with another. The dialogue form enables a public conversation around identity – of "who" the protagonist "is", both for the subject and the work's viewer.

The emphasis on picturing a relationship with someone else also suggests a focus on the gap between one's notion of one's own identity and its representation out in the world; this involves a movement away from fusion, towards a split subject and object and towards a character for whom the look of others is constitutive of him- or herself. Likewise, the sublimation of this body into a digital avatar or acted character underscores the transition away from the body as a site of authenticity and towards an aesthetics of representation. This occurs in two ways: first through language and second through the accumulative temporality of identity's presentation on the web, where the "full picture" is never available.

Dialogue also suggests the need for viewership online or the audience as constituent of being online; we can also think back to Jesse Darling's *Habeas*

Corpus Ad Subjiciendum (2012) here, in which they alleged they were nothing without the audience. Similarly, one cannot exist, these works of dialogue suggest, without a public watching, reading, or listening. Or, to put it differently, one only exists through a public watching, reading, or listening. The concept of the dialogic, developed by the Russian literary theorist Mikhail Bakhtin in the 1930s as a means to acknowledge the fluidity of language's meaning, is salient to these works not just for the conspicuous link to the formal device of the dialogue that they use. Looking at the form of the novel, and especially the writings of Fyodor Dostoevsky, Bakhtin used the term "dialogic" to show that an utterance implies a response in its very construction; or, as Michael Holquist, who helped introduce Bakhtin to Western readers, writes: "Language, when it *means*, is somebody talking to someone else, even when that someone is one's own inner addressee" (Bakhtin 1975, xxi). All words are in conversation with past and future words, and thus their meaning is never stable. The dialogic thus reveals the inherent intertextuality or heteroglossia of language and the relational construction of meaning, and shows how the becoming of the self through language is dependent on context – something that, suddenly, is under threat online.

The speed and context collapse of communication on the internet – where images and texts are traded so quickly that their original context becomes irrelevant – means that the internet has become a microcosm of the centrifugal nature of language that Bakhtin saw as both its defining characteristic and its ideal. The surprisingly prevalent move of contemporary artists to picture foils to themselves suggests a desire to resist this obliteration of context, to push not for a synthesis of self and surround but rather for a specificity and authored characterisation of both. As Bakhtin's diagnosis of heteroglossia shows, language will always exceed one's grasp, but I would argue that the move to fix it, motivated by its connection to one's own identity, is itself indicative of the tensions within digitality. The dialogic communicability of language on the internet mirrors the contradictive stance occupied by the digital image, as seen in Chapter Three, which is stretched between representationality and networked circulation. This is slightly to conflate language's inherent relationality with the more specific metaphor of circulation on the internet, but I would like to argue that this relationality is both thematised – in a slightly anxious spirit of tamping down its effects – and ramped up and performed.

Personations

Language is of utmost importance to one of the most visible post-internet practices, that of Ryan Trecartin. The US artist makes videos, which he calls movies, in a quite conventional manner: they are written scripts, performed by a team of actors and edited into discrete, finalised, medium-length videos. He works with the same team of actors in various videos, and, though they are scripted by him, his working method is collaborative. (His frequent close collaborator, Lizzie Fitch, is co-credited on some of them.) Fitch appears in most of his work, as does Trecartin, from his first major video – the 2004 *A Family Finds Entertainment*, which was also his degree show work at the Rhode Island School of Design (RISD) – to the more recent *Priority Innfield* (2013), a four-movie project in which characters appear like players in a video game. The aesthetic of the videos and their subject matter have stayed relatively constant over his decade-long career. They show characters – whom Trecartin calls "personations", rather than "impersonations" (Norden 2011, 14) – in various scenes of social inhabitation: chatting in bedrooms, talking to the camera on a yoga mat, running at the mouth in a DIY-built set of an airplane. These sets are often complemented by installations in which viewers can sit in order to watch the movies; Trecartin and Fitch call these physical environments "sculptural theatres". My rather sober characterisation here belies the intense fractiousness of their aesthetic, which is what he is best known for. They appear to mimic the short-attention span of online existence and the disorienting chaos of pop platforms such as quickly edited music videos and advertising and sitcoms directed (or seen to be as such) at a youth market.

Trecartin emerged within the mainstream art world as one of its first artists to work with YouTube as subject matter and mode of dissemination, and has in some ways become a public spokesperson for post-internet work. He has received attention both within the art world and without,[2] and he curated with Lauren Cornell the New Museum Triennial of 2015 that encapsulated a US branch of post-internet work. Trecartin's work has been particularly influential to an understanding of how identity is conceived of in the online imaginary: as fungible, shaped by images and commodities, with a dispersed authority and authorship. Language is crucial to this presentation. Speaking, for Trecartin, is tantamount to visibility, even to existing within the diegetic frame; characters gain the attention of the camera by talking. The fact that Trecartin's movies have only the loosest claim to a plot means that characters – though all are named and credited at the end of the movie – rarely exist in the imaginary of the viewer once they have left the frame. The effect is one of incessant amnesia and instantaneity, which belies the careful attention given to the shape-shifting of language within his work.

The self is a major subject, and characters frame most statements as opinions or as self-descriptions, constantly directing a constitution of the world back to their own imagining of it. A sample from *Ready (Re'Search Wait'S)* (2009–2010) includes:

> I'm sick and tired. . . . I'm restructuring this. . . . I realise love was behind me the whole time . . . I'm channelling Miami Beach. . . . Someone just flashed an image of me; I am so sure of it. I am such a free download. . . . I'm finally just an "as if". Sense me now.

The only partly sensical language of these characters gives the impression of language mutating in front of the viewer, as well as the identities of the characters they form. The fluidity of character portrayal is underscored by the fractured narratives and the breaking of the visual field into various pop-out screens and graphics, as well as the high-pitched and digitally altered voices in which the lines are uttered. If this is a representational idiom, it is not one of naturalism.

Cornell has suggested that the universe as conjured by Trecartin simply has no centre: no means to structure Otherness. He thus accomplishes, she argues, a radical undermining of binary identities (Cornell 2011, 56). Characters freely mix gender and racial signifiers: Fitch, Trecartin's closest collaborator, regularly appears topless, like a boy, with shoulder-length hair, like a girl. Her skin is orange, as is the case for many of the characters, as if she is the victim of an overly enthusiastic spray-tan. A series of Photoshopped images that Trecartin made for the fashion magazine *W* in 2010 exemplify both the use of performative excess and the desire to complicate signifiers of identity. In the C-print *Again Pangaea + Telfar Clemens* (2010), Telfar Clemens, a member of Trecartin's rotating cast, is portrayed as mixed race. That is, his right arm is white, his left arm is black, and his torso is a shade in between. His face, looking directly at the viewer, is pixelated – almost as a mosaic – in different shades of skin colour. His hands have the texture, colour, and black markings of basketballs – a reference to black culture – while a black face peers from the picture on his iPhone. His hair is long, held in place by a hairband–like belt, but his face masculine. A dark pony-tail cascades from the phone. His trousers are covered in a cartographical map. His elbow has a pierced hoop dangling from it. A logo lies on his raised heel like a fake tattoo. His foot, in a flip-flop, is standing on what appears to be a men's razor. The background is an indeterminate city, superimposed behind him. His torso is covered in plastic, with small IUDs – forms of birth control – stuck to him. A zipper dangles down his chest but zips nothing up. He wears a cut-off tank top with a recycling emblem emblazoned on it. On his lips are superim-posed the words "Agree Inn". The image is saturated by socially significant emblems: the person emerges as not one or the other, or even all at once, but a process leading away from coherence.[3]

Trecartin refers to individuals as "situations and "clusters": identity as an aggregate of signifiers and representations. In many ways, this is also a clas-sical means of representing characters. Privately commissioned portraiture, from the Renaissance to the present day, presents identity as a legible agglom-eration of signs pointing to character traits (patience, avarice, kindness) and profession (writer, explorer, sovereign). (Think of the portrait of the current Earl of Spencer, in which he clutches the notes for the eulogy in which he condemned the Prince of Wales and the press for the death of his sister, the former Diana Spencer.) Trecartin works in this vein but suggests these traits as in the process of mutating, liable to change into another iteration or form. The tension between legibility and illegibility is crucial. *Again Pangaea* is *excessively* literal: the surfeit of signifiers overwhelms one singular reading. In the same way, Trecartin's videos reflect a sense of being overwhelmed by digital media and cultural expressions online as well as by what Fredric Jameson identified as the unrepresentability of global capitalism. The tenor of Trecartin's work is

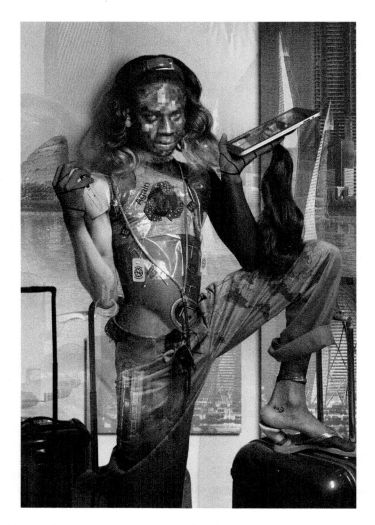

Figure 5.2 Ryan Trecartin, *Again Pangaea + Telfar Clemens*, 2010, C-print, 91.4 × 61 cm.
© Ryan Trecartin. Courtesy Andrea Rosen Gallery, New York

not simply anxiety but of a fight – a constant attempt to define oneself amidst a colonisation of identity, objects, and language by marketing and consumer capitalism.

The insecure visual and linguistic presentation of personhood extends beyond characters to material objects, images, and even words themselves, all of which often detach from the picture plane and float across the screen, vying for our attention. Bodies distend, logos levitate, and green-screen effects promiscuate.

Dialogue works both to confirm a fluidity of identity and to create a plane of equivalence among words, bodies, objects, logos, commodities, and emotions. As Michael Wang has noted, about the *Any Ever* series, Trecartin's

> transformations mirror the strategies of late-capitalist marketing whereby, for example, an emotion becomes a word, a word an image, an image a product. Marketing speak, a language in which Trecartin and his characters are fluent, is replete with examples of "nominalisation": The conversion of adjectives and verbs into nouns. This grammatical convention is a slight of hand that transforms qualities or actions into seemingly physical entities – the easier to productize, buy, and sell.
>
> (Wang 2015, 404–45)

Trecartin's affinities with the language of capitalism suggests a bleeding of consumerism into the constitution of the self, a critique which is also grounded in an awareness of class and the closed horizon of social mobility in the US. His characters' milieu is that of lower-middle-class and middle-class America, on Spring Break in Miami Beach, making YouTube movies in new builds. Class signifiers are common; indeed the genetic enhancements of Deitch's posthuman bodies – Botox lips, mid-winter tans – now suggest an economic precarity that is intranscendable: short-term indulgences that detract attention from a larger economic stagnation. "I need to tell ya'll, We in the PastNow. 'cause I'm practicing a new kind of surgery called: History Enhancements. I think acceleration is fuckin Slow, it's takin way too long to get where We Are!", says a character in *P.opular S.ky (section ish)* (2009). The myriad choices offered by consumer capitalism never end up being much of a choice. "I'm gonna name my first born VISA", says another, "&Then I'm going to abandon her".[4]

Foul perfections

The focus on the commodity and the person as equal subjects of the camera adds a new gloss to the history of objects in Chapter Three: a way of understanding the commodity object and commodity image that moves beyond art's conventional position of critique. I want to look at this move in detail, both for what it says about the commodity object and for how it informs a genre of performative inhabitation that recurs in post-internet art, which I would like to call "personation", adapting Trecartin's neologism to suggest a mode of full inhabitation and immersion rather than mimesis, and underlining the lack of the external standpoint inherent in this genre and its consequent obviation of immanent critique. Trecartin's inductive mode of thinking about identity – as a grouping of signifiers – mirrors the actual presentation of identity on the web, in which identity appears through various instantiations, accumulated and evaluated by the viewer over a period of time. A number of post-internet artists have used this temporal and performative mode to create fake identities, reprising a genre prevalent in net.art. Compared to net.art, however, these personations are more invested in affect and in the aspirational styling of an authentic identity. I want to focus on two examples of this work and then draw out its larger implications for the relation of the internet user to commodity culture.

YouTube space is commonly described as a "glass bedroom", in that viewers are able to see directly into the bedroom of the performer. With resonances of the fourth wall, the glass bedroom suggests a mode of theatricality in which fiction is knowingly suppressed. The personality performed by vloggers, for example, is "authentic" with many layers; the fiction – acknowledged as such by both performer and viewer – is that the activity pictured on their webcam, of the figure dancing or chatting or doing his or (more likely) her hair, would be the same even if unseen, or that one approaches the vast internet public with the same level of familiarity as if they were a known friend. The fact of the bedroom also suggests the levels of intimacy, both personal and sexual, suggested by YouTube users: the typical first-person address to the camera has confessional overtones, allowing the speaker to be more emotionally or sexually free. (That this is pure fantasy is also reflected in the way it has become a genre on online porn.) Though it traffics in fictional personae, much of the work of personation on YouTube (both artistic and general) is motivated more by the performance or evocation of the shared affective relations that characterise the YouTube universe: the loneliness, voyeurism, scopophilia, desire, and binge-watching boredom. For artists who use YouTube or other social-media venues to create a role, this tethering to authenticity also means that performance's ludic possibilities – the camp portrayals of Jack Smith's *Flaming Creatures* (1963), for example, which allowed not only gender trouble but tropicalism and the exploration of different cultures – are curtailed. For artwork that inhabits this mode of impersonation, even if creating a fully fake identity, the work formally aims to fit in to the internet genre; any ontological aspect of being an "art project" lies not in the execution but in the intentionality of the artist.

The artist Ann Hirsch, for example, explores the role of women online and tests the extent to which a woman can be sexual without becoming exploited or trolled. Her first major project in this regard was the character "Caroline", in *The Scandalishious Project* (2008–2009). Caroline was a "camwhore" on YouTube – a woman who produces mildly sexual material to get as many followers as possible – and Caroline's videos, made over the course of two years, were first-person addresses to the web camera by a young woman. They are indistinguishable from much YouTube fodder: there is some bed-writhing, a song about her butt, faux-faux innocence, and general narcissism. *Scandalishious* sets off a chain of imitation: Hirsch imitating a camwhore who is imitating media performers, who are imitating socially constructed notions of attractiveness. Later projects, such as *horny lil feminist* (2014–2015), addressed the fact that one of the main representations of women online is in pornography and offered a compendium of videos of vaginas (both hers and others) in which the note struck is one of humour rather than visual exploitation. (The vaginas break out in song, for instance.) "Caroline" was taken as real by the YouTube audience,

Figure 5.3 Ann Hirsch, *The Scandalishious Project*, 2008–2009, performance on YouTube.
Courtesy the artist and Arcadia Missa, London

and the project was summarily ended without, I imagine, most of its viewers knowing its experimental nature.

Similar to *Scandalishious*, in *Excellences & Perfections* (2014) Amalia Ulman created an unnamed persona via Instagram. Over the course of several months, Ulman uploaded images to the social-media site – mostly selfies but also memes, motivational sayings, and cartoons – to tell a story about a character breaking up with her boyfriend and rebounding from this loss. The idea of a woman performing for the gaze of others was integral to the narrative as well as the conceit. Pictures showed her apparently getting breast augmentation surgery, as she made her attractiveness both a commodity in the attention economy of the Internet and within the story she impersonated. To (real) friends and acquaintants, for example, she noted that she was deliberately setting out to be a "hot babe" and to create images that garnered the most likes (Kinsey and Ulman 2013). Ulman has underlined that a major focus of her enquiry is class, and the project carefully parses different signifiers of socio-economic level, particularly in their intersection with sexuality and femininity. She dyed her brown hair blond, which with her dark eyebrows had the effect of making her look slightly tacky, a character reading she explored through an episode in the project that suggested prostitution as inherent in the role of assiduously attractive woman. She began posting more sexually explicit images of herself – in bed, in her underwear, for example – as well as text-images like a checklist reading "single / taken / busy getting money", with a tick in the box next to "busy getting money". At a certain point, she reverts to her natural hair colour and posts more upscale pictures of herself: handbags, house porn, fancy hotel shots as well as uplifting messages like "namasté". The work is a deft reading of how people consciously and unconsciously trick out their social-media profiles to signal their inclusion, or their desire to be included, in different subcultures or social brackets.

Indeed, Ulman's personation is in many ways simply an amplification of how people use Instagram, in the same way that Hirsch's *Scandalishious* amplifies the mimicry at the heart of representations of sexuality. *Excellences & Perfections* imitates Instagram images in the way that Instagram users have internalised the ability to create images out of their own lives. Like *Scandalishious, Excellences & Perfections* was taken for real by the online public, who now expect authenticity rather than passing, and both were widely viewed. (Ulman's Instagram account had over a hundred thousand followers; Hirsch had hundreds of thousands of views.) It is not terribly difficult to understand why they were popular: people like to look at sexual images of women. There is, of course, a foul imperfection to Ulman's and Hirsch's projects, which is their own self-exploitation – even though they are aware of it – in the process of the projects.

This mode of fully inhabiting another crops up repeatedly in post-internet art and art concerned with digital technologies (and often in projects by women). There is little space for reflection within these works, nor any critical standpoint beyond their stated intentions. The work is a self-commodification in an economy of attention. In some sense, this self-commodification is not far from the hybridisation of art practices under the sign of post-internet art, which happily accommodates commercial ventures. Indeed this commercialism is one of the hallmarks of post-internet art, and is often a lightning rod for critique (or rolled eyes), both because it goes against art's typical mode of critique, and – on the flipside – because it claims commercialism as something new and radical, when art history is awash with experiments in commerce. (One apposite example would be Andrea Fraser's *Untitled* [2003], a transaction in which the work's collector, in buying the work for $20,000, received in return sex with Fraser, and a sixty-minute video of the act.) Under this heading of commercialism we can think of DIS, the New York-based art and fashion collective that publishes a magazine, curates shows, and sells fashion and design items, or K-HOLE, the art collective that provides consulting to companies that wish to expand into the youth market.

Post-internet work often frames the commodity status of the art object as transactory (again, as in Fraser's *Untitled* or the consulting that K-HOLE provide) and a direct function of finance capitalism, rather than, say, the objects sold by Sarah Lucas's and Tracey Emin's East End shop of the 1990s, which looked back to the local economy of a village store.[5] Christopher Kulendran Thomas, for example, has investigated the ways that the art object could become so closely aligned with its commodity status that it would become, only, a financial asset. In the project *Real Flow* (2015, in collaboration with Victoria Ivanova, Suhail Malik, and Diann Bauer), he attempted to create a financial instrument particular to the art world. *Real Flow* segued into *New Eelam* (2015–ongoing), a work shown in the – DIS-curated – 2016 Berlin Biennial that focuses on the town of Eelam in Sri Lanka, whose population was decimated in the country's civil war and now exists as largely dispersed. *New Eelam* questions the idea of territorial belonging by proposing an AirBnB-like housing arrangement, where those who have signed up to Kulendran Thomas's scheme will have the use of different apartments in whatever city they are flying to next – a territory of access rather than national belonging. A brochure produced for the work mimics the glossy stock photography and industrial loft aesthetic of hipster aspirations and focuses on the housing market as a primary site of inequity. The work exists as paraphernalia, genuine proposal, and conceit: at the biennial an "experience suite" of sculptures relates to the brand and a film announces the scheme; Kulendran Thomas is also working with website developers and real-estate agents to assemble a portfolio of properties, for which he is fundraising, to create the project as a real concern. Indeed, I have difficulty gauging whether *New Eelam* is a mode of accelerationism or a critique of the systemic iniquities of the current housing market. Kulendran Thomas wrote me,

> [T]hrough a genuine share economy (i.e. collective *co-ownership* rather than private property), we think it may be possible to go much further than existing disruptive platforms and perhaps resolve one of the classic dilemmas of capitalism – between the flexibility of renting and the equity benefits of property ownership. *New Eelam*'s model is an attempt to enable the greater luxury of communalism (rather than of individually owned property) through a more liquid form of citizenship, where it's possible to live anywhere in homes that are as streamable as music or movies.
>
> (pers. comm.)

The work furthers the deterritorialisation within the model of AirBnB or Uber, in which items are transformed in purpose by the nature of one's access to them (homes into hotels, cars into taxis).[6] These models' connections to the exploitation of labour, the lack of unionisation, and even safety problems for their users is well known, and I am sure not lost on Kulendran Thomas, an astute reader of art and politics. Rather, its liminal nature seems to me symptomatic of accelerationist aesthetics in practice, where disavowal again comes into play.

The relation between the use of the internet and self-commodification is also real, not notional. Online activity is packaged and sold as commodities to consumer companies for new product development and more tailored advertising: the circulatory network of the internet makes commodities of us all. More importantly, the circulation of the internet itself produces the user as a commodity. This is similar to the network created among celebrity, advertisement, and commodity object of post-World War II, pre-internet TV. Television enforced heterosexual social norms in a mode opposite to the way in which the internet enables multiplicitous identity, but these nuances matter little to the eventual self-commodification that the internet engenders. Advertising made commodities of the celebrities whose fame it created, such that the celebrity selling an object on TV became him- or herself the commodity being sold, transmuted into the televisual unit of currency, the image. On the internet, the circulation of the user as image travels along a network that users themselves motivate and which attracts attention back to the image. Daniel Boorstin's insight that celebrities are famous for being famous is tightened online, where viewers contribute to the circulation that renders and amplifies this visibility.

If it is important to remember that the circulation and commodification of identity was part of television, it is also crucial to note the differing stance of artists vis-à-vis this rendering. David Joselit contrasts TV's characterisations of normative identity roles with artistic televisual experiments of the same period, as by Nauman, Jonas, and Vito Acconci, that seek to disrupt the transformation into character by placing a wedge between identity and image (Joselit 2007, 162–63). In her 1972 *Organic Honey's Visual Telepathy* performance (and later video of the same name), Jonas created a female alter ego, a masked double in a feathered headdress. Her performance uses mirroring and the doubling of video into real and representation to create a split image of herself, one as Jonas and the other as the showgirl Organic Honey. Jonas and her image oscillate in this in-betweenness, figuring identity as a process of becoming. (This is a different nuance to Krauss's reading of work of the same period, focusing on the productive impossibility of synthesis rather than the ambition for it.) This is a split or, again, possibility for immanent critique not directly explored in the work of Hirsch, Ulman, and others. Despite the temporal nature of their projects, they create not a performance of becoming but images to be seen and forwarded on: units along a circuit that they do not control, which lead them towards being images in a gallery or subjects of trolling or masturbatory fantasy.

This is not to call them out for naïvety; rather, what is striking to me is why this activity is accomplished, despite the evident self-exploitation the performances and commodification of their bodies entail. The move to self-commoditise reflects the internet user's alienation from his or her labour – in this sense, from his or her identity and image, where identity and image are understood as the product of one's labour. Internet activity entails a vast amount of immaterial and unpaid labour: we are all out there working on Facebook for free, our linking and liking turned by others to profit. The notion of the social-media platform is that of a hyper-reality, both in a popular, immaterial sense and in the closer Baudrillardian reading, where commodities are profoundly distanced from use value and from an authenticity of self. Like Rabih Mroué's Syrian protestor, who believes the world of images to be reality, the sheer level of exploitation of some of these works might be rationalised as a by-product of extreme alienation: it is as if the trolling is happening to another. One becomes a figure uncanny to oneself – a revolting Facebook profile with inane comments about Donald Trump and cliché images of children on their first day of school. Making that figure explicitly other might be the most sane way to cope with life on the internet. Or, perhaps, noting that this terrain is overwhelmingly populated by women artists, in a sacrificial vein – as a means to show by their very own experiences the commodification of self and exploitation of all images of women that is general to internet use.[7] "Now, as a woman", Hirsch has noted, "how do I show myself online [in a way] that feels like it's moving a conversation forward, doing something new and showing women in a way that they're not normally seen?" (Hirsch quoted in Saner 2016).

Affirmative action

This shift towards commodity affirmation is also reflected by the tendency of post-internet artists and artists concerned with the internet to identify with the norm, rather than the counterculture. This propensity, particularly for the New York, net.art-inflected, post-internet community, was best expressed in the satirical table *Hacking vrs. defaults chart*, made in 2007 by the artist Guthrie Lonergan and first published on his blog. Lonergan was a member of Nasty Nets, one of the so-called "surf clubs" that found and posted, in the early to mid-2000s, wild things from the web on different bookmarking sites. He was one of the first artists to use the emerging face of the Web 2.0 as material, anticipating the direction towards private over-sharing that it would take; *Babies' First Steps*, a video made in 2005, for example, is a compilation of videos parents have posted of their children's first steps. The schematic *Hackings vrs. defaults chart* is a product

Hacking	Defaults
Hacking a Nintendo cartridge to make images	Using MS Paint to make images
	12 point Times New Roman
Net.Art 1.0	???
 Anxiety	 Banality
"The Man is taking away our privacy... that's lame!"	"We willingly give up our own privacy (i.e. endlessly talking about ourselves on our Myspace profiles)... why?"
Empowering The People by subverting The Man's power	Being and critiquing The People by using the tools made by The Man
Rock & Roll attitude	Exuberant humility
Jodi's blogs	Tom Moody's blog
Sophisticated breaking of technology	Semi-naive, regular use of technology

Figure 5.4 Guthrie Lonergan, *Hacking vrs. defaults chart*, 2007, web page.

Courtesy the artist

of this hinge point between net.art and post-internet concerns, setting out the differences between net.art and what Lonergan, in one of the early competing definitions of post-internet art – its Betamax, if you will – called internet-aware art, by contrasting net.art's hacktivist and DIY stance to the normcore aesthetics and complacent attitude of 2000s work. Where there was anxiety over privacy rights, the table shows, there is now the willing divulgence of information on MySpace. Where there was coding, there is now the use of the default Microsoft Word font of Times New Roman in 12 point – or, indeed, the use of the default WordPress setting, which Nasty Nets used.

The term "normcore" was coined by a report produced by the collective K-HOLE in which they analysed the increasing specialisation of lifestyle signifiers and their co-option by anyone and everyone in a mode they call "Mass Indie". Under the heading "Trust the Cargo Shorts", they observe, "When the fringes get more and more crowded, Mass Indie turns toward the middle. Having mastered difference, the truly cool attempt to master sameness" (K-HOLE 2013). As for personation, the mastery of sameness as a mode of differentiation is, perhaps, an appropriate response to the hypocrisy of artisanal or authentic lifestyles, in which one's handlebar moustache pomade may still be made in Bangladesh with by-products that pollute rivers and retard children in utero. The much-cited comment of Slavoj Žižek's that there is no imagining an alternative to capitalism is powerful. There is a feeling of no means of articulation beyond a default setting, so one might as well cosy up to it, inhabit, or accelerate it.[8] Normcore is also born of necessity: artists do not have the luxury to "drop out" in a 1960s manner, in an era of dizzying rents, student loan debts, and few grants. In some sense, artists must play the game.

The sheer scale of the number of images on the internet, and the erosion of the idea of the original, also engenders a reversal towards the commodity. The theory of the commodity fetish endows the commodity with a latent life, returning a sense of uniqueness to the commodity object and marking it out as special to the consumer. The validation of default culture, by contrast, looks for meaning in the mass rather than the unique item – following the cybernetic logic of the algorithm, which sifts through vast quantities of information to find the strongest pattern. Stock images, for example, rather than being discounted, speak more about collective desires and hopes than the subcultural long tails of targeted marketing: they provide a bridge to the public that is foreclosed by the individuation of personal experience on the internet. DIS, for example, has amassed a stock image bank, accessible from its website, in which cultural assumptions become startlingly legible. (Again, Aby Warburg was born a hundred years too early.) A surprising number of images, for example, show a woman laughing alone eating salad – a fork poised in mid-air, smiling at apparently nothing, just happy to be eating healthy lettuce – a revealing performance of class, gender, racial, and body ideals. The collective social imaginary decried in critiques of television returns almost as a subject of nostalgia: a collectivity inherent within the common knowledge of jingles and sitcom characters.

Stock images become a shared history. I don't want to push this slightly senti-mental reading too much, but want to note the level of craft that is often associ-ated with stock images and with digital media in general. Despite the impression of its ease of use, digital techniques such as Photoshopping, video editing, and sound mixing are incredibly time-intensive, and the labour they entail is highly skilled. In Constant Dullaart's *Jennifer_in_Paradise* (2013), for example, Dullaart re-built the image that was initially used by the software program Adobe Pho-toshop as it booted up. It showed Jennifer, the then-girlfriend of the founder of Photoshop, John Knoll, on a beach in Bora Bora in 1987 – the same day, in fact, that he proposed to her. When Knoll was demonstrating what would become Photoshop to Apple engineers, he happened to have that photo with him and scanned it and used it for the demonstration: the world's first Photoshopped image, and an iconic image of 1990s and 2000s computer use, as anyone using Photoshop had to stare at that image and the long, tiny-font list of engineers while the program slowly got started. When Dullaart began the work, rather remarkably, the image only existed online in low-res jpgs. Dullaart re-built the image, as in a mode of care for the collective past of the internet. He exhibited this reconstructed image in a variety of aspects, blown up and pixelated as wall-paper and given different, often hammy Photoshop effects, such as the imitation of a whirlpool in which the image is seen as swirling, or the image as raked by

Figure 5.5 Constant Dullaart, *Jennifer_in_Paradise*, 2013. Restored digital image re-distributed online, holding a steganographically encrypted payload within the code of the JPG file, which can only be revealed by a password.

waves. Rather than the high production values or ability to make pictures "lie" often associated with Photoshop, the technique here becomes a picture of craft and nostalgia-laden effects.

Such resonances are key to the presentation of the commodity and of stock imagery. Rachel Reupke, for example, focuses on the norm for how it might offer a means of representing situations of emotion and commonality: the art-directed representation of the social that becomes truer than its individualised or naturalistic portrayal. The use of stylisation in art to speak more truly than the true is an old one, but rather that seeking to amplify affect, Reupke reduces it, working in a Warholian vein. The video *Ten Seconds or Greater* (2010) explores the kind of stock footage used as backdrop filler for insurance or bank ads, which Reupke came across when researching material for pop music videos. She was struck, she says, by its coexistence of the banal and the emotional extreme:

> Ill health, family arguments, financial crisis – moments of acute emotional stress – happen in everyone's lifetime, but we don't see them represented very often. What I found surprising about stock footage was seeing these events actually represented, because of the nature of its market – e.g. health insurance.
>
> (pers. comm.)

Mimicking the stock footage allowed her to create scenes of genuine emotion, through banally staged representations: this was amplified in the final product of her video, which focuses not on exceptional scenes of emotions but on the everyday emotions of boring normal life. In *Ten Seconds or Greater*, generically good-looking people in generic preppy clothes do generic, run-of-the-mill activities, such as chopping vegetables or checking emails (notably together – transformed in this happy universe into a collective rather than atomising activity) in a sterile set comprised mostly of IKEA furniture. The characters re-perform the same actions as if for different takes, making them look stuck in a particularly acute syndrome of the return of the repressed: a mode of alienation that renders them supremely sympathetic. The video *Wine & Spirits* (2013) also arrives at affective portrayal via flatness: it takes dating as its subject, staging a series of encounters of typical figures in pubs with wine and lager in front of them. Each scripted episode is based on a still image, either from print advertisements or from news imagery, and the video echoes the staged quality of its pre-represented source. As in *Ten Seconds or Greater*, the desire of the characters is never fulfilled; we see the same two characters across five different scenarios, as if always at square one, never seen actually taking a sip from their drinks. Collapsed into stock types, their activity invites our identification with them – they could be anyone, and we could be anyone – and this recognition of our banality is framed both as abhorrence and relief: everyone, after all, dreads dates.

The mass production that Adorno saw as barbaric is here seen as an index of social relations – a signal of community or affect. One way to think through this is to return to the "comrade object" of Boris Arvatov in the Soviet Union of the 1920s. Arvatov's work provides a counterfactual history to that of our first chapter, privileging the object over the image. Arvatov worked alongside the Russian Constructivists to re-conceive the commodity as a particularly powerful object in which the social relations with which it was invested were not reified but were a form of agency. Christine Kiaer, in the study *Imagine No Possessions*, shows how the Constructivists' commercial work, such as Rodchenko's graphic design shop or Liubov Popova's dress designs, are not to be understood as compromised entries into commercialism or even as an undoing of the categories between high and applied art, but rather part of a theoretical project to create a "socialist" object, one which would be the comrade to whomever used it. The new role would entail making the consumer aware of the material production that went into the object and would recirculate the libidinal desire provoked by the commodity fetish into a form of friendship (Kiaer 2005, 38).

Commodity aesthetics

Such a liberation of the commodity's desire can also be seen in the work of Elizabeth Price. Her video *The Woolworths Choir of 1979* (2012), structured in two parts, explores unison, with the repeated motif of hands clapping in unison and the phrase "We Know" punctuating its footage. The first part – the "*Choir*" – opens with images of religious statuary (a non-commodity example of a fetish) and looks at the architectural feature of a church choir, where the clergy and church elders sit during services. She uses this term to suggest other modes of unison: the choir in ancient Greek theatre, which narrates the play but does not appear as actors within it, and back-up singers, who complement the main performer. The second part of the film looks at a fire in the Manchester branch of Woolworths in 1979, in which women strapped in a second-storey window made an enigmatic hand gesture of help that mimics the choreography of back-up singers in the footage of the first part of the film. Commonality is here thus equated with marginalisation – the back-up singers, the choir who narrates but does not act, the women trapped, the clergy who legitimate the church service – and with femininity. The "back-up" nature of women, the choir to the main event, is repeatedly challenged by the "WE KNOW" that flashes across the screen, endowing this group with the crucial and never divulged position of both omniscience and commonality that the video's varied cultural forms yearn for.

The commodity is, again, another means of engagement with commonality. The art historian Tamara Trodd has used Price's work to identify a mode of "commodity aesthetics", in which fetishistic desire is deepened rather than critiqued, which she speculates runs throughout the twentieth century. Trodd shows, for example, how the sheen of Neue Sachlichkeit photographs of the 1920s, which expressed the commodity as fetishistically gleaming objects, is reprised in the metallic glossiness of Price's *Welcome (The Atrium)* (2008). The video is the first of two that pictures an imaginary museum, comprised of projected and circulating images. It chronicles a machine of sensual curves built of car parts, dripping fondue pots, and oil fountains, presented against a perspective-less black background. The contraption is designed to represent the atrium of the museum, almost an establishing shot for the larger series, proposing redundancy and excess as consitituent to the archive, as the viscous fluid moves through different iterations of recyclable movement. The second video in the project, *USER GROUP DISCO* (2009), quotes from Adorno's "The Form of the Phonograph Record" (1934), situating its presentation of household items specifically in the lineage of the commodity fetish that Adorno develops in his essay. Assorted objects appear devoid of human contact or use, again presented in chiaroscuro against a black background. They spin across the screen, visible only in parts or levitating as of their own accord – the truncated stem of a faucet, the biomorphic shape of a Beaux-Arts candlestick, the spin of a milk frother, mugs, jugs, bowls – often with New Aesthetic-like geometric patterning.[9] Later, as the pop song *Take on Me* begins in the background, text scrolling across the video enumerates the brands of the objects, underlining the aspiration encoded within their very names: "the COSMOSTAR clock radio . . . the STAR-UNITED cappuccino whisk . . . a PERFECT SOLUTION magazine rack . . . and a MASTERS PRO-SERIES crystal souvenir golf-ball". Trodd argues that *Take on Me* enacts a particular relationship towards the viewer, one in which he or she "speaks the language" of the commodity fetish even as it is made ironic by the enumeration of the products' own promises. The viewer, she writes, almost subconsciously supplies the words to the song; he or she becomes culpable, part of the increasing circuit of fetish and desire evoked by the presentation of the objects:

> Price photographs objects in such a way as to intensify their allure for us: the gleaming lip of the ceramic mug here arousing a desire in us to raise it to our mouths. Yet Price's frequently comic use of text, to make the objects 'speak' their promises, draws out. . . . [the] fantasy concerning industrial design and manufacture: that it will be perfect, that it will never grow dull, that it will satisfy us forever, completely – and she exaggerates this, making it explicit, to the point where it becomes alarming and ridiculous. . . . Intensifying our libidinal investment in commodity fetishes, she releases this energy from its rational uses to become more free-floating, unfixed and unpredictable: taking up what confronts us as alien in the commodity and rendering it as a new and vivid form of life.
>
> (Trodd 2014)[10]

The commodity is not simply switched to a position of affirmation but becomes something other, "new and vivid", calling to mind the explosions of Benjamin's dialectical images. It is transformed from an object of alienated labour into one in which this alienation becomes ecstatic, a drunken performance of bad decision-making and short-term thinking, of splurging money on things one

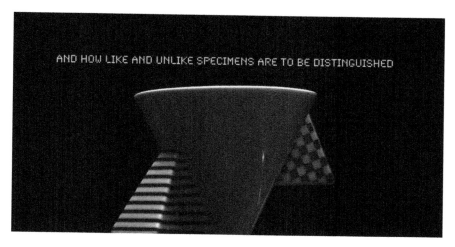

Figure 5.6 Elizabeth Price, *USER GROUP DISCO*, 2009, video still.

Courtesy the artist and MOT International London and Brussels

doesn't need. The new and vivid conditions of the commodity – the enlivening of its alienation – resemble those of the catastrophic time of digitality, abutting the glorious self-determination of neoliberal capitalism but facing a reality in which "the future and its possibilities . . . seem to be frozen" by the ubiquity of debt, as Maurizio Lazzarato writes in his assessment of the current period, *The Making of Indebted Man* (Lazzarato 2012, 49). As with digitality as a mode of imitation, the closed-off horizon shuts down the possibility of progression.

Works like Kulendran Thomas's *New Eelam* and Hirsch's and Ulman's person-ations can also be seen an updating of capital's recuperation of any position of critique, specifically in their suggestion that immanent critique is limited to accel-erationism, which proposes the only way out of capitalism as through capitalism. Primarily associated with Benjamin Noys, in an economic mode, and Steven Sha-viro, in an aesthetic one, the notion is that capitalism's internal contradictions must be pushed through, so that we can arrive at an equal distribution of resources in society: it welcomes the crisis. In aesthetics, it communicates itself through excess and immanence, which Shaviro draws in counterpoint to modernism: "Where transgressive modernist art sought to break free from social constraints, and thereby to attain some radical Outside, accelerationist art remains entirely immanent, mod-ulating its intensities in place" (Shaviro 2013). There is, as Shaviro notes, following Antonio Negri and Michael Hardt, no outside to power. Transgression is the key mode that accelerationism defines itself against. Shaviro, notably, explicitly refrains from making political claims for accelerationist aesthetics; rather, he simply says that former modes are inauthentic to the current lived experience. They are modes of "*aesthetic inefficacy*". Accelerationism, that is, is a crucial mode of digitality: the qualified acceptance of a compromised position – "I wish it were other, but this is how it is". Artists are playing the hand they have been dealt, as capital has moved voraciously to consume any historical critique of the twentieth century that has been levied against it.

Art is in a particular position vis-à-vis these questions of immanence and critique, given that as a field, it is partially (or majority) funded by the luxury purchases of the 1%.[11] The proliferation of biennials as content-making mechanisms has been accompanied by the proliferation of art fairs as money-making mechanisms. The two may not be causally related, but they lie on the same circuit, traversed by artist and artwork, and this is a difficult fact to ignore. In the next chapter, we will look more closely at theories that have attempted to make sense of the change to the economic scale of the art world and its relation to the art object; I wish, in this section on the commodity, simply to put a note or perhaps a linguistic hyperlink here to underscore that art's connection to hypercapitalism is not only notional.

The language that belongs to so many others

I want to focus in the closing of this chapter on the contradictory and privileged position that the voice plays within certain, more explicitly politically engaged works about cultural representation and identity. The voice becomes a means to signal political representation: embodying past histories while also being a means of disembodiment. It is privileged for its connection to the body, to contest digital or "un-real" existence, but also, as disembodied and digitally rendered, to allow new discourses to circulate. The emphasis on the voice occurs both on the level of subject matter and formal articulation: oral speeches, linguistic speech patterns, and sounds are frequent subjects.[12] Oral speech is conceived both as a function of embodiment and as the political other to written speech: the discourse of the margins or the dispossessed, a means of existing between the cracks of different dominant discourses – gypsy patois, urban slang. This notion of "existing between the cracks" brings up a second other to speech, that of visibility, which as we have seen occupies its own vexed position with regard to internet culture: visibility enables participation in the politics of representation – but also enables control, surveillance, and censorship. In many ways, oral communication emerges as a response to the theoretical aporia presented by this new version of visuality, which no longer functions as a straightforward symbol for political representation.

One clear way this is done is through live performance, particularly the lecture-performance. The lecture-performance appears throughout the twentieth century, and by the 2010s, it becomes a genre of its own. I want to argue that it does so as a means to contest hierarchical regimes of knowledge formation, supplementing them with a body-led discourse. The lecture-performance typically takes the format of an artist speaking on a stage and/or behind a lectern to an audience, aping the register and display tactics of academia or corporate presentations.[13] In this sense, it reflects the hybridisation of the artist as a discursive content producer, coming out of the so-called educational turn in the art world and the wider knowledge economy: the artist as researcher, academic, archivist, as well as producer (Frank 2013). This is particularly so for artists belonging a generation slightly older than that of post-internet art who have made this work a hallmark of their practices, such as Mark Leckey, Hito Steyerl, Sarah Pierce, Andrea Fraser, and Rabih Mroué.

The lecture-performance extends authority beyond academe to the interpersonal and artistic realm, knighting that as an equal place of knowledge production. The first-person singular is used to structure many of the statements, and a thematisation of the process of research for the project often forms their narrative. Everyday or defiantly non-high art examples are ushered in: Steyerl, in *Duty Free Art* (2015), recounts a dream where she was talking to the philosopher Peter Osborne and reproduces in the article generated from this lecture the image of a schematic of art history that she remembered while asleep. In *I Dreamed a Dream: Politics in the Age of Mass Art Production* (2013), she screens Susan Boyle's rendition of *Les Misérables* ballad "I Dreamed a Dream", when the matronly Scotswoman wowed the audience of *Britain's Got Talent*. Lecture-performances are often knowingly camp, delighting in a feeling of transgression in occupying the role of high content producer. As the example of Steyerl's subconscious suggests, a main means this is accomplished is by privileging affective relationships, as well as the body itself as a source of knowledge. Leckey's *In the Long Tail* (2009) lecture-performance, for example, structures its argument via an allegory of orgasm and release; the lecture culminates in a crescendo of the whirring sound of Leckey's makeshift digitisation machine, while Leckey, shouting, enumerates the nine historical stages in the allegorical life of Felix the Cat, the first image to be broadcast on television (that is, the first image to be digitised). Rather than a perfectly maintained system, the body here is a desirous subject, leading towards erotic self-destruction (notably, another way we could read accelerationism). Darling's *Habeas Corpus* likewise hinges on the interpellation performed by their hyper-articulate slides projected against their mute body.

The voice is often used to evoke a community of people in a number of works from the 2000s onwards, both in those that take on board digital concerns and those which primarily signal a performative or research focus. (Sharon Hayes's work on the queer voice or Rod Dickinson's historical re-enactments would be two examples here.)[14] The factor of digitality widens the problems staked out by this territory, as digitality allows oral discourses to circulate beyond their tethering to the body, reading embodiment symbolically as well as by being a live instantiation in space.

Bouchra Khalili's *The Speeches Series* (2012–2013), a video trilogy about African, Middle Eastern, and Latin American migrants in Europe and the US, suggests language as tantamount to ethnic identity, and the right to speak publicly as tantamount to political power. The first in the trilogy, *Mother Tongue* (2012), shows five migrants in France reading historical anticolonialist speeches – most originally written in French – in their native languages, of Moroccan Arabic, Dari, Kabyle, Malinke, and Wolof, all of which, except for Dari, have no written script. The performers recall the history of racist oppression – the work demonstrates how little progress has been made since the mid-twentieth century – while suggesting that these migrants are excluded not only from the seat of power but also from the privilege inherent in its now institutionalised critiques, which likewise exist in the language of their colonisers. *Words on Streets* (2013), the second video, shows long-term migrants in Italy who, because of their non-Italian ethnicity, are always taken as other. "I'm an Italian disguised as Chinese", says one who has grown up in Italy.

> As if my skin was not my skin, my eyes, my nose, my hair, as if they were only a useless dress. I got used to you, was changed by you. But how many times have you called me 'the Chinese girl'? What is your country when you don't feel like you belong to one or the other?

Language becomes equivalent not just to identity but to embodied identity, a factor underscored by the *mise-en-scène* of the third film, *Living Labour* (2013), in which immigrants in New York speak about the exploitation and racism they

Figure 5.7 Bouchra Khalili, *Words on Streets*, 2013, digital film, HD video, 4:3, 18 minutes, from *The Speeches Series* (film trilogy, 2012–2013).

Courtesy the artist

encounter in the low-wage jobs they work. Echoing the language of the body used in *Words on Street*, *Living Labour* focuses visually on the bodies of the speakers; the camera isolates their hands, their chests, their necks. The precarity of their existence is written on the fatigue and labour of their bodies: their lives are reduced to bare life, in a term here borrowed from Giorgio Agamben, and they are seen by others as exemplars of their race. Their testimonies, in this final instalment, focus most directly on the workers themselves; these are delivered unscripted and in their own languages or dialects.

Throughout the *Speeches Series*, the ostensible subject is the extent to which language delineates an ethnicity: the long-term Moroccan migrant in Paris who is still seen as other because of his Arab language, by which he connects to other Arabs of the diaspora. Focusing on linguistic discourse allows Khalili to frame language as a means of oppression, as well as a potential for self-representation – the right to speak publicly. She has said, for example, that *Words on Streets* refers to the historic Italian tradition of soapbox speeches as a political tactic. But as the work unfolds, the question of the body gains in prominence, exhibiting a tension between language as the mark of otherness – a facet that could be appropriated by the immigrants, turned into a weapon on their behalf – and their appearance as the mark of otherness: "my skin, my eyes, my nose, my hair". Their skin is

Figure 5.8 Bouchra Khalili, *Living Labour*, 2013, digital film, HD video, 4:3, 25 minutes, from *The Speeches Series* (film trilogy, 2012–2013).

Courtesy the artist

the source of the racism they encounter, something that they, nor Khalili, can do little about.

This tension between speech and the body is also addressed by Nsenga Knight, who for the project *X Speaks* (2015) commissioned different collaborators to collectively read famous speeches by Malcolm X on the internet, using Google Hangouts and live-streamed on YouTube. The purpose was, as Knight says, to embody speeches that are still relevant now, during a time of heightened awareness of police brutality in the US towards people of colour. Like *The Speeches Series*, *X Speaks* reflects the power of the postcolonial body as a cypher for a history of oppression, refracting this enquiry through immaterial, vocalised language and its further disembodiment online. The project swings between the anonymous public of online circulation and the specific public targeted by activists. For the performance of the speech "The Oppressed Masses of the World Cry Out for Action Against the Common Oppressor", read by Cristal Truscott and Amir McMillan at Texas Prairie View A&M University, Truscott, the director of the university's theatre program, organised her students to respond to the speech in a separate feed. She gave them signs saying "Speak" that they were instructed to wave whenever they wanted to signal agreement, placing the performance, as Knight says, "in the tradition of call and response or even 'testifying' in the Black community, where people in the audience, if they agree with and are moved by the speaker may simply say 'Speak!'" (pers. comm.). The reading of the speech was streamed online, with responses to it in PIP (small pop-out) boxes on the Google Chat screen, and others were encouraged to respond live via hashtags on Twitter (the PIP boxes and Twitter hashtagging were used for all eight of the project's speeches, though no others had the staged signs). The work, thus, is deeply invested in using the internet's circulatory mechanisms to help the speeches travel as widely as possible – but is also concerned with a specificity of response, such as its deliberate situation in the black community, or via the inclusion of conversations between the readers and Knight herself elaborating on the meaning of the speeches within the documentation of the event. (We can think back here to our reading of dialogue as a way to ground interpretation as much as letting it proliferate.) Moreover, as much as they are concerned with the circulation of speech, they also go to lengths to signal embodiment; Knight's use of members of the black community as the readers situates the discourse in a context of racism that is based on reactions to the black body (which is also, of course, the original context of Malcolm X's work). However, I wish to read "embodiment" here as more than a contextual siting in a body, and as something that signifies "offline". *X Speaks* is concerned to show speech as signifying in both an online and offline demos, as the staged mirror of offline conditions in "The Oppressed Masses" makes clear.

That is, the use of the voice to signal political agency demonstrates a relationship between power and nonvirtual communication, in which power is figured as phenomenologically indexical. Returning to Baudrillard's claim about the Gulf War, the war's mediation on the level of spectacle suggests an alienation for the Westerner from its real effects. Embodiment works as a way to contest this

alienation, to redirect a focus onto real living conditions – but only allegorically under the sign of digitality. As such an allegory, embodiment thus appears
both as the sentence of those for whom the body is exceptionally significant,
by its departing from the privileged norm, and its potential, the way in which
migrants and dispossessed minorities might be re-valorised. That this allegory,
in the endless enfolding of internet imaginary and real effects, also speaks to
the deterritorialisation and alienation of the internet is significant. The cultural
critique of neoliberalism has centred on its individuating effects at the expense
of the collective. And, particularly in an internet context, confidence in the
state as protector and judiciary has eroded after the Snowden revelations. Even
Angela Merkel, the embodiment of the German state, is surveilled by the NSA
bureaucracy. A well-known pop-cultural hero is Jason Bourne, from the *Bourne
Identity* films, who has to and can move between the cracks of power structures.
In this context of general surveillance and the erosion of the power of the state,
the dispossessed or those who function within a state without adequate state
protection reflect a new form of precarity, but also, perhaps, new models for
political agency.

The connection between the voice and embodiment and the state of exception is seen clearly in Lawrence Abu Hamdan's video and lecture-performance
Contra Diction: Speech Against Itself (2014), in which the artist discusses an
articulation of a phoneme that exists particularly among the Druze, a Levantine
ethno-religious minority spread out across Syria, Lebanon, and Palestine/Israel,
who have, throughout history, been persecuted and who have suffered terribly
at the hands of IS. Depending on whom they are speaking to – Druze or not
Druze – the Druze fully pronounce the Arabic letter "ق" (qaf), which in
standard spoken Arabic is replaced with a glottal stop, similar to the New York
accent's pronunciation of Manhattan ("Manha'an"). Abu Hamdan underlines
the physicality of the sound "qaf", which in classical Arabic, and in the Druze's
enunciation, is pronounced deep in the throat. (It does not have a corresponding
English sound.) He reads the Druze's pronunciation of the letter not as a factor
of language but as one of the body itself, opening his mouth wide and pointing
to his throat to show where the sound originates from, far down by his Adam's
apple. Language and ethnicity have here altered the vocal cords themselves: if you
have not learned to make this sound as a child, you will have trouble doing so.

Abu Hamdan frames this distinguishing vocal facet as something that allows
the Druze to operate in between the cracks: to pass as both generic Arabic
speakers and, to other Druze, as members of the same group. He uses this to
bridge two concepts: freedom of speech in a surveilled age and the tactics of
a minority.[15] He begins his lecture with a discussion of a computer software
program whose existence was made public knowledge by Snowden in his NSA
Wikileaks. The program, LVA 6.5, analyses the vibrations of the vocal cords to
gauge the sincerity, emotion, and tenor of a person speaking – a technological
re-embodiment of the voice – and is used essentially as a highly sophisticated lie
detector. The Druze selective pronunciation shows a people so used to surveillance and persecution that even their language has evolved to avoid detection – a

tactic of evasion that is also enshrined in the Druze version of Islam through a piece of jurisprudence called Taqiyya.[16] "Taqiyya", Abu Hamdan explains, "is an old and obscure Islamic law. In its simplest possible articulation, Taqiyya is a legal dispensation whereby a believing individual can deny his faith or commit otherwise illegal acts while they are at risk of persecution or in a condition of statelessness". Taqiyya legitimates acts against the faith in a state of crisis; it is a strategy for a permanent state of exception.

The video of Abu Hamdan's lecture-performance uses, as illustrations for the sound "qaf", amateurish drawings of an open mouth and a schema of the head that shows how the sound is made. Again, the body is overly pointed to, supplied here in the format of a drawn image that signals indexical gesture. At other times, Abu Hamdan's portrayal underlines a posthuman aspect; he wears a voice synthesiser, and for his aural example of the pronunciation of "qaf", Abu Hamdan (who here assumes the role of "Wissam Abu Dargham", a Druze specialist) plays a clip on his iPhone of a Druze woman speaking to a non-Druze friend. Her conversation is interrupted by a phone call from her mother, and in speaking to her, she articulates the sound "qaf" and then resumes her enunciation of standard Arabic to her friend. To illustrate this, he holds out his iPhone, on which the audio clip plays, like a piece of proof he is submitting, hopeful that though what he shows does not prove his point, it will perhaps prove the honesty of his intentions: *believe me,*

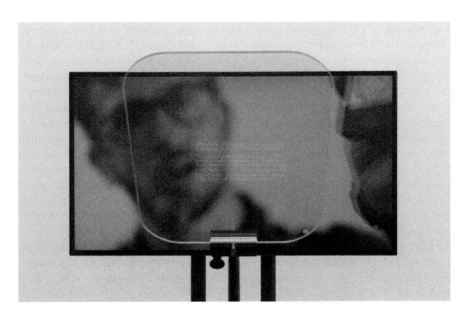

Figure 5.9 Lawrence Abu Hamdan, *Contra Diction (Speech Against Itself)*, 2015, live audio essay. Installation view at Kunst Halle Sankt Gallen, 2015.

Photo: Stefan Jäggi. Courtesy the artist

his gesture says. The woman's voice, so important throughout in its physiology, "appears" here as bars of sound on the iPhone screen, held horizontally towards the viewer. Most of the performance's audience will not understand her words in Arabic, and Abu Hamdan does not bother to translate the entirety of what she says. Instead, he looks to the visual representation of the modulating sounds as if it were her voice itself, transferred under the meta-sign of the digital to another state. The gambit is only partially successful. He seeks to prove visually that this sound exists and that Taqiyya is the strategy it represents. But how can you prove what you don't know how to hear? At the very moment Abu Hamdan tries to introduce the Druze to the public of the art world, they disappear into digitality.

The body politic and states of exception

As these examples of modes of public speech suggest, the "public" means rather more than out loud, audible, and not private but is an arena of political and human rights, freedom, and sovereignty. This draws from the equation in antiquity between the right to speak and participation in the demos, where a citizen was branded as a free man (i.e. distinguishing him from being a slave, an animal, a child, or a woman) by his right to speak publicly.[17] Public speech is entry into the demos – indeed the use of visual metaphors for political representation, which I have been arguing is newly compromised, is itself a modern phenomenon. The conception of public speech and power as embodied and offline also reflects its classical constitution in the nation-state, in which a seated, national state exercises authority over a bounded geopolitical territory. This has been challenged not only by the notional deterritorialisation of the internet but also by globalisation more broadly and the rise in migration over the past twenty years. Abu Hamdan, in an article on the use of the voice in determining nationality, has suggested, for example, thinking of identity not as national but as temporal. He uses the term "cartography of a voice" to suggest the dialogic character of vocal communication, where the speaker, like the Druze, adapts his or her speech for whomever is listening. In the way that the postcolonial body has become legible, here the embodied voice shows in its accent the traces of migration and movement:

> [D]ue to issues of mimicry, contagiousness, and survival, the life of an accent is possessed to a greater or lesser extent by every living person it has ever come into contact with, especially influenced, of course, by the one voice with which it is presently in dialogue.
>
> (Abu Hamdan 2014, 73)[18]

The geographical metaphor points to the fact that Abu Hamdan has in mind a process of becoming as it unfolds across different territories. Language here functions both as a symptom of deterritorialisation and as a means to suggest deterritorialisation as taking place across different, actual territories, in the path of a migrant, for example – a subject of no small historical importance to this period.

The three works above address figures in what Agamben has called, following Carl Schmitt, the state of exception – a condition that has also proliferated during the years that overlap with post-internet art and the emergence of the digital and the internet as daily concerns. In what has come to be known as his *Homo Sacer* project, Agamben shows that democracy has at its core the state of exception, or legalised lawlessness, when the state arrogates to itself exceptional powers. The twelve-year reign of the Third Reich, for example, was one such state of exception, as is Guantánamo Bay and its classification of its inmates as enemy combatants, where they are deprived of the rights of citizenship of their own countries as well as the rights accorded to prisoners of war under the Geneva Convention. Since the project began, with the publication of *Homo Sacer* in Italian in 1995, and the English translation appearing in 1998, the state of exception has grown as a geopolitical reality: from the CIA's practice of extraordinary rendition, in which "enemy combatants" are taken to countries in which torture is legal, thereby circumventing the US's injunction against torture under the Geneva Convention, to the increased movement of migrants from Africa and the Middle East into the holding camps of Europe, where they are held in between the laws of their countries of origins and destination. The contamination of democracy represented by the state of exception is also mirrored in Agamben's figure of the *homo sacer*, a term from Roman law that Agamben revives. Agamben distinguishes between the life of the polis – *bios politicos* – and bare life, his conceptualisation of a state of life that is both excluded from and included within the community through its exclusion. The *homo sacer* is a figure outside of the law, who has no political rights but who, because he cannot be juridically condemned, cannot be killed. The *homo sacer*, in a homoeopathic dynamic that might by now seem familiar, exists both within and beyond the law: he shows the power of the law in determining life by his existing as an exception within it.

Since the Snowden revelations, in the context of the internet, the mismatch between nation-state jurisdiction and the deterritorialised flights of power enabled by the internet have weighed heavily on those who think critically about new technologies. James Bridle's *Citizen Ex* project, which he began developing in 2014, for example, notes that one's internet searches create an algorithmic citizenship, a quotient based on the national incorporation of the sites one visits. If one's quotient drops beneath 50% for "American", he alleges, one is considered by the NSA to be non-American, and thus one's private communications can be accessed without a warrant. One's search history in this very real sense overrides the protections afforded by citizenship – to say nothing of the mass abrogation of rights the NSA surveillance program entails for people who are not US citizens to begin with.

Silicon Valley corporations such as Amazon and Facebook likewise variously attempt to evade national sovereignty first for tax purposes and second to avoid local laws and customs. They are also the beneficiaries of another form of surveillance, of data mining. As mentioned before, internet users freely surrender information pertaining to themselves: purchase histories, political proclivities, specific hours of internet activity, medical records, communication on corporate email servers. The ease with which this is given up has been extensively remarked upon – even though, as the digital theorist Douglas Rushkoff says, the alternatives of secure email systems and data shielding are easily available (Rushkoff quoted in Tucker 2016). The individual surrenders information, the thinking goes, and in return puts up with targeted ads that appear in his or her feed. This is the price that is apparently paid for deterrence against terrorist acts. But, as the *Guardian* journalist Glenn Greenwald testified in Laura Poitras's film *Citizenfour* (2014), speaking about the Snowden leaks (which he helped disseminate), this is itself a false perception: much of the data surrendered by both US and non-US companies to the US government has been in the service of helping corporations set up monopolies or compete with foreign corporations.

It is likewise understood that, if for the law-abiding citizen ads are a nuisance, the non-law-abiding citizen – the potential terrorist, whom the government dragnet is designed to catch – will end up in Agamben's bare life: an extra-territorial state of exception where they are excluded from the possibility of claiming a right. Or, in Hannah Arendt's formulation, they don't have the right to have rights. The support of extraordinary rendition, Guantánamo Bay, the US drone program, and other contemporary examples of this state of exception vary among the populace and among different countries, to be sure, and it is not exactly fair to say that by tolerating data mining, one tolerates states of exception. But, as I intimated in the previous chapter, data mining, surveillance, and bare life are linked in the internet imaginary, and one further way to gloss the representation of violence online is a response to the part the internet plays in extra-territorial states of exception. The body is the bulwark against the endless proliferation of data and its unseen surveillance and is also the means, through its association with the demos, to challenge its wrong usage. This is why, I would argue, you see within post-internet and internet-aware art a push to *signal embodiment* when the political stakes are high: for the marginalised populations of Khalili's undocumented and illegal migrants, the stateless Druze minority, or people of colour in the US. If language is the reigning mode of representing identity on the internet, the importance of the bodily vocalisation of language suggests an understanding of power as material, sited, and actual.

Notes

1 By "written", here I simply mean words that exist on a page or on an internet forum, rather than spoken out loud. In another sense, one could contend that much of written language on the internet can plausibly be taken for oral: it is intended purely as ephemeral, instantaneous communication and is often stylised to be as close as possible to spoken speech, with indications for non-verbal responses such as facial expressions via emoticons and physical reactions via acronyms such as "lol" ("laughing out loud") or even "rofl" ("rolling on the floor laughing").

2 See, for example, the round-up of rapture in Calvin Tomkins's 2014 profile of Trecartin, "Experimental People: The Exuberant World of a Video-Art Visionary", *The New Yorker*,

24 March 2014, http://www.newyorker.com/magazine/2014/03/24/experimental-people (last accessed on 7 September 2016).

3 One can think also here of the Juliana Huxtable's self-styling as a cyborg, particularly in the sculptures of her body that the artist Frank Benson exhibited, alongside work by Huxtable herself, in the New Museum's 2015 triennial, where she appears tinted in dark silver paint, her braids – a signifier of her race – falling down as she lies on her side, arms resting on her raised knee, both breasts and penis visible. She inhabits not only the posture of odalisque – the genre of the reclining prostitute that Manet famously mocked in his *Olympia* – but also, in her metallic sheen, of a technological object, which the work is (it is a 3D print of a photograph of her taken by Benson). Through the deployment of various legible signifiers, then, she is able to be read as a series of unstable and oscillating binaries: man/woman, subject/object, artist/artwork, human/thing, erotic/untouchable.

4 Quotations (and orthography) reproduced from *Popular S.ky (section ish)* as reprinted in *Ryan Trecartin: Any Ever* (exh. cat.), New York: Skira Rizolli, 2011, pp. 31, 30.

5 This attempt to represent the flows of finance capital is a steady subject in art, from the 1970s, as Jameson shows, onwards and post-2008 especially in a variety of curatorial and theoretical endeavours. See, for example, Alberto López Cuenca, "Artistic Labour, Enclosure and the New Economy", *Afterall*, no. 30, Summer 2012, pp. 5–16. What differs here, I argue, is the normalising of the standpoint of affirmation.

6 Another example might be *RMB City* (2007), a Chinese city in Second Life that Cao Fei made in collaboration with the non-profit exhibition site Vitamin Creative Space in Guangzhou. One was able to invest in RMB City with real cash, and the city became a site of property speculation much like Asian cities have been in real life.

7 In this way, the *ewig Weibliche* – Goethe's Romantic conception of sacrifice as part of the "eternal womanly" – does not seem far off as a standpoint or subject of critique. Other female artists who have made similar projects include Faith Holland, Tabita Rezaire, and Angela Washko. A number of the concerns touched upon here have also been explored under the banner of "selfie feminism", which the writer Sarah Burke has summarised as the belief that "selfies are empowering because they reclaim the male gaze by allowing women to flip their own gaze onto themselves and let it be publicly known that they're doing so" – a reading that for her and others underplays the fact that selfies are another form of self-commodification (Burke 2016). Her article includes a good round-up of other think pieces on the subject.

8 Art Club 2000, a New York collective in the late 1990s who in many ways prefigure the style of much post-internet art, anticipated normcore with their images of the collective's members, all students at the Cooper Union School of Art, lounging in clothes from the Gap in furniture showrooms.

9 The New Aesthetic is a term coined by James Bridle in the early 2010s and explored via his blog and Tumblr feed that looked at examples of the digital styling in popular imagery: motifs such as grids, rough pixelation, and surveillance imagery.

10 See Tamara Trodd, "Elizabeth Price's Commodity Aesthetics", 2014, given at the conference "Shimmering World", University of Manchester, 25 April 2014. I am grateful to Trodd for sharing this paper with me.

11 For a reading of the relationship between contemporary art and the 1%, see Andrea Fraser, "Le 1%, C'est moi", *Texte zur Kunst*, vol. 83, September 2011, pp. 114–28.

12 My contention is that orality signals embodiment within the codes of digital culture. This is not to say that speech is always delivered by a human figure; indeed, a common feature of post-internet art is its use of voice simulation. I would argue, though, that even here its connection to the body is salient, because the context for this technology is often a corporeal one or an investigation of speech pattern specificity. Stark, for example, locates her *My Best Thing* dialogue *in* the computer by using vocalisation software, underscoring the disembodiment of her figures in contrast to the potential for cybersex and real intimacy on chat rooms that she explores. In the project *Penetrating Squid* (2014/2015), Anna

Barham asked a group of people to read a story aloud into a voice recognition software program. The program's inaccuracies created a second text, which a second group of people then read aloud, creating a third text which a third (and final) group then read. This material informed score-like works that she has exhibited, and Barham has also used this format for live performances. *Penetrating Squid* marked the ebbs and flows of real vocal instantiations versus the software program's desire for normalcy. I participated in the second group, and the software was nearly perfect in transliterating my US accent. British accents fared worse, particularly regional and working-class ones.

13 Despite this interest in the form of the lecture, artistic mimicry focuses on academia and corporations, and not the arena that might seem most obviously suited to techno-logical critique – Steve Jobs's theatrical unveilings of Apple's new product lines or the middle-high-brow infotainment of TED talks, which often focus on technology. Indeed, throughout post-internet art and art responding to digital technologies, there is relatively little concern with Silicon Valley and the tech industry.

14 Dickinson's work *Closed Circuit* (2010), made with Steve Rushton, explicitly addresses states of exception, for example. In the performance, two suited male performers – in their 60s and clean-cut – stand at lecterns and read out alternating sound bites from two screens positioned behind the audience, as if they are reading from autocues. The speeches they form, much like the presidential speeches and governmental press briefings they satirise, use a lot of words but manage to say nothing at all: "I know it is hard to understand, but sometimes painful things like this happen. It's all part of the process of exploration and discovery. It's all part of taking a chance and expanding man's horizons. The future doesn't belong to the fainthearted; it belongs to the brave". *Closed Circuit* is a compendium of different speeches given to declare and maintain states of crisis and emergency, shorn of identifying material like specific names and dates, that are well nigh seamlessly woven together. Drawn from the US, the EU, Soviet Russia, and Latin America, from democracies and dictatorships, the same propagandistic rhetoric and nationalistic dictations are utilised, making the phrases' idioms almost indistinguishable from each other. (The quotation is from Ronald Reagan on the *Challenger* explosion in 1986.) Language precedes individual usage: political rhetoric produces its subject regard-less of the system of governance. In reducing political contrasts to a function of discourse, moreover, crisis and its abrogation of rights is seen as an effect of language, created and instituted by it.

15 Abu Hamdan's example has chance overlaps with a Biblical story quoted by Agamben in *Homo Sacer*: "We refer to the episode in Judges 12: 6 in which the Galatians recognize the fleeing Ephraimites, who are trying to save themselves beyond the Jordan, by asking them to pronounce the word 'Shibboleth', which the Ephraimites pronounce 'Sibboleth'. ('The men of Gilead said unto him, "Art thou an Ephraimite?" If he said, "Nay"; then they said unto him, "Say now Shibboleth": and he said Sibboleth: for he could not frame to pronounce it right. Then they took him, and slew him at the passages of Jordan')". Giorgio Agamben, *Homo Sacer: Sovereign Power and Bare Life* (1995; trans. Daniel Heller-Roazen), Stanford: Stanford University Press, 1998, p.21.

16 The word "Taqiyya" (تقية), quite nicely for the argument's formal resolution, contains the very letter "qaf" that the Druze can selectively pronounce, as do the Arabic words for truth, in the sense of fact ("haqiqa", حقيقة), and in the sense of honesty or integrity ("sidq", صدق). This is significant to the legitimation of Taqiyya as Islamic jurisprudence, as Abu Hamdan notes. In Islam, the Arabic language is a divine creation – not a repre-sentation of things but another mode of their existence.

17 The classicist Mary Beard, addressing the misogyny of the hate speech – trolling – she receives as a public figure on Twitter, notes that free women had the right to speak in antiquity but only on topics that concerned female life. See M. Beard, "The Public Voice of Women", *London Review of Books*, vol.36, no.6, 20 March 2014, pp. 11–14.

18 Abu Hamdan is part of Forensic Architecture, a research agency run by Eyal Weizman at Goldsmiths in London.

Bibliography

Abu Hamdan, L. (2014) "Aural Contract: Forensic Listening and the Reorganization of the Speaking Subject". In: Forensic Architecture ed. *Forensic: The Architecture of Public Truth*, Berlin: Sternberg Press, 65–82.

Agamben, G. (1995) *Homo Sacer: Sovereign Power and Bare Life*. Heller-Roazen, D. trans. (1998) Stanford: Stanford University Press.

Bakhtin, M. (1975) *The Dialogic Imagination*. Holquist, M. ed., Emerson, C. trans. (1982) Austin: University of Texas Press.

Burke, S. (2016) "Crying on Camera: 'Fourth-Wave Feminism' and the Threat of Commodification". *Open Spaces* [online magazine], 17 May, http://openspace.sfmoma.org/2016/05/crying-on-camera-fourth-wave-feminism-and-the-threat-of-commodification/ (last accessed on 18 May 2016).

Butler, J. (1990/2006) *Gender Trouble: Feminism and the Subversion of Identity*, London: Routledge.

Cornell, L. (2011) "Medium Living". In: *Ryan Trecartin: Any Ever*. McGarry, K. ed., Exh. cat., New York: New Museum and Skira Rizolli, 55–57.

Frank, R. (2013) "When Form Starts Talking: On Lecture-Performances". *Afterall*, 33, 5–18.

Fraser, A. (2011) "Le 1%, C'est Moi". *Texte zur Kunst*, 83, 114–28.

Goffman, E. (1959) *The Presentation of Self in Everyday Life*, New York: Random House.

Gronlund, M. (2014) "From Narcissism to the Dialogic: Identity in Art after the Internet". *Afterall*, 27, 5–16.

Joselit, D. (2007) *Feedback: Television Against Democracy*, Cambridge, MA: MIT Press.

Kendall, L. (1998) "Meaning and Identity in 'Cyberspace': The Performance of Gender, Class and Race Online". *Symbolic Interaction*, 21 (2), 129–53.

K-HOLE (2013) "Youth Mode: A Report on Freedom". *K-HOLE.net* [website], http://khole.net/issues/youth-mode/ (last accessed on 27 April 2016).

Kiaer, C. (2005) *Imagine No Possessions: The Socialist Objects of Russian Constructivism*, Cambridge, MA: MIT Press.

Kinsey, C. and Ulman, A. (2013) Conversation Hosted by Arcadia Missa Gallery, London and Post Media Lab (Leuphana University of Lüneburg) at Limehouse Town Hall, London. 17 July 2013. https://www.youtube.com/watch?v=ifbRYL6By4k (last accessed on 2 May 2016).

Knight, N. (2016) Email. 8 April.

Krauss, R. (1976) "Video: The Aesthetics of Narcissism". *October*, 1, 50–64.

Kulendran Thomas, C. (2016) Email. 16 April.

Lazzarato, M. (2012) *The Making of the Indebted Man: An Essay on the Neoliberal Condition*. Jordan, J. D. trans. (2012) Los Angeles: Semiotext(e).

López Cuenca, A. (2012) "Artistic Labour, Enclosure and the New Economy". *Afterall*, 30, 5–16.

Massumi, B. (2002) *Parables for the Virtual: Movement, Affect, Sensation*, Durham, NC: Duke University Press.

McHugh, G. (2011) *Post-Internet: Notes on the Internet and Art 12.29.09 > 09.05.10*, Brescia: Link Editions.

Norden, L. (2011) "When the Rainbow Is an Option". In: *Ryan Trecartin: Any Ever*. McGarry, K. ed., Exh. cat., New York: New Museum and Skira Rizolli, 11–15.

Poitras, L. (2014) *Citizenfour* [film]. HBO Films, Participant Media, Praxis Films.

Proust, M. (1913) *Correspondence*. Kolb, P. ed. (1984) Vol. 12, Paris: Plon Éditions.

Reupke, R. (2016) Email. 27 April.

Ryan Trecartin: Any Ever. McGarry, K. ed. Exh. cat., New York: New Museum and Skira Rizolli, 2011.

Saner, E. (2016) "Digital Artist Ann Hirsch on Why Her 'Singing Vagina' Empowers Women – and Terrifies Men". *The Guardian.* 21 March, https://www.theguardian.com/lifeandstyle/2016/mar/21/digital-artist-ann-hirsch-singing-vagina (last accessed on 9 September 2016).

Shaviro, S. (2013) "Accelerationist Aesthetics: Necessary Inefficiency in Times of Real Subsumption". *e-flux journal* [online journal], 46, http://www.e-flux.com/journal/accelerationist-aesthetics-necessary-inefficiency-in-times-of-real-subsumption/#_ftnref13 (last accessed on 1 May 2016).

Tomkins, C. (2014) "Experimental People: The Exuberant World of a Video-Art Visionary". *The New Yorker.* 24 March.

Trodd, T. (2014) *Elizabeth Price's Commodity Aesthetics. Paper given at the conference Shimmering World*, University of Manchester, 25 April.

Troemel, B. (2013) "Athletic Aesthetics". *The New Inquiry* [online magazine], 10 May, http://thenewinquiry.com/essays/athletic-aesthetics/ (last accessed on 27 April 2016).

Tucker, I. (2016) "Douglas Rushkoff: 'I'm Thinking It May Be Good to Be Off Social Media Altogether'". *The Observer.* 12 February.

Wang, M. (2015) "Made of the Same Stuff". In: Cornell, L. and Halter, E. ed. (2015) *Mass Effect: Art and the Internet in the Twenty-First Century*, Cambridge, MA: MIT Press, 401–12.

6   The art world infrastructure post-internet

In the past our technologically-conceived artefacts structured living patterns. We are now in transition – from an *object-oriented* to a *systems-oriented* culture. Here change emanates, not from *things*, but from the *way things are done*.

(Jack Burnham, "Systems Esthetics", 1968)

How has the art world been changed by the internet? The question is repeatedly posed in the broadsheets and by the enormous attention given to post-internet art. In the following chapter, we will move away from the close readings of the previous two chapters to consider the art object's context, often returning to issues we have explored before, but looked at here in a more brass-tacks sort of way. We will discuss how the two main means of ascribing value to artwork – the art market and the discipline of art history – have been affected (and not) by the internet's changes to art's circulation, and, particularly via David Joselit, how the discourse around rights and ownership becomes increasingly significant. We will touch on the deepening importance of the figure of the artist in determining an object's status as art, alongside further theoretical changes to the art object ushered in by the internet: the way circulation itself has been theorised within art practice and the artwork's shift from unique object to circulating image.

The short (and perhaps disappointing) answer to whether the art world infrastructure has been fundamentally altered by the internet is "not really". The art world has changed dramatically in the last half century and even since the turn of this century: it has vastly exploded in terms of participants, money, and profile; it has bifurcated into two largely separate strands (the commercial and the discursive); the curator has eclipsed the critic as the chief public assignor of intellectual value; and non-art-making discourses and forms have become integral parts of art practice. All these are linked principally to a number of conjoined factors, such as the growth of art as an asset, the privatisation of public museums and their reliance on donors, cheap airfare and the establishment of biennials as the major platform for critical engagement and thesis-making, and art's own questioning and widening of the parameters of what an art project can be. While some are affected or intensified by the internet, the internet cannot be said to answer for them.

Indeed, despite initial hopes or musings, the art world has been remarkably effective about reasserting its border patrols onto the field of work made and distributed on the web; commercial gallerists, critics, scholars, and both institutional and independent curators are still in charge of ascribing and parsing its value. On the market side, the idea that collectors buy work after seeing it on Instagram is a tabloid ruse – it happens (and collectors certainly do buy work after simply seeing jpgs of it emailed to them), but in no way is it a significant enough phenomenon to change the established primary and secondary market means of buying art. If anything, the fact that there are enough collectors with the money to make such a big purchase on the back of a digital viewing shows not the reach of the internet but the vast amount of capital looming within the hyper-rich and the popularity of art as an ultra-high-end consumer good. The online auction houses that have been established since the mid-2000s – most notably, Paddle8 – likewise mostly serve to speed up activities that already take place offline. Greater data on past market performance, and greater ease of being able to look at the works, makes it easier to buy them but does not substantially change the way in which it is done.

The dream that the internet would eclipse the authority of gallerist and curator suggested that the art field would become more democratic. It was a means of eliminating the middlemen and the keen need for access to them. However, while the gallerist and the curator remain as important, the internet has effected changes – not in the initial phase of bringing the artwork to a public viewing, but rather in how the work is later historicised, both analytically in a scholarly framework and practically within archives.

Everything is (not) different

It is common among writing about on or after the internet to say that the internet has changed the very definition of art. An article in the *Economist*, for example, on the Whitechapel show "Electronic Superhighway (2016–1966)", which (like this volume) set out a historical context for the present post-internet moment, came out with "The internet has continued to erode established notions of what qualifies as art, and who can claim to be an artist" (*When the New Grows Old* 2016). The internet years of 1989 to the present, however, are not particularly fraught with art-ontological angst, if we consider things historically. In the 1960s, art weathered the triple onslaught of the rediscovery of Duchamp's readymades (which were first executed in the 1910s but were given renewed attention in that decade) and its negation of craft; the dematerialisation and challenges to the very physicality of the art object of Conceptualism; and the convergence between high art idioms and commercial and commodity advertising and packaging of Pop. It is no surprise that the 1970s saw the development of various theories of art that transferred aesthetic ontology from the art object to its context. Under the institutional theory of art, the US philosophers George Dickie and Arthur Danto argued that it was the institutional parameters of the white cube and museum that decided what should and should not be counted as art. Pierre Bourdieu, working at a similar time in France, re-formulated this distinction as one of cultural capital: objects were transformed into artworks by those who had the knowledge to read an object for an artwork.

The internet provides – at least notionally – a major challenge to these ideas, in that artwork presented directly online, on platforms such as Vimeo, YouTube, or Tumblr, which are widely accessible and not coded or conceived of as "art spaces", will often have little to distinguish them from other creative projects online. This is exacerbated by work, such as we saw in Chapter Five, that actively seeks to align itself with internet genres, such as Ann Hirsch's impersonation of a camwhore in *The Scandalishious Project* (2008–2009). Indeed – and this is one of the important questions asked by popular writing on net.art and post-internet projects – what is the difference between Ann Hirsch initiating a meme or anyone else initiating a meme?

This question is asked by artworks themselves, framed largely as a question of circulation: an image travels from context to context and thus loses whatever ontological specificity is given by its surroundings. We can think back to Claude Shannon's theory of information here, which attempted to find a way for information to travel through different channels without being changed or corrupted. The idea of testing an image from context to context within practices of appropriation is similar: indeed circulation is the link of post-internet work to previous discourses of appropriation, rather than some apparently radical gesture or a simple shared use of the technique.

As we have seen, circulation was a central concern to early post-internet art, sociologically theorised as one of the major disruptions of the internet. One of the first critiques in a "post-internet vein" – that is to say, about the internet's impact on the everyday – was Seth Price's *Dispersion* (2002/2008), which addresses how the internet as a circulatory mechanism changed the notion of the "public" as a mass audience. Written for the Ljubljana Biennial of Graphic Arts, and distributed freely from Price's website as a PDF, *Dispersion* looks at historical artworks that stepped outside of the "carefully structured" system of art, such as Conceptualist projects that were printed in mass-media magazines or artworks released as pop commodities, and set these against the field of the internet where the binary of mass media and art system – the tension that animated these earlier circulation projects – no longer inheres. This, Price argued, alters both the constitution of the audience and the character of the experience of the work. The "direct communal experience" of appreciating art in public space stands in contrast to the private consumption of artistic production on the web, determining an ad-hoc, accumulative, and appropriative practice within

> the production of social contexts, using existing material. Anything on the internet is a fragment, provisional, pointing elsewhere. Nothing is finished. What a time you chose to be born!
>
> (Price 2002/2008)

The communal and public spirit of art's erstwhile mode of exhibition translates in the internet age into art's preoccupation with the "production of social contexts". The art world, he rightly speculates in 2002, will expand ever outwards to take on new types of production: the "redemptive circulation of allegory through design, obsolete forms and historical moments, genre and the vernacular, the social memory woven into popular culture: a private, secular, and profane consumption of media. Production, after all, is the excretory phase in a process of appropriation".[1] Duchamp, as ever, is the model figure to this border-crossing, cementing the link between his first radical gesture of the readymade and its evolution into a mode of deictic appropriation and contextual, social concerns.

In his artistic practice, Price also focuses on circulation, often framing images as the empty shells of a content that has disappeared (sometimes quite literally so). In a series of vacuum-packed commodity items he made in the mid-2000s, he encased iconic and regular items in plastic, such as bomber jackets, fists, masks, and skeins of rope, exhibiting the vacuum-packed plastic cases instead of the objects themselves. The production of the case reproduces the outside of the objects in minute detail, in the way that a death mask reveals the flaccid wrinkles of a face. The hollow encasing is often coloured in gold, mimicking a commodity fetish, while also paying attention to the basic fact that his artwork participates in a luxury market, on which it circulates as a physically empty signifier. Price investigates this place of non-meaning – as he says, two motifs for the vacuum-pack series, the fist and the breast, were "appealingly blank" (Price quoted in Wiley 2014, 11). That a fist and a breast should be taken as "blank" is quixotic – and should be taken with a grain of salt. Indeed, Price often tests the possibility to empty out meaning in contexts that are particularly, almost unassailably meaningful. We might recall the video *Digital Video Effect: "Holes"* (2003), for example, in which punched-out holes appear across footage of the Israeli massacre in the Jenin refugee camp. A video made the subsequent year, *Digital Video Effect: "Spills"* (2004), uses footage from a home movie taken by Joan Jonas in 1970, in conversation with Richard Serra and Robert Smithson, about the effect of money on art production. In the art world, this is practically the primal scene: three great artists at the high point of Conceptualism talking about what many feel to have eroded art's criticality and potential since. Price shot through this conversation with digital media effects where black ink seems to spill across the screen, effacing the video by adding to it. He renders it dumb, attacking its ability to speak but also transforming into a third text: a compromised symptom of historical and market forces. Price works with images to show how they are always in a state of flux, investigating how they can be changed, can recirculate, can recur, can re-signify, can close off all meaning to an original referent, or can carry the referent like a kernel inside it (though such a sentimental reading does not often occur). This mode of appropriation and detournement also characterises a second strand of Price's practice; he makes video works for YouTube that use appropriated songs and media, collaging these and re-circulating them under his name.

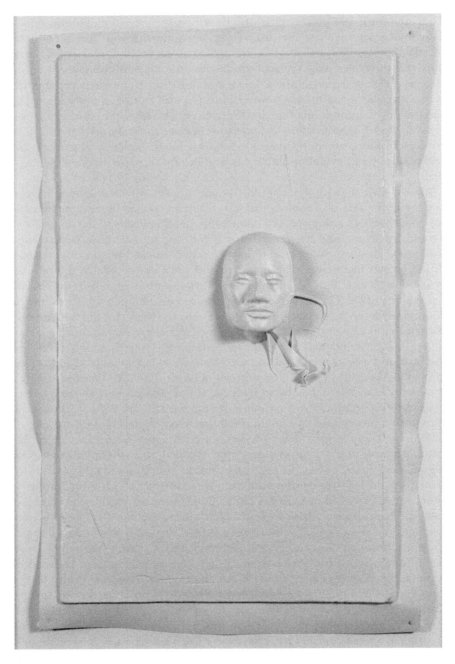

Figure 6.1 Seth Price, *Untitled*, 2006, Vacuum-formed high-impact polystyrene over mask, 125.1 × 77.5 cm (SPR 16/026).

Courtesy the artist and Petzel Gallery, New York

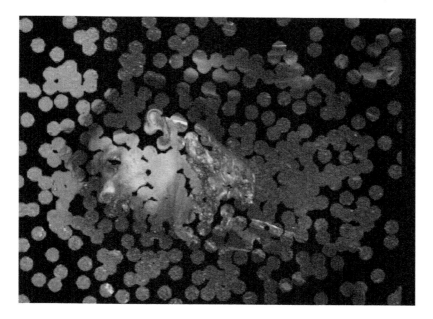

Figure 6.2 Seth Price, *Digital Video Effect: Holes*, 2003, DVD, Combination TV/DVD player in its own packaging, 12 minutes.

Courtesy the artist and Petzel Gallery, New York

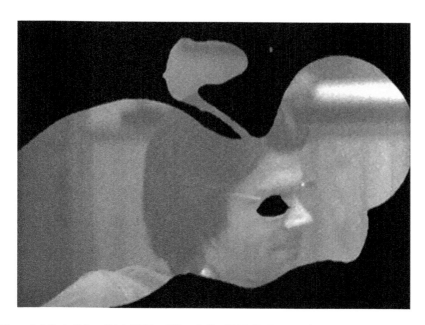

Figure 6.3 Seth Price, *Digital Video Effect: Spills*, 2004, DVD, Combination TV/DVD player in its own packaging, 12 minutes.

Courtesy the artist and Petzel Gallery, New York

Price's use of YouTube as both a genre and a means of dissemination for some of his video work is not at all uncommon and returns us to the question of the liminal character of social-media work. One key characteristic of post-internet art is its integration of everyday usage of the internet – an artist's participation in memes and blogs, or on social media – into art practice, in a reflection of how life is lived today. A number of post-internet artists have substantial online presences, with audiences that far exceed the limited art public. Jesse Darling, for example, created a gif of their having a nervous breakdown in IKEA that now circulates as its own meme. The idea of "serious play" is one way to approach this question: the internet as a ground of testing and a source of material, in which questions can be explored but from which answers are not necessarily desired.

Blogospheres

As a caveat, each artist naturally has a different relation to his or her social-media activity, with some seeing it as integral to his or her practice and others not. For critical purposes, however, this information is often not legible in the work itself, and though the two are commonly dissociated in casual or curatorial discussions around work, nascent post-internet scholarship and the more substantial body of scholarship on net.art has mostly decided to take this kind of activity into account as part of artists' practice. The bookmarks on del.icio.us, a site for sharing and bookmarking different links, that were made by the net.art collective JODI.org, are analysed as part of their work. Their "work", in this sense, does not mean discrete outputs but rather the sum total of activity online. This understanding extends the performativity that is seen to characterise identity online onto the practices themselves: one's practice is one's life online. It is also consonant with the notion of art as versions, or as an unfolding process that occurs performatively through time. Laric, for instance, has made *Versions* three times, each with the same title. James Richards, whose work includes making what might be considered digital versions of found footage films, re-uses different clips in different works, making his overall oeuvre a rolling compendium as much as a series of discrete videos.[2] Erica Scourti, as we also saw in Chapter One, edits a different version of her work *Life in AdWords* (2012–2013) to adapt to different screening contexts.

This equating of social-media or all regular activity and artistic work opens artists up to profound potential exploitation. How can artists be adequately remunerated if they put in all these hours for free? This question is intensified by the feeling that artists must keep up their social-media activity to maintain their profile in a competitive marketplace (a pressure felt by art professionals and those in other fields as well). It has become standard for artists to set up websites, manage their back catalogue, provide Vimeo or embedded video snippets of their moving-image work, jpgs of sculpture, and categorise and excerpt press material – all work that was formerly done by a gallery, or not at all. This also reflects the larger-scale hybridisation of practices that has been motivated by the internet's capacity to disseminate information, allowing a small organisation to have enormous publicity outreach, and of economic changes after the 2008 crash, where money in the art world has been redistributed upwards, squeezing the bottom and flooding the top commercial tier. The effects of the latter are numerous: cash-strapped museums have had to look to galleries for funding for retrospectives, a conflict of interest (blue-chip gallery underwrites canonising museum exhibition for its own artist) that would have been discrediting for both museum and gallery just a decade ago. In the absence of decent funding for emerging non-profit spaces, younger galleries have begun to function as both commercial and discursive networks, selling work and also hosting conferences and publishing periodicals. Other younger non-profit art "spaces" act as art collectives, light on their feet and able to move from site to site and project to project without overheads. Within this mixing of roles one might also put the oft-remarked-upon tendency to think of artists as brands, relentlessly promoting themselves.

That this self-promotion also abuts against social-media activity, which itself abuts against "proper" artistic activity, suggests one reason why blogging and participating in feeds within post-internet work is often considered different from the internet activity of net.artists. Some of it is intellectual engagement, and some of it is frantic profile-chasing. The pressure to keep it all going is totalising, not to mention exhausting. We can also recall here that the artist Brad Troemel used the analogy of athletics to describe the level of engagement needed to maintain a social-media presence (Troemel 2013). And where is the "back stage", to use Erving Goffman's term, where artists can hang up their hats and not be productive? Darling has, by contrast, noted that the frequent denigration of social-media work vis-à-vis one's exhibited gallery practice carries with it a note of misogyny, in that life is seen as the province of women's art, and still not on an equal plane with other artistic concerns. A number of cases in which social-media practices are explored as extension of the self are made by women, a reading that is either knowingly explored by the artists (as in the social-media work of Ann Hirsch, Amalia Ulman, Jennifer Chan, and Erica Scourti) or which derive through the perception of others (Petra Cortright, Darling).

The overlap between online activity and artistic performance also relates – and most importantly so – to the revamping of the role of the artist, who assumes priority over the artwork. As Troemel notes elsewhere, images travel but brand remains (Troemel 2014): the artist's name unifies disparate activity on the web. Referring to an artist as a brand suggests something more objectively referential – foreign, object-like – than the flesh-and-blood persona of someone working, and this seems to characterise the affective feel of one's avatar online. Social-media profiles and their activity become signs themselves, circulating beyond spatio-temporal or physical contiguity to the author: when I tweet, my Tweets circulate beyond myself and are read at points when I may no longer be online. This, of course, has always been so for the published author (who knows when and where people read articles I have written – or what they do with them afterwards), but it is now the case for everyday, non-professional activity.

Looking to the author to delineate the type of activity is a heightened version of Foucault's author function, which addressed many of these questions of what is considered work and non-work in 1969 (Foucault 1969/1998). Foucault showed how the sign of the author determines the type of discourse, distinguishing literary text from laundry list, in his famous example, and prescribing the behaviour of the text. It sets up a tension between the author's ownership over a text and the appropriative quality of all discourse; it stands, that is, within a juridical framework of possession. It's important to note that Foucault's analysis focuses on how the author function works; he was writing it in a situation where the "medium", so to speak, of a text was largely clear from in its context. It's evident what's a book and what's a laundry list, though we should thank the Conceptual Poetics exponents Craig Dworkin and Kenneth Goldsmith for making even this territory slip under our feet. The literary theorist Stanley Fish similarly underlined the importance of the author in determining the state of the text, equally famously performing an experiment on his students in which he kept a list of five names of well-known linguists on the chalkboard of his class from a previous lesson. He told his next class that it was a poem and asked them to interpret it (Fish 1982). (They did, in winning and sophisticated ways.) Fish's chalkboard is closer to the ground zero of existential confusion of the kind of activity on the web, where institutional parameters are absent or diversely theorised.

Indeed, the question of the ontology of the art object online was also prompted by net.art, and many of the queries within post-internet art are churning in its wake. Ed Halter, in the essay "The Centaur and the Hummingbird" (the catalogue essay for "Free", a 2010 exhibition of net and post-internet art at the New Museum in New York) argued that

> given the proliferation of creative activity online – amateur, corporate, and otherwise – it is difficult, and sometimes impossible, to tell when something online should be thought of as art, or indeed to image in purely formal criteria that would distinguish art from any number of art-like creations.
>
> (Halter 2010, 236)

This ontological confusion was both incidental to the medium of the internet and part of the project of its users. Net.art, a field less connected to the world of commercial galleries than post-internet art, eroded the foundations of what could count as art, both polemically – to counter the classist, money-obsessed, and exclusionary system of the commercial and institutional art world – and simply out of lack of interest for what had been laid down as established artistic parameters. The contributions of net.art, as understood both by practitioners and largely in scholarship, are the titled "works" as well as infrastructural elements such as servers, codes, and platforms that individuals and groups developed so that net.art culture could flourish. The strong connections between activist groups and net.art practitioners, such as Ricardo Dominguez, who agitated for immigration rights in the 1990s, more befits a category of artist-activist – a term that is now often used to describe figures such as Hito Steyerl and Trevor Paglen, despite both having blue-chip gallery representation and participating in established biennials. Net.artists' "erosion" of traditional artistic parameters owes to the fact that their own goals and aims lay outside the established framework of production, exhibition, and collection of the art world, but also has not altered their standing as an art movement: the art world happily subsumes various practices under the category heading of contemporary aesthetic production.[3] Post-internet work acts within a similar open terrain but is, again, less oppositional to the art market.

For work on the internet, whether of net.art or post-internet, the institutional models of Dickie and Danto do not hold. In its place is the name of the artist. Halter addresses the online work *Legendary Account* (2007–2010), a series of gnomic questions the artist Joel Holmberg posed in chat forums, which was shown in "Free":

> In the decades-long discussion around the centrality of the readymade to contemporary art, the nomination of an object to the status of art is classically thought of as occurring in the space of the gallery, as if the white walls themselves were necessary for this transformative magic. But for *Legendary Account*, the paper print-outs on view at "Free" comprise merely one version of the piece, and arguably a nonessential one – any number of platforms could be used to show it, in an "art space" or not. The status of Holmberg's *Legendary Account* postings as art is primarily supported by Holmberg's assertion of his own professional status as artist. Put another way, *Legendary Account*'s status as art can't be separated from Holmberg's own self-authored online presence.
>
> (Halter 2015, 236)

The artist is thus not only promoted into a brand but becomes foundational to the ontology of the artwork as such. The phenomenological context of the work's first instantiation or the nature of its reception by an audience are, by contrast, of limited importance.

It is through the artists' name that we can understand a social-media art project as operating both as "art project" and as social-media activity. Holmberg, for example, acts within internet culture, and his work is also taken as part of the art world, that triangle of commercial galleries, institutions, and biennials. The difference inheres in the fact that he can signal his belonging within the art world and have his online activity looked at by the "right" (art) people. Holmberg did an MFA, can link to art-world people, speak the art language, and generally possesses the necessary cultural capital to signal himself as an artist. This is to rely on Bourdieu in a moment when Danto and Dickie's parameters are lost: these are questions of intention, class, and education, each of which functions as an inclusionary and exclusionary mechanism. It is perhaps worth noting that the best contemporary commentator on art, finance, and power – Andrea Fraser – has long subscribed to a Bourdieusian framework, that is, far before the internet as it exists now was conceived.[4]

While the question of the erosion of established definitions of art seems to exemplify the disconnect between popular and art-world notions of art, it also reveals problematic biases within the art world. It doesn't matter if an online enterprise is *art* itself – or if it's "internet folk art" or some insane thing that someone did which has come to light thanks to the internet. "Art" has been so deconstructed as a set based on class and language, or so broadened as an ontological category, that its appearance in a credible text smacks of sentimental humanism. Who really cares if something is "art" or not? This is in itself radical, considering the way that art has been understood within the Western tradition as so important to the soul, to the capacity for empathy, and to the sensation of joy in beauty – notions that are all curtailed in current art rhetoric. This is partly a problem of discourse: many artists, of course, remain invested in notions of formal transformation and the expression of the inexpressible; we could look here to Magali Reus's battened-down, puzzle-like sculptures of overlapping locks or the waves of longing and hope produced by Richards's videos of collaged and ripped footage, though these affective relations are often played down in the critical reception of the works.

The market

Of course, it matters financially whether something is "art". The market is the elephant-in-the-room when talking about networks: the artwork is also constituted by its taking place on a network of capital, and the question of "representationality" that I argued in Chapter Three as a contested element of digitality could be equally framed as a question of market circulation. It not as determinant in a critical sense as doomsday scenarios have it: it is not the case that scholarship, on this question and others, follows what the market knights as ontologically worthy like some obedient and over-keen lapdog.[5] (Though some museums have more to answer for here.) And though it is conventionally assumed that selling one's work is a kind of reification and, deeply problematically, participation in a compromised circuit of capital (again, who is this 1% and where have they gotten that money?), being able to make a living from one's work is also the dream for artists – it means being able to concentrate on one's practice rather than making up the difference with "money jobs" such as teaching or working as an art technician. The art market, on its side, has long been able to accommodate trends, such as the fact that most post-internet work circulates freely on the internet, that would seem destabilising. Once you're able to monetise Robert Barry's puff of gas, I suppose, you're not going to be held back by iterations on YouTube. The market's strategy for selling non-unique post-internet work – that is, work that exists as a reiterable file – is by artificially limiting supply. Galleries also often ask artists to produce physical effects from immaterial projects that they can sell, in order to support production costs for a long-form or expensive video or installation, and for basic income and profit. This mirrors the strategy has emerged, after a number of fits and starts, in regards to moving-image work, which is likewise a technologically reproducible file or print rather than a unique object and which is instructive as a point of comparison for digital production.

In Hollywood, the solution has been one of licencing: studio films licence the capacity to screen a movie to cinemas and home viewers. When one buys a DVD, one buys the permission to watch it, a fact that has become even clearer with movie streaming, where a purchase of a DVD often also includes a password for watching it online. (The internet's changes to the structure of the feature film world, via illegal downloads and more frequent home watching, have been deeper.) Historically, for analogue artist's film, this model of licencing for exhibition was complemented by political intention – a facet that often inhered on the side of production as well as the point of sale. Filmmakers in New York and London in the 1960s and '70s organised into co-op structures in response to the high costs of production and exhibition of film, a collectivising of resources that offered a practical as well as ideological solution to an expensive medium.[6] The New York Film-Makers' Cooperative, founded in 1961 and the London Film-makers' Co-operative, founded in 1966, owned cameras, developing, and projection equipment that they offered for hire to their members; screened films (of their members and others); published journals and film writing; and operated as distributors for members' films. As such, they sought to create a model for the financing of films that would not be dependent on their sale – and indeed, this notion of selling rather than hiring a work seemed logically contrary to the iterable technology of film itself and the political way in which they conceived of it both as a medium and in their particular usage.

While artists' film of the 1970s deliberately stood against the art market, many video artists of that period – the remarkably productive years of Joan Jonas, Vito Acconci, Bruce Nauman, and others – were made within the support of the commercial art world, which attempted to create a market for video. The dealers Leo Castelli and Ileana Sonnabend, for example, set up Castelli-Sonnabend Videotapes and Films (CSVF) in 1972 to distribute videos made by their artists for hire and for sale, but the venture was unsuccessful. The bulk of the work they offered was in unlimited quantity, which reflects less a strategy (or lack thereof) for selling video work in particular than the fact that limited editioning was not yet a general mode in the art world. It only grew later into a mode for selling moving-image work as well as "sculpture, prints, and other art multiples", as Noah Horowitz writes in his history of the contemporary market (Horowitz 2011, 40). Video art struggled to find a market till well into the 1980s, by which time photography had also begun to sell for high prices; methods of conservation and quality had improved; and more fundamentally video was seen as an established practice – though video is still less popular with collectors than paintings or other more conventional media.

The strategy that was eventually hit upon for video – and for analogue artists' film, which moved from the film festival circuit and film financing into the art world, both in terms of public funding sources and of gallery representation – is the same that exists for post-internet work: again, artificially limiting supply and selling physical effects. This is so despite the fact that contemporary iterability is twinned with a potential for circulation impossible for works on film and video-tape. Most moving-image artists put their works online, free for public distribution either in part or in full, and online sites such as VDrome offer month-long online exhibitions where one can see a curated selection of moving-image work. This has not impinged upon artists' ability to place their works in institutional or gallery shows, whose remit was once simply of public exhibition (rather than thesis-making) nor to sell them to collectors. Ryan Trecartin posts his videos for free but is still able to sell them in the region of the tens of thousands of dollars (Tomkins 2014). What one buys, as when one buys an ephemeral work, an instruction piece, or a performance, is the social and cultural capital of being a supporter of Trecartin as well as the nebulous but deeply felt sense of intimacy and duty of care towards an artwork in one's possession. One is also the holder for those images when they are loaned out to institutions – another source of cultural and social capital. In effect, this echoes the Hollywood model of licencing; one buys a system of legal permissions that designates you as the "owner" of a work that everyone else can see on YouTube.

In a deeper sense, the way the market has been able to accommodate internet work is another in the internet's string of failures of democratisation. The art market, which privileges the unique work as the most coveted, and thereby expensive, might seem to contravene the logic not only of how to sell a non-unique object but also of how images accrue value in an internet age – which is by prevalence and connections to other images, rather than by uniqueness or value in context. Here we can return to David Joselit's analysis in *After Art*, from Chapter Three, in which he considered the valuation of images in a ciculable age. Joselit refers to the presence of connections as "buzz" and uses it to deconstruct the historical relation between the unique image and the proliferating copy. It should be underlined in this assessment that the poles of his debate are not unique/copy but, rather, contextually situated/circulating. The more an image circulates and connections it builds, the more powerful it is. Buzz is thus not a factor of the image itself but an emergent behaviour among its viewers: echoing our discussion of how certain kinds of artistic practice emerge on the web, buzz derives from events that are "'distributed' over several small acts that, taken individually, may have no intention, or consciousness of a bigger picture" (Joselit 2013, 18). It denotes a mode of becoming rather than a static quality: an image's popularity (and hence power) is dynamic and always in the state of being performed, emerging, or perhaps slipping away.

The privileging of buzz over the contextual image reverses not only the logic of the market but also the way that unique objects have been theoretically valorised, specifically in the wake of Walter Benjamin's immensely influential definition of the aura. Benjamin identified the loss of aura as an effect of the exhibition–value image, or the image that could travel, thanks to new technologies, in contrast to the cult image, which derives its power from being in situ. Subsequent scholarship has ratified Benjamin's insight of the aura – though at times contradictorily, affirming the aura as a function of an art object but allowing for its disconnection from uniqueness. Aura has been repeatedly ascribed to iterated images as well as unique ones: it becomes a function of reception rather than the image itself. Artistic practice has likewise valorised the copy: the 1980s Appropriation artists detourned the fear of the iterable into a critique of authority. Mike Kelley related the many to a celebration of working-class culture against the elites of high culture. And, for post-internet art and art concerned with the internet and digital technologies, the notion of the original or unique image is often irrelevant or taken as a deliberately anachronistic standpoint. Joselit reformulates Benjamin's terms, using cult value for the "fundamentalist image" and exhibition value for "the neoliberal image" (Joselit 2013, 71) and setting the neoliberal image as (newly) the privileged category. For the neoliberal image, again, meaning is supplied not by context but by buzz – by the number of its iterations and by the different networks it connects to. It thus takes into account the mode of the web in ascribing image power: crowd-sourced intelligence rather than the rarefied knowledge of cultural gatekeepers. Though, as one may guess by the labels he has chosen, one is not to be seen as better than the other. And, in practice, the market has so far been able to accommodate the contradiction too that would seem to emerge from the neoliberal image's ascendency: in many ways, it simply works to support the fundamentalist image. Trecartin's popularity online (with the "right people") to a certain extent boosts his market value.

Finally, we should also note that one reason moving-image work is expensive to collect is a function of the labour and time inherent in its production. It is primarily bought by institutions, whose mandate of cultural patrimony makes the paradox of the work being freely accessible but also "owned" by someone easier to square. Museums have been – some might say, finally – taking on board the challenges that come with exhibiting and storing time-based media, digital arts, and performance as well as the possibilities of new media one can't conceive of yet. The high costs of making moving-image work also help locate it in the realm of the institution on the production side as well, as film and video work is more often executed as a commission for a future show or biennial, for which a commissioning budget becomes available, or whose invitation can be leveraged to access funds in the form of grants.

Still, making moving-image work is relatively cheaper with new software – which is as much a change to the art world as the ease of its dissemination. While co-ops had to collectivise the means of production and distribution, thus creating both an audience and delimited community for filmmaking work, the barriers to working with digital are lower. It can be part of any art practice, shown to any art audience. At the same time, it is too easy to be sanguine about the lower costs of production: the skilled labour involved in techniques such as CGI animation is inordinately expensive, and though a film can be shot on equipment far cheaper than celluloid and edited on cheaper software, artists are working in an environment with fewer opportunities for public funding and more competition for these opportunities.[7] The immaterial labour costs borne by artists are tremendous, and young artists face situations of extreme precarity, particularly in countries where a social welfare net is eroding or non-existent. One "change" coincident with the rise of the internet, for artists, is a regression of social mobility.[8]

Historiography

The shift from the 1990s to the present is one of self-built websites giving way to mass engagement with Facebook and Snapchat: a widening of the audience who engage on the web but a radical curtailing of what they may do once there. The failure of democratisation also inheres on the side of historiography, though the picture is – as Joselit's choice of two equally compromised terms suggests – not uncomplicated. The internet's archives and databases operate according to the logic of indexing and crowd-sourcing, of re-posting, and of algorithmically generated search results that erode the power of the specialist. These new logics will affect how digital art and cultural online forms more broadly are historicised.

Google's museum project, for example, involves digitising walk-throughs of museums. This seems slightly farcical considering that Google Image search could be considered the world's most interesting data bank, drawing from a far greater pool of images than a museum ever could. The great proliferation of material on the web allows for the emergence into visibility of marginalised histories and practices as well as for voices connected with these practices – which might have otherwise languished in non-English language articles or not had access to any academic power structures or means of visibility. This is the internet as a democratising medium at its best. The ethos, carried over from the beginning of the internet in the 1990s, that information should be free has aided the circulation of these new discourses, and, for the art world, material has been collected and re-posted in a number of invaluable sites, such as aaaaarg.fail, VVORK.com, Monoskop.org, or ubu.com, which re-post out-of-print texts; texts pertaining to critical theory, Conceptual Poetics, and art practice; digitised artists' film and video works; avant-garde music; and other material. The websites repeatedly fall afoul of copyright laws. Aaaaarg.fail has had a lawsuit brought against it and has had to change its name a number of times. Ubu.com has to migrate servers every couple of years, as they are hosted for free and their illegal re-posting of material puts those who host them at risk; they were last based in Zagreb and are currently hosted in Mexico. The copyleft movement has emerged as advocacy for the free circulation of information, as well as a means of systematisation that takes on board the criticisms against free information, such as protecting the rights (and remuneration) of authors. Creative Commons' menu of standardised licences, for example, allow cultural producers to choose for their work different balances between authorial control over uncredited republication and circulation and visibility for the work.

At the same time, putting too much stock in data banks discounts the role of curators and scholars in setting out a hierarchy of importance of objects and a coherent narrative of events. One may disagree with the valuations in the hierarchy produced, or the exclusion of or weighting given to events in the narrative, but they are important means of transmitting cultural knowledge from one generation to the next. They also safeguard against some of the worst effects of the internet's means of accessing information. Google's ranking of search results by popularity algorithms, rather than by valuation, rewards the winners – those with the most links to their pages – and then reinforces their places at the top.[9] Though I have suggested that the montages of atlas works approximate and presage the reproduced quality and lateral hierarchies of the internet's images, they do little to communicate the kinetic feedback and self-fulfilling mechanisms of search-result generation.

The internet's privileging of the wisdom of crowds over institutional gatekeepers, as can be seen by the highest-ranked YouTube videos, is often a race to the bottom. And on a different note, sites such as VVORK.com, aaaaarg.fail and Monoskop.org are perhaps less ground-breaking than they might seem. Their editorial choices, as that of any blogs or social-media accounts one might follow, provide channels through the vast and overwhelming amount of information on the internet. They do not function as gatekeepers but play a quite similar role for many of adjudicating what is seen and not seen, and their partial or undeclared mandates differ from the collecting ethos of public or university libraries, which chased the impossible dream of the universal collection (*Toute la mémoire du monde*, as Alain Resnais's film about the Bibliothèque Nationale de France had it). This compounds a problem for incomplete historiography that is already within disciplines that are conceived as marginal, such as experimental film and video, digital art, net.art, and media arts. Often, the histories that exist of these practices are written by not by art historians but by practitioners, who tend to explore and analyse within their own niche rather than creating crossovers between areas. Such obvious connections as the link between Michael Snow's rule-based films and the rule-based sculpture of Minimalist artists like Carl Andre are only now being fully explored, the two disciplines – artists' film and mainstream art – having been historicised separately. (The increasing specialisation within academia does not help.) This is the art-historical version of Hito Steyerl's argument of the "poor image", which reads this problem – the under-resourced nature of archives in shaping national narratives – on the state rather than the academic level.

The problems of historiography are further complicated by those of the archive of the web itself, which mirrors the move from institutional repositories and towards various individual enterprises. The internet has a paradoxical relationship to the archive: it may document everything we say on it, but who documents the internet – pages that have been taken down, Tweets that have been deleted, and sites that have gone out of business? Britain and France have public internet archives, run by the British Library and the Bibliothèque Nationale de France, which cover .uk and .fr addresses respectively (effectively, a sliver of the internet). In the US, the Library of Congress must seek permission before it archives any page, so it contractually relies on a private non-profit, the Internet Archive, as a repository. (It is characteristic of the web's development that this private company has come to serve as our collective online memory.) The Internet Archive, based in San Francisco, is the largest of a number of private and public archives of the web. It uses the Wayback Machine, a crawling tool that saves every page on the internet about every two months. The Archive is also supported by users; anyone can save a page themselves by going to the Internet Archive and copying and pasting the page's URL or by installing a program onto their browser. It is now, by default, the go-to archive for the internet.

The fact that the archiving function is an add-on to web pages – or, rather, the lack of any notion of "history" as palpable on the internet – contributes to the sense of the internet's being an eternal present, in a reading similar to that of digital technologies. Other, earlier models for the internet incorporated a time axis or a timestamp that would date each page. Brewster Kahle, who founded the Internet Archive, developed the Wide Area Information Service (WAIS), a protocol for accessing the internet that was superseded by Tim Berners-Lee's hypertext transfer protocol (HTTP), developed in 1989.[10] WAIS would allow you to see all the previous versions of a website, in the same way that all of Wikipedia's versions are accessible to the viewer (click on "view history"). Berners-Lee's more simple protocol eschewed a time axis, giving way to the strange paradox of the web as a constant present that also functions in the public imaginary as a looming materialisation of the past. "I'm so lucky I didn't go to college when Facebook was around" is a common refrain, at least for people of a certain age. "Never post photos of your children online or they'll never escape them" is another. The internet shows you first what is newest, but if you want to go deeper, you can find more material on a person's past than he or she might feel comfortable with.

Moreover, the fact that the major platforms on the internet are private companies, and headquartered in a country with a low appreciation of (or willingness to finance) the public sphere, means the reverse of this looming archive: the internet is too liable to evanescence. For artists whose blog and Tumblr posts are part of their practice, there is the real threat that one day Wordpress, for example, could go out of business, taking down all their work with it – as happened with Geocities, a website hosting service that was shuttered in 2009 and which was an important site for early cultural activity on the web. (Geocities was bought by Yahoo! at the top of the dot-com bubble in 1999.) As with the Internet Archive, interested private parties are moving in to archive the past that is important to them, particularly those associated with net.art – reflecting again the DIY spirit of that movement and the equal weight it gave towards artwork and its hosting platforms, here displayed in a more mournful, recuperative mode. The artists Olia Lialina and Dragan Espenschied host the Geocities archive, which was captured in a torrent file before the site was taken down.[11] The Photographers' Gallery in London staged an exhibition of 16,000 Geocities home page videos and has aided Lialina's and Espenschied's *One Terabyte of Kilobyte Age* (2009–ongoing) project. Rhizome hosts the archive of the VVORK blog,[12] which ran from 2006 to 2012, showing the organisation taking in a new role of digital conservation alongside analysis, advocacy, and community building.

Of course – what about the past that is important to those without the tools to archive it? This is again the question of Steyerl's "In Defence of the Poor Image"

(Steyerl 2009). For art, digital and internet technology presents specific problems. Trying to adequately convey the precise temporality of internet projects has already been a challenge for net.art. The mediated performances of internet activity have a dispersed audience who arrive at the performance at different times, and, in multi-authored projects such as *Brandon* (1998–1999), onto different sites. From whose point of view will the documentation arise, and how does one document a shifting narrative except in translation into a third form?

For traditional film and video repositories, archiving digital videos also inverts their economy of production. While the shooting and production costs for digital video are significantly lower than for analogue film, the costs of archiving digital video are greater. Technology moves so quickly that digital master copies have to migrate every few years in order to keep pace, and if the trail is broken, the original data becomes inaccessible. When one considers the budget cuts that many film archives, particularly in the US, are facing, the cost of keeping up with technologies inherent in storage becomes more acute. In this way, the questions of "what is art" will matter for archiving, as the ancillary material of blogging, Tumblr posts, and bookmarks might well be cut for budgetary reasons.

These two problems, of archiving and partial scholarship, arguably make the role of the institution in the digital age ever greater, despite a current antipathy within the art world for its museums. While in the UK, for example, university library budgets are stagnating, large museums have become incredibly popular, both with the public in general and with the donating few. They have the mandate to be the institution that sets out the narrative of art history as it happens. It is thus more crucial than ever to disentangle the public interest from the influence of donors who have large collections – which museums are always courting – even as museums are increasingly under pressure to attract patronage. Collecting policies are as important as front-of-house exhibition programs. Again, the problems facing museums (such as a playing field that privileges the large over the medium-sized museum; a need for blockbuster exhibitions and demonstrable public engagement; and, most importantly, the budget-forced tendency of museums to track the commercial art world at the expense of other types of artistic production) are not due to the internet. Nor are their solutions – such as the use of networking across borders to share resources and complicate single national narratives, as is exemplified by the museums network L'Internationale. But they could play a key role in answering some of the challenges singularly posed by the internet and digital technologies.

Public/private versus transactions

Another way to frame these questions around the role of traditional scholarship, archives, and the museum is that of the role of the public sphere amidst increasing privatisation. The internet imperils the public repository in all its various forms – the public museum, the public archive, the public university – by either doing the repository's job better or in different ways, with there being little political will behind the concept of the public. The public sphere is also imperilled by its own limitations. The Enlightenment idea of universal man was not quite universal, though to be fair it was chiefly about men. The notion of these public initiatives was to preserve the cultural patrimony of a nation – a remit that is now even linguistically suspect. Which patrimony? Whose? Of what nation? The terms of privatisation versus public sphere seem ill suited to a discussion of how information and power actually travel on the internet – which is to say, along networks and according to visibility. Reframing public/private as access/non-access focuses on who is accessing what information and for what reason, and reflects the undermining of grand narratives that have been bound up in the dismantling of the public project. It is hard to maintain the notion of one historiographic narrative in the face of the long tails, geographically marginal cultures, and subcultures brought to light on the internet – or, if unknown, notionally existent.

This is perhaps the reason that reports of changes to the art public vaunted by art's engagement with the internet are misplaced. Different publics presuppose different modes of engagement; the engagement of the non-art public in art itself matters little to the art-world processes of assigning intellectual and financial value, whether this is done online by viewership, appropriation, or comments or in person at a museum or fair. The art world's sequestration from other social and economic milieus means it remains its own arena online as in the physical world, and indeed the network that matters is the art network, not the virtual network. Actor-network theory and Deleuze and Guattari's rhizome have become such important tools because they offer means of reflecting on the structure of artistic engagement as dynamic and as overlapping networks, rather than inhering to older forms of binaries.

As we have seen, cybernetics augured both the shift to networks and the accompanying understanding of the broadening of art's discourse and formal possibilities – as well as what is stake in this change. For Jack Burnham, in "Systems Esthetics", the artist moved from being a maker of objects to a maker of aesthetic decisions, a reconsideration that ultimately calls into question the entire category of art.[13] As Burnham noted, this entails a value judgement (Burnham 1968). Is art as in its contemporary form worth holding onto? Similarly, part of David Joselit's project has been to protest forces that move against democracy, political justice, and freedom of expression; his book on radical television, *Feedback*, ends not on a pro-forma scholarly summary but on a manifesto-like call to arms. This is important to take into consideration when we look at his *After Art*, which is as much an analysis of the end of art as an attempt to enable contemporary art to take stock of its own internal contradictions and to use the power it has amassed positively. Networks, of course, are of primary importance to one, amoral area in particular: the circulation of commodities and capital. One of the key insights of *After Art* is that it offers a means of discussing art's imbrication within hyper-capitalism beyond the understanding of the art object as a commodity, to which the only possible reactions are affirmation, rejection, or co-option. Joselit understands the image as a function of the circulation of information, which allows him to show financial circulation as endemic to the notion itself of the image.

Joselit shows how art facilitates a currency of exchange that is not cash but is *transaction*: art allows connections among its public to become visible. Through the museum, art is translated into cultural capital, which is translated into cash, which is translated into power for the museum itself, specifically in its current heightened role of standard bearer for a city's brand or part of a municipal regeneration strategy. As Joselit writes,

> there is a lingering tendency to regard art's power as *virtual* – as an epiphe-nomenal reflection of other kinds of "real" power, such as capital . . . on the contrary, the organization of the art world – its format – is as real as it gets when it comes to capital's effects. It's not just the purchase of artworks, but the self-image of entire nations, the transformation of neighbourhoods and cities, and the fashioning of diplomatic identities that art is capable of accomplishing. In fact, its power has never been greater.
>
> (Joselit 2013, 93)

It is in this compromised and vexed terrain of the museum and the eclipse of the public sphere that Joselit's titular claim – being "after art" – emerges. Joselit's claim of the end of art hinges on the relation between the neoliberal and the fundamentalist image and on the role of museums in the current understanding of art. Museums, he argues, are compromised by their anti-democratic concentration of capital and power and, as such, expose a contradiction at the heart of the neoliberal image, which – though power accrues to it through buzz and circulation – still believes its rightful place is in the repository. Images with real power are those that remain outside the institution, and to shut art up in duty-free storage or the vaults of a private collection is to radically diminish them. This is not power in the sense of aesthetic transportation but actualising might: the power of an artist to make things happen – to buy 100,000 followers on Twitter, to ask a man to re-scan himself, to start a new international housing scheme. This is a power predicated not on the unique image and yet contravened by the museums that support it. By following power away from the museum and towards the circulating image, Joselit affirms the situation of "after art", one in which the art image circulates along a path that does not trespass in the funds of oligarchy, nor serve to reinforce class distinctions in the name of democratic access. The demise of the public sphere is nothing less than the demise of the models that rose up within it, including the system and philosophical understanding of art as a mode of private experience, public collection, and commodification.

What next? Rights and networks

My three-year-old told me the other day that ponies can't use phones because they have no fingers. I was a little surprised, because I still think of phones as a means to talk to other people, even though I spend the majority of time texting and on the internet, fingers jabbing at the screen. I say this to suggest, again, the problem of immanent critique and perhaps to betray some reluctant sympathy for accelerationism – what *is* next? Once we say good-bye to the public sphere, the alternative isn't great either. The "network" is already often simply a watchword for "privatisation": the erosion of the public sphere, the body politic, or the common good. Rather than a group of people exploring a notion together, networks signify alienation and atomisation: the evasion of taxes by offshore incorporations, the superficial contact allowed by social media, and the exploitation of the new spirit of capitalism. The move away from mass media and public institutions has been technologically enabled, but it has also been motivated by a decreasing amount of money in the West's public purse and an unwillingness to use that money for public institutions, whether for culture, health, or public infrastructure. Networked forms are the inexpensive tactics of the under-resourced opposition. They are born of and signify precarity, and they are also a function rather than a politics, whose potential can be used within the sphere of scientific debate and rationalism, by grassroots organisations – such as the *Whole Earth Catalog* – or by non-state armed groups.

It is worth noting that a public internet is not notional but historical. In an influential report in 1978, two French government ministers, General Simon Nora and Finance Inspector Alain Minc, urged the French president to create a public communications network so that the French public would not have to solely rely on the US company of IBM, then the largest service provider (*L'Informatisation de la société: Rapport à M. le président de la République*). The pamphlet was widely popular and helped spur on the establishment of the Mini-tel, the networked public computer system that was accessible via phone lines throughout France. Launched in Brittany in 1978, and across France in 1982, the Minitel was similar to the internet in the functions it enabled: email, online purchases, weather, stock price, train schedule information, etc. (It remained in operation until 2012.) It is a source, naturally, for the French claim that they preceded the internet over their Anglo-Saxon rivals. The Minitel's terminals were lent for free to telephone subscribers, and the network itself was owned by PTT (Poste, Téléphone et Télécommunications), and after PTT's division, by then-public France Télécom. (France Télécom was privatised in the 1990s.) Many of the ministers' predictions about the privatisation of communications technologies have come true. As Nora and Minc foresaw, today one doesn't "telematically conference"; one Skypes. One doesn't "search online"; one Googles. The potential liberatory effects of media engagement are tempered by the fact that any engagement with digital media is engagement with a corporation and often one – such as with current platforms of WhatsApp, Facebook, or Twitter – that archives and owns the information you post or which have tax mitigation policies you might disagree with.

Though these facets have been acknowledged by artists, particularly in the "anti-internet aesthetics" we looked at in the end of Chapter Four, post-internet art's willingness to work inside these parameters is a further reason for the dissatisfaction about post-internet art on the part of net.art practitioners. Net.art, which firmly took as an ethos that information should be free, used the ability to code as a means for autonomy on the web. The problem of complicity with the internet's programs also inheres within its hardware. It is well known that computers and other technological items are often made under inhumane conditions in factories in countries such as China, within an outsourced supply chain that allows companies such as Apple to disavow full responsibility for the long hours, substandard wages, and environmental and health toxins associated with their production. Again, this is acknowledged within the art sphere – we might look to the Belgian artist Herman Asselberghs's film *Dear Steve* (2010), in which Asselberghs methodically dismantles his computer while addressing Apple founder Steve Jobs about the conditions of its production – but without the real drive to move beyond it. Today's is the state that Steyerl identifies as *November* in her film of the same name (2004): "November is the time after October, the time when revolution seems to be over, and peripheral struggle has become particular, localist, and almost impossible to communicate".

As the copyleft movement shows, and as our study has hopefully suggested, a crucial balance on the web is between circulation and rights: what are the rights afforded to subjects when the protective power of the state falls away? This is so in the implementation of the NSA leaks, the extreme situation of stateless people, and notionally – though only notionally – in the deterritorialisation of the web. It is worth remembering that Foucault situated his essay on the author function in a framework of authorial rights, and I would like to focus on this last subject in our final example, which again turns to Joselit, who uses Foucault's author function in a paper given on the "cloud" as an insufficient metaphor for information plasticity. Joselit suggests replacing it, instead, with the profile (Joselit 2015).

Joselit underlines how the author function enables the discourse's circulation: an authored text circulates. A published text travels but not a private letter or anonymous poster (or a laundry list). Joselit highlights this relation to circulation as a key part of the author function, which he refines as a particular mode of organising information, submitting it as a "profile". Profiling, he notes, – particularly as a verb, to profile, or to provide a representation external to oneself – also characterises data mining, ethnic profiling, labour profiling, and of course the user's own activities as profiles on social-media sites, where one maintains a social-media profile. The profile function thus determines the type of discourse but also the fact that one is oneself quantified and circulated as a form of information.

His analysis of what the profile means for freedom and visibility draws from Balibar's understanding of property and alienation, in his text "'Possessive Individualism' Reversed: From Locke to Derrida" (2002). Balibar argues that the possession of property also involves a dispossession, in that the legitimation of private property is also the legitimation of the state. Private property is thus linked to political rights, as freedom entails retaining a measure of self-possession. As Joselit says, "We must sell ourselves, but there must be something that we can't give up". Joselit reads this through the work *Antoine Office, Antoine Casual* (2014) by Artie Vierkant, for which Vierkant bought a hologram of a person,

Antoine, who had scanned himself and iterated this two-dimensional representation into a three-dimensional avatar. He dressed this "Antoine" in office clothes and casual clothes, showing the video projections on two back-to-back screens – a recto and a verso, as Joselit calls them. The figure's movements are by turns funny and mesmerising: they traffic in the uncanny and in a doubling (work self, home self) but are puppet-like enough to elicit empathy from the viewer.

Figure 6.4 Artie Vierkant, *Antoine Office, Antoine Casual*, 2014, two-channel HD video, flatscreens, custom steel mount, 17 minutes, 46 seconds (looped).

Courtesy Artie Vierkant Studio

Figure 6.5 Artie Vierkant, *Antoine Office, Antoine Casual*, 2014, two-channel HD video, flatscreens, custom steel mount, 17 minutes, 46 seconds (looped).

Courtesy Artie Vierkant Studio

Vierkant's practice is concerned with the effects of the visual in a proprietary regime. His well-known series *Image Objects* (2011–ongoing) produces work in between the established categories of image and object, both formally and legislatively. Vierkant understands the image or object as modes in an iterative chain: not a third category, but a reflection of an oscillating process, rather like light is both particle and wave. He creates objects from images by rendering them as prints on Dibond (the trade name for two aluminium sheets that sandwich a lightweight, sponge-like material, which is often used as a mounting board for presentations) so that they achieve sculptural presence. He then documents these objects, and re-touches the images of them, finally re-circulating these photographs, so that the image objects exist both as the physical sculpture and as new images on the art-world media circuit and the internet. The images are not reproductions of the objects, nor vice versa, but bear and are changed by the network they circulate within. Watermarks, for example, are often left in place, highlighting legal parameters of a process that begins with appropriation from the web.

Negotiating rights is an integral part of the process of his work, thematised and signalled in the final product. For the project *Air filter and method for constructing same* (2014), he made a contract between himself and a patent-holder for an air filter that allowed him to make seventy-five derivative works of the device, provided they were within artistic usage. This, of course, was unnecessary – he is covered by copyright law that allows him to quote the originals if using them in a new and creative way, but Vierkant's engagement with juridical parameters allows him to question both the rights of the maker and, more interestingly, the rights of the images or subjects themselves. To make *Antoine*, for example, he bought a full-body hologram of Antoine, but since he wanted to use and manipulate the entire body for his work, he had to ask Antoine to be rescanned, as he had been captured with his hands in his pockets. Antoine agreed, provided that Vierkant did not do something lewd with the image. Joselit uses this detail to show how Antoine has lost the agency to his own image: Vierkant, of course, could do whatever he likes with the image (to a certain extent). For the project he had in mind, he did not have to agree to Antoine's terms. For Joselit, Antoine's loss of control over the circulation of his image is "an alienability that is the epitome of unfreedom", again here using Balibar to link property with freedom. We might think here of privacy as a sphere of freedom in the way that Jacob Appelbaum explains it or, again, as the legal precedent that has been relied upon in the US to safeguard rights such as freedom of sexuality or a woman's control over her own body: privacy as a realm of jurisdiction that Antoine's image has travelled beyond.

This notion of who owns one's image differs from region to region, and the question often relates to privacy rights, which Europe, for example, more strenuously defends than the US. Legislation rests on two interrelated elements: first the public attitude towards privacy, and second the private attitude towards legislation. In the US, which is more libertarian than the EU, the instinct is for less legislation. In other countries, the relationship is less straightforward. The Sharia system of law, parts of which are in place in Muslim countries, is both religious and civil, where "religious" also means the set of social conventions that govern being a proper Muslim. (Though it is often seen as extremist, Sharia is in place, in part or full, in a variety of Muslim countries on a spectrum of illiberality, including Afghanistan, Brunei, Iran, Iraq, Mauritania, Pakistan, Saudi Arabia, Sudan, the United Arab Emirates [UAE], Qatar, and Yemen.) Many Muslim countries thus bring legislation to bear on social norms beyond what would be considered the norm for legislation in the West – in the UAE, for example, it is illegal to post a picture of someone on social media without asking his or her permission first. These nuances are important to underline not only as a counterpoint to the illusion of the internet a fully globalised, non-national enclave, but also because it is within these laws that we begin to see a legal reaction to the insight of philosophical shifts towards objects and systems: how do we legislate for the rights of images as they travel?

In the US, it is illegal for someone to use your image in a deeply offensive manner, for commercial purposes, or in a defamatory or false way. What one can do with the image online rests on what "commercial, defamatory, and false" mean – no one has successfully won a case against the widespread practice of Photoshopping the heads of famous actresses onto other bodies in porn, though this could plausibly be considered defamatory. The strongest protection for image rights is in the field of child pornography, which is one of the few cases where even doctored images are illegal: that is, the mere instantiation of them is illicit, whether or not the images are based on actual children as referents. Child pornography protection, similar to the UAE's social-media law, criminalises the image as a function of representation, as much as its use in its circulation.

The question of the "rights" of images pertains to how closely we perceive the identity between the image and the person who is shown – an identity that Antoine, despite his decision to go into hologramming himself to make money, seems to perceive as absolute. The idea that one "travels" like an image hangs in the background of the contemporary conflation between one's profile on the web and oneself. Public figures of the internet also seem to exemplify the extra-territoriality of images on the web. Whistle-blowers such as Edward Snowden and Julian Assange are said to belong to the "international community", for whose benefit they argue they have acted, rather than to a particular state. In this way, they have been compared to Agamben's *homo sacer*, as well as being seen as emblems of a qualified freedom. In "Dark Cloud", for example, Joselit argues that Snowden's revelations were enabled by his operating in the cracks between different knowledge regimens – of NSA access, the press, and the dark web: his freedom is secured by his undiminished access to public platforms.

I have argued throughout this book that post-internet art reflects on images as they move through different networks of circulation: literally so (on the internet, in the art world, and as capital); formally (from the image to the object and back again); or in the mode of digitality (which thematises the ephemerality and mimicry inherent in movement along a chain). This takes place against a background of the circulation of capital and image, and of circulation of migrants from Latin America, Africa, and the Middle East. Philosophies such as actor-network theory and the new materialisms address this matter in terms of ascribing agency to an object or image – a query that is not notional but, in light of the above, crucial. What are the rights of subjects and images in a system, and how might they be adjudicated? We might think, for example, of images' accruing a *droit de suite* – the French right where an artist receives a percentage of a works' value when it is sold at auction, beyond the primary market, essentially enshrining a system of authorial ownership even as the image circulates. How to parse this enfolding between image, author, subject, and rights of all without equating different kinds of rights is the signal challenge here.

A cheap and false version of the true

The years of post-internet art, from the mid-2000s to the mid-2010s, map out a time when the internet has gone from being a technology to a condition. This sets, as we have seen, its strictly technological predecessors in uncertain relation to it and cements a move into Bishop's "mainstream" of contemporary art as well as into everyday life. This is one reason why I have found digitality to be such a helpful heuristic, as it recognises the way that the digital refers to more than the sum of its binary parts and takes on board the persistent illusions of life online as much as the realities. The image of life online seems to exceed our capacity to imagine it, perhaps because one can not reach a total picture of the internet. This is a function of the quasi-materiality of cyberspace as well as of time: digitality reflects the temporal aspect that is so important to the performative, accumulative versions practices that have developed within post-internet art. As Vierkant and others have noted, the participation in the life of these ongoing versions is also collective – and thinking of this dimension of production is perhaps a way to reclaim some of the promises of the internet that have soured during the corporatised 2010s.

If the internet suggests a deterritorialised landscape, this notion of unfolding through time – so similar to modernist queries, particularly of the *longue durée*, that we began with – further inhibits our ability to fully conceptualise life online. There is a remarkable, though slightly grouchy, line in one of Barthes's essays on the photograph in which he laments the fact that film does not allow for private scansion (it was written in 1970, before the VHS or DVD pause button) (Barthes 1970/1977, 66). He explains that he often prefers stills from a film to the film itself, as one cannot stop the reel when one wants to nor gaze upon the image for as long as one needs to in order to fully contemplate it. In many ways, this is another means of lamenting the shift to systems over static artwork; today, one method for representing systems is the translational impulse I described within cybernetics, which tracked the transition of information from one form to another. Another is to embody the artwork oneself, moving with it through time and argument. Ascribing rights to the object as it shifts from context to context is another such method: a tethering of the object to a framework of jurisdiction, at a moment when movement, capital, and the workings of the internet itself threaten the sense of nation-state governmentality. Thinking of digital technologies not simply as a factor of technology, moreover, reminds us that its key concerns are those of its social and political context: in so many ways, this will mean re-thinking how rights are established and secured, and whom, exactly, they protect.

Notes

1 Mark Leckey's lecture-performance *In the Long Tail* (2009) likewise addressed internet circulation in this same manner, suggesting a reversal of the mass-media pop culture publication and distribution strategies of twentieth-century television, newspapers, and magazines. The "long tail" theory, which was first given by the *Wired* writer Chris Anderson in 2004, argues that the internet allows for the flourishing of different subcultures as opposed to mass pop culture.

2 For a nice reading of this, see Ed Halter, "Will You Be My Version? James Richards", *Afterall*, no.38, Spring 2015, pp. 41–50.

3 The incredible growth of the contemporary art sector in the last fifty years is not only accomplished within the size of the art world economy but in the number of participants within it and the purview it extends. The Serpentine Marathons, run by the curator Hans Ulrich Obrist, have treated a number of non-visual art topics, such as poetry, map-making, and ecological disaster, since their inception in 2006. What have these, an annoying broadsheet (or indeed a small art space in want of funds) might ask, to do with art? The conjoining factor is critical theory or an attitude of cultural critique: it depends on the kind of questions asked of the subject rather than the object of enquiry produced.

4 See her collected writings in Andrea Fraser, *Museum Highlights: The Writings of Andrea Fraser* (ed. Alexander Alberro), Cambridge, MA: MIT Press, 2005, and in work since.

5 I have mentioned throughout the book that the work under discussion here is market-aligned, which is significant not in the sense of disqualification – that these works are simply luxury commodities produced for high-brow consumption – but in thinking through how the artwork's network of circulation produces the work itself. The art world consists of two strands: the commercial strand and the intellectual strand, and at the very height of each, there is little crossover. At the top of the commercial strand, we find the artists who command the highest prices at auction and who are traded by mega-galleries such as Gagosian, White Cube, or Barbara Gladstone. The peak of the intellectual strand is inclusion in Documenta, affiliation with top curators and the major biennials they organise, and with more cerebral galleries. This bifurcation is new and reflects the amount of money that has flooded into the system in the past twenty years. It also belies the way that, due to the constriction on resources for smaller spaces and biennials, most artists now rely on their galleries to foot the bills for their inclusion in biennials. (This means an exhibition cannot afford a Richter as much as being unable to afford too many unsigned artists.) To be "outside" the commercial system is very difficult – this is so for people who deliberately do not sign on to it and for those who have not been picked up by galleries. That these artists circulate in the market is less a remark on their commodity-alignment, or a certain lack of radicality or desire to placate rather than challenge (though that could be alleged of some), but rather the pervasiveness of the market in the art world today – which makes critiques that understand the market as integral to the art object itself (rather than systemic critiques such as institutional critique) so important.

6 Collectivising equipment and specialist knowledge remains a common strategy in the context of scarce or ever more specialised technological resources and access. In the early 2010s, for example, the Andy Warhol Foundation supported the digital development of small-scale independent art journals by hiring a CMS (content management system) website development team who could be used by five selected organisations, offering them a much more advanced site than each could have afforded individually. In countries where broadband access to the internet can be sporadic, internet users re-create a digital network in what might be called an analogue fashion: the Post Gallery in Manila, for example, hosts file-sharing nights where users share videos, images, and texts from their hard drives.

7 These programs may be cheaper, but their costs are often borne elsewhere. One pays for the program, computer, internet connection, etc.

8 The Arts Council in England, for example, announced in February 2016 a survey into the material conditions of working as an artist in England. See "Arts Council Launches Survey into Visual Artists' Livelihoods", (press release), *Arts Council*, 22 February 2016, http://www.artscouncil.org.uk/news/arts-council-launches-survey-visual-artists-livelihoods (last accessed on 2 May 2016).

9 Social media also rewards the winners, something that has been the subject of critique by the artist Constant Dullaart. In the work *High Retention, Slow Delivery* (2014), he purchased 2.5 million Instagram followers to level the playing field of visibility for different art figures: 100,000 followers for everyone. "Audience is a commodity", he writes in a

manifesto accompanying the work (http://dismagazine.com/dystopia/67039/constant-dullaart-100000-followers-for-everyone/), and *High Retention* is a form of income redistribution: understanding that the size of an audience is tantamount to visibility and opportunity, he set out to give everyone a fair shake. He bought the fake followers from the site "buysocialmedia.com" for a reported $5,000, distributing them to the likes of Zach Feuer and Gagosian galleries as well as post-internet figures such as Petra Cortright, Karen Archey, and Brian Droitcour. *High Retention* posits a 1% theory of the internet: in the same way the rich get richer, those with more influence get more influence – and more opportunities, more resources to pursue more opportunities, and so on.

10 For more on the Internet Archive see Jill Lepore, "The Cobweb: Can the Internet Be Archived?" *The New Yorker.* 26 January, 2015, http://www.newyorker.com/magazine/2015/01/26/cobweb.

11 See "One Terabyte of Kilobyte Age: Digging through the Geocities Torrent", *Blog Geocities Institute,* http://blog.geocities.institute/ (last accessed on 29 April 2016). The artist and designer Richard Vijgen also used Geocities for his virtual project *The Deleted City* (2011), which imagined the site's structure as if it were a street map.

12 See VVORK.com, now available at http://webenact.rhizome.org/vvork/20141006184357/http://www.vvork.com/ (last accessed on 29 April 2016).

13 Danto (and others not already mentioned in this volume) also argued for the "end of art", though on more philosophical grounds. Though Danto's philosophy is by and large analytic, in his *After the End of Art,* he strikes a Hegelian note, arguing that, with Warhol's *Brillo* boxes, subject and object had become one: representation and the thing itself closed together. Once this has happened, the project of art as traditionally conceived comes to an end. See A.C. Danto, *After the End of Art* (1995), Princeton: Princeton University Press, 2014.

Bibliography

Anon. "When New Grows Old: Artists Working with Technology Struggle to Stay Current". *The Economist.* 6 February 2016, http://www.economist.com/news/books-and-arts/21690014-artists-working-technology-struggle-stay-current-when-new-grows-old (last accessed on 7 September 2016).

Balibar, E. (2002) "'Possessive Individualism' Reversed: From Locke to Derrida". *Constellations,* 9 (3), 299–317.

Barthes, R. (1970) "The Third Meaning". In: Heath, S. trans. (1977) *Image – Music – Text,* London: Fontana Press, 52–68.

Burnham, J. (1968) "Systems Esthetics". *Artforum,* 7 (1), 30–35.

Fish, S. (1982) *Is There a Text in This Class?* Cambridge, MA: Harvard University Press.

Foucault, M. (1969) "What Is an Author?" In: Faubion, J. D. ed. and Hurley, R. trans. (1998) *The Essential Works of Foucault (1954–1984): Aesthetics, Method, and Epistemology,* Vol. 2, New York: The New Press, 205–22.

Fraser, A. (2005) *Museum Highlights: The Writings of Andrea Fraser.* Alberro, A. ed. Cambridge, MA: MIT Press.

Halter, E. (2010) "The Centaur and the Hummingbird". In: Cornell, L. and Halter, E. ed. (2015) *Mass Effect: Art and the Internet in the Twenty-First Century,* Cambridge, MA: MIT Press, 231–42.

——— (2015) "Will You Be My Version?: James Richards". *Afterall,* 38, 41–50.

Horowitz, N. (2011) *The Art of the Deal: Contemporary Art in a Global Financial Market,* Princeton: Princeton University Press.

Joselit, D. (2013) *After Art,* Princeton: Princeton University Press.

———— (2015) *Dark Cloud: Shapes of Information: Lunch-Bytes*. Talk given at the Haus der Kulturen der Welt, Berlin, 20 March, as part of the Lunch-Bytes programme, organised by Melanie Bühler.

Lepore, J. (2015) "The Cobweb: Can the Internet Be Archived?" *The New Yorker*. 26 January, http://www.newyorker.com/magazine/2015/01/26/cobweb (last accessed on 7 September 2016).

Nora, S. and Minc, A. (1978) *The Computerization of Society*. Bell, D. intro. (1981) Cambridge, MA: MIT Press.

"One Terabyte of Kilobyte Age: Digging through the Geocities Torrent". *Blog Geocities Institute* [website], http://blog.geocities.institute/ (last accessed on 29 April 2016).

Price, S. (2002/2008) *Dispersion*, New York: 38th Street Publishers.

Steyerl, H. (2009) "In Defence of the Poor Image". *e-flux journal* [online journal], 10, 2009, http://www.e-flux.com/journal/in-defense-of-the-poor-image/ (last accessed on 23 April 2016).

Tomkins, C. (2014) "Experimental People: The Exuberant World of a Video-Art Visionary". *The New Yorker*. 24 March, http://www.newyorker.com/magazine/2014/03/24/experimental-people (last accessed on 7 September 2016).

Troemel, B. (2013) "Athletic Aesthetics". *The New Inquiry* [online magazine], 10 May, http://thenewinquiry.com/essays/athletic-aesthetics/ (last accessed on 27 April 2016).

———— (2014) "Art after Social Media". In: Kholeif, O. ed. *You Are Here: Art after the Internet*, London: Cornerhouse, 36–43.

Index

Italic numbers denote reference to illustrations